Tales *of the* Field

SECOND EDITION

Tales of the Field

On Writing Ethnography

SECOND EDITION

John Van Maanen

THE UNIVERSITY OF CHICAGO PRESS
CHICAGO AND LONDON

The University of Chicago Press, Chicago 60637
The University of Chicago Press, Ltd., London
© 1988, 2011 by The University of Chicago
All rights reserved. Published 2011.
Printed in the United States of America

20 19 18 17 16   4 5

ISBN-13: 978-0-226-84964-5 (paper)
ISBN-10: 0-226-84964-3 (paper)

Library of Congress Cataloging-in-Publication Data

Van Maanen, John.
    Tales of the field : on writing ethnography / John Van Maanen.—
2nd ed.
        p. cm. — (Chicago guides to writing, editing, and publishing)
    ISBN-13: 978-0-226-84964-5 (pbk. : alk. paper)
    ISBN-10: 0-226-84964-3 (pbk. : alk. paper) 1. Ethnology—
Authorship. 2. Sociology—Authorship. I. Title. II. Series: Chicago
guides to writing, editing, and publishing.
    GN307.7.V36 2011
    306—dc22
                                                    2010049460

For Colleen

Contents

Just the place for a snark! I have said it twice:
That alone should encourage the crew.
Just the place for a snark! I have said it thrice:
What I tell you three times is true.

In the midst of the word he was trying to say,
In the midst of his laughter and glee,
He had softly and suddenly vanished away—
For the snark *was* a boojum you see.

LEWIS CARROLL

Prologue
2010

Long before I wrote *Tales of the Field*, there once was a time—a dreamtime—when I read ethnography as a leisurely cultural description based simply on the face-to-face, soul-to-soul experience an author had with a strange (to both author and me) group of people. Those who wrote ethnographies may have had doubts about just what their adventure in the field had taught them and just how "being there" could be conjured up in an ethnography, but few doubts of the authorial sort were put into print. It seemed as if ethnography emerged naturally from an unassuming stay in the field. One staked out a group, lived with them for a while, took notes on what they said and did, and went home to write it all up. If anything, ethnography appeared to be a rather pleasant, peaceful, and instructive form of literary journalism or travel writing.

As a naïve and rather gullible reader of ethnography in this dreamtime, ethnography promised an apparent freedom from rigid methodological rules and a blissful disregard for high-flying theory. It seemed to offer a wonderful excuse for having a jolly good time under the pretext of doing serious intellectual work. I figured it would all come together in the end as long I could cozy up and settle into some slightly odd but intriguing community facing problems I thought significant. All that was required, it seemed, was access, a steady gaze, a sturdy and thick notebook, and plenty of time to spare.

This pleasant dream was of course broken—shattered—by the time I sat to write *Tales*. Not only had I been to the field several times and struggled mightily with the pragmatic but intractable demands of ethnography such that whatever innocence I once possessed was long gone, but the trade itself was under attack. The master trope when I was writing *Tales* was *J'Accuse!* Ethnography was no longer pictured as a relatively uncomplicated look, listen, and learn procedure, but rather as something akin to an intense epistemological trial by fire. The field and its approach, its concepts, its justifications were all being taken to task—by some of its most respected practitioners no less—for its reliance on unquestioned cultural conceits ("ours," not "theirs"), for its unwarranted claims of objectivity, for its treacherous subjectivity, for its racial and gendered silences and partiality, for its failure to abandon the scientific posturing associated with modernism and essentialism, for its links to colonialism and the empire, and, most damning, for its inability (or unwillingness) to critically reflect on its own practices.

Now, twenty-some years later, it is apparent that the restlessness and determined critique that swirled within and around ethnography did not bring the enterprise down. If anything, ethnography has endured, moved on, and spread far and wide. It has also changed as a result of its own loss of innocence brought about by the ethnography-of-ethnography work that began in earnest in the 1980s and continues today. *Tales* was written in the midst of heated controversy and serves now as something of a period document. I wrote it not so much to add my own two cents (or less) to the debates of the time but more to try to sort out how ethnographers were able to forcefully critique what they were doing while they were doing it, a reflexive practice I much admire (and still do). That they were doing so in part through inventive and serious textual play was to me a revelation that I wanted to pass on to readers in an inviting way.

Now, re-reading *Tales*, I can easily find some stilted, rather cringe-worthy passages that I could erase in a minute (and then rework in the weeks and months ahead). But, perhaps not altogether shocking to a reader, I find most of the book holds up reasonably well to current practices and thus still provides a supportable survey, if breezy and introductory, of ethnographic voices. I have not messed with or touched any of the original text—even the cringe-worthy segments—not because I am lazy (although there is that too) but because I think it still does the job I wanted it to do. The ethnographic exemplars I put forth in the text—excluding my own—seem to me to have aged well and remain informative and helpful. What I have done here is work up a fairly lengthy epilogue—a new chapter more or less—that tries to summarize what I think has changed and what has not since *Tales* was published. There is a certain conceit involved, of course, in trying to squeeze my reading of some twenty years of morphing ethnographic history into a chapter, but it is maybe less a conceit than the one that attaches itself to *Tales*.

The last twenty years in ethnography have been lively ones to say the least. The critique continues while new work appears. A good deal has occurred, and our readings of ethnography as well as the meanings we take away have surely altered. Exactly how they have done so is a bit harder to determine. I would like to think we are now more sophisticated readers, more willing to take chances, more inventive in our writing practices, and a bit less harsh and evaluative when others experiment in print. I doubt much of this has come to pass, or if it has, a lot of it escaped me in my reading of this period. Of course, change of this kind in any time-honored, on-going, and more or less successful practice would be of an institutional sort and is likely to come about only at a glacial and uneven pace. But maybe this is the way it should be. As I suggest in the epilogue, despite the problems it faces, the need for ethnography—away and at home—is greater than ever before. And, given the broadening of interest in ethnography, it now seems to me that demand outruns supply. What I wish this second edition of *Tales* to do is add to the strength of those ethnographies yet to be written. May there be an abundance of them.

To wrap up this prologue and get the reader on to a proper preface, a ceremonial task is in order—the ritual thanking of others for their help, advice, and comfort. Much of the epilogue comes from various talks and papers I've written over the last three or four years. Some of these presentations and writings were prompted by the twentieth anniversary of the publication of *Tales of the Field*. At the University of Colorado in 2006, I gave a talk on "The Power of Wonder" at the Center for the Arts and Humanities at the invitation of my friends Chris Braider, Dennis McGilvray, and Patti Adler, all of whom I must thank for the gentle critique they provided me on my performance. At the Telling Tales Conference sponsored by the University of New Mexico in 2008, I delivered a paper I called "A Song for My Supper," which fellow conferees Ann Cunliffe, Bud Goodall, Mike Agar, and John Johnson read. After the dishes were cleared, they helped me sort out some of the "new" ethnographic tales I'd just put forward. Finally, at the foot of Mount Fuji, in Mishima, Japan, I gave a talk in 2009 on "Ethnography, Then and Now." This conference was sponsored by the Mitsubishi UJF International Foundation, who generously paid my freight (but could not stop the rain that halted my once-in-a-lifetime climb to the top of Mount Fuji before it began). The paper I presented at the conference was graciously taken apart by Toshihiro Kanai-san and Ikuya Sato-san, who then urged me put it back together again more carefully. Bits and pieces of these talks and papers appear in the epilogue.

To my family must go, as always, my greatest appreciation for simply being here (and there). Several of my clan chained me to my writing desk this summer so I could get this second edition of *Tales* into print. To Kyla, Nicole, Patrick (and Nicole Harper), Casey, and especially Colleen (my no-nonsense editor), a heartfelt thank you. But this second-generation book most appropriately belongs to Harper Lily Van Maanen, my magnificent granddaughter who is about to take her first step.

John Van Maanen
AUGUST 2010

Preface

This is a book about culture in black and white. It is about how one culture is portrayed in terms of another in an ethnography. It rests on the peculiar practice of representing the social reality of others through the analysis of one's own experience in the world of these others. Ethnography is therefore highly particular and hauntingly personal, yet it serves as the basis for grand comparison and understanding within and across a society.

How social reality is conveyed through writing involves, among other things, authorial voice. The author's perspective exhibited through voice marks particular ethnographic styles and genres. But, reader beware. Voice varies within and between ethnographic narratives, and the voices classified and displayed here are not exhaustive of the possibilities. Indeed, as students of cold print know, matters of voice can quickly grow complicated.

This is not, however, a book written for technical specialists, literary critics, or scholarly insomniacs. This is a survey of ethnographic voices, and it is meant to be informal, readerly, light in spirit, and above all, introductory. It is addressed primarily to fieldworkers of a sociological or anthropological bent, be they prospective, practicing, retired, or manqué. In a vague way, of course, we are all fieldworkers whenever we must make sense of strange surroundings and pass on our understandings to others. But ethnographic fieldworkers who mix the art and science of cultural representation are the obsessional professionals of the social sense-making and translating trade. They publish their understandings.

Ethnographers occupy a literary borderland somewhere between writers who reach for very general audiences and those who reach for a specialized few. To the generalists, ethnography often seems pinched and inelegant, its standards stiff and restrictive. To the specialists, the same writing may seem imprecise and unfocused, its standards loose and unfathomable. Versions of these borderland skirmishes are played out within ethnographic circles as well. Ethnographers have never been at ease with such matters, and this discomfort seems to be growing of late. In fact, a number of formerly routine and taken-for-granted tricks of the trade are now very much up for grabs and widely discussed. Unsettled and contested notions of what constitutes high- and low-grade ethnography are being brought to the surface. Some ethnographic scribes are testing the waters by publishing some stylistically unfamiliar and sometimes quite startling fieldwork accounts. Other scribes, notably the high priests of cultural theory, are questioning in print the previously unquestioned epistemological assumptions on which cultural representations rest. My aims in what follows are, first, to examine some of the problematic (and virtuous) features of different ethnographic genres and, second, to keep the pressure on ethnographers to continue experimenting with and reflecting on the ways social reality is presented.

Much of this material may interest a wider audience than might have been possible ten or so years ago. Fieldworkers of all varieties are now putting to use novel representational forms in their studies. Some forms are trendy, some are classical; but one result is that the distinction between literature and science in ethnography is shrinking. I think this is good, although I realize it may violate some of the normative conventions certain readers hold dear. Put simply, many familiar ethnographic conceits have had their day and are no longer very persuasive. To wit, the glacial clarity once attributed to, say, functional, structural, materialist, cognitive, or linguistic theories have all withered. Nor is there to be found the cheerful optimism once carried by adventurous bands of self-defined cultural scientists out to steadily refine our formal understanding of human behavior through the relentless compiling of cross-cultural observations. During their ascendancy, such conceits may have had a rather beguiling and, no doubt, pleasing narcotic effect on fieldworkers, but the effect has now worn off.

My own view is that the accumulation of ethnographies indicates and enhances an enduring domain of human discourse more than it signals any advance in our formal understanding of cultural affairs. Looking backward, for example, it is relatively easy to see that during particular periods (and within particular theoretical circles) ethnographers were able to more or less agree on what kinds of cultural representations were acceptable and authoritative for their ordinary purposes. Yet these largely implicit agreements were hardly fixed or timeless, since they eventually broke down as new ways of handling previously unseen representational difficulties emerged. We seem now to be in a period of considerable uncertainty and change, for what was once "good enough ethnography" seems to many not so good any more. New voices are audible, new styles are visible, and new puzzles are being put forth.

Much of this intellectual restlessness was only dimly grasped when I first put pen to paper to write this manuscript. While I had long been aware of the practical troubles I faced when trying to convince readers of the authenticity and worth of my writing, I had little inclination to do much more than shrug my shoulders and get on with solving representational problems piecemeal as I faced them passing across my writing desk. I now regard these problems as downright central to the ethnographic enterprise, certainly as central and consequential as any problems faced in the field. In a sense, to consider these writing issues seriously and systematically pushes conventional notions of method—including the overrated criteria of reliability and validity as well as the underrated criteria of apparency and verisimilitude—both forward and backward in time. Minimally, I now think that method discussions of ethnography must explicitly consider (1) the assumed relationship between culture and behavior (the observed); (2) the experiences of the fieldworker (the observer); (3) the representational style selected to join the observer and observed (the tale); and (4) the role of the reader engaged in the active reconstruction of the tale (the audience).

I did not start out to pursue such lofty matters. This monograph began several years ago simply as a frivolous celebration of the often informal, profane, ludicrous, and mock-heroic stories fieldworkers privately tell of their research adventures. I wanted to make public a little of the corridor talk of fieldworkers as a way of deflating, not inflating, the ponderous and preachy pronouncements on method put forth by the initiators and propagandists of ethnography. The manuscript I imaged would reflect the quirky and unpredictable moments of my own history in the field and lightly spoof some of the maxims of the trade. The intent was to be less instructive than amusing. Along the way, however, things grew more serious.

Such solemnity results largely from my readings of the literary wings of current anthropology and sociology. Stories and spoofs are still cobbled together in this manuscript, but they are now the two-penny nails of a final structure that conveys a more general view of ethnography. Those readers familiar with the recent writings of Clifford Geertz, George Marcus, Howard Becker, George Stocking, Joseph Gusfield, and particularly James Clifford will note that the concerns of these writers serve as the focal point for much of this book. Their writing has provided a touchstone for what began as a few tales in search of an excuse for their telling.

This academic posturing announces, of course, personal prejudice and propensity. Not all is pompous peculiarity. My own training as an ethnographer of a sociological sort reflects, I think, the training of many ethnographers and would-be ethnographers whose professional teeth were cut outside the more prominent and justly famous centers of fieldwork practice. For better or for worse, we lack a formal apprenticeship in the trade and perhaps the proper respect for our ancestors and the comfort their representational devices might provide. Without mentors or cohorts, our appreciation and understanding of ethnography comes like a mist that creeps slowly over us while in the library and lingers with us while in the field.

This lack of tutoring is perhaps most telling at that still point in our studies when we have returned from the field and sit before the blank page that must eventually carry the story of what we have presumably learned. Aid, comfort, and confidence may be difficult to come by at this lonely and sometimes terrible stage. For instance, when returning to the university after a stay in the field that was to serve as the basis for my dissertation, I was told by my worthy academic advisors, whose interests and skills lay well outside ethnographic traditions, to simply "write up" what I had "discovered" in the field as if what was then in my head (and field notes) could be uncorked like a bottle and a message poured out.

My thesis was eventually written over a two-year period around some survey work I had accomplished in the field. My fieldwork-based materials were used sparingly to embellish and provide local color for a thesis straight from the land of multiple regressions and chi-squares. Since then I have managed, largely through trial, error, and the generous support of friends who were the unlucky readers of various drafts, to publish a respectable amount of what I naturally regard as reasonably competent ethnographic writing.

Yet like so many fieldworkers, I have never been particularly attentive to the writing conventions I follow in practice. By and large, my writing style, such as it is, developed by paying close attention to those ethnographic works I admired and then used as blueprints for my own work. Like other ethnographers, I have read a good deal about the methods and aims of fieldwork and have found this writing attractive (perhaps because of the many charms etiquette discussions and in-house gossip hold for the perpetually anxious). But I have also found this writing curiously silent on matters of narrative representation and style. My recent encounter with the incisive, but appreciative, literary critics of my trade, as displayed in the materials that follow, has been both impressive and helpful. As indicated, however, it has not been reassuring or calming. But as the reader will presumably gather from the text, I will not be able to read or write ethnography in quite the same way anymore.

The encounter was also an encouraging one—although the reader will note a slight touch of dismay here and there in the book. It was encouraging from the standpoint that I think most ethnographers have achieved a very high level of cultural expertise and sophistication through long-term topical, theoretical, and domain specialization of the sort that presupposes historical knowledge, linguistic competence, and deep personal experience. Occasionally such expertise may dampen intellectual daring or inhibit the trying out of new ways to solve old problems. But, nonetheless, I think ethnographers, especially those in the vanguard of the new ethnographic genres, are learning to write better, less soothing, more faithful, and ultimately more truthful accounts of their fellow humans than ever before. By debunking some of the conventions associated with fieldwork accounts, I am not suggesting the abandonment of the craft. Indeed, I think we need now, more than ever, concrete, sharp, complex, empathetic, and politically sensitive portraits of what others might really be like if we are to learn, tolerate, balk, help, confront, instruct, or otherwise adjust to the uncountable ways of living and being that surround us.

Ethnographies are portaits of diversity in an increasingly homogenous world. They display the intricate ways individuals and groups understand, accommodate, and resist a presumably shared order. These portraits may emerge from global contrasts among nations, societies, native histories, subsistence patterns, religions, language groups, and the like. Or they may develop from the more intimate contrasts of gender, age, community, occupation, or organization within a society. I take it as self-evident that there is as much deep and divisive cultural misunderstanding and frighteningly real conflict of interest among people within our own society as there is between our society and others. While I have no prophetic or utopian words to splash across these pages, I do hope the book furthers the spread of intensive fieldwork by making some of its distinctive reporting practices more visible and hence less daunting or mysterious to the uninitiated.

To this end, I try in this book to erase some of the rather arbitrary lines that currently separate anthropology from sociology. I recognize that both fields are now so thoroughly balkanized into esoteric theory and method groups that to think of either as a single discipline in confident possession of some grail-like paradigm is at best a passing fancy or at worst a power play. The paradigm myth, however, dies more slowly than the post-paradigm reality, for there remain those fieldworkers who still salute a tattered disciplinary flag and rarely venture beyond their traditional campsites. Yet a fair amount of competent, self-reflective ethnography attending to some very similar problems is now being produced under both flags, but seldom are the two literatures set side by side. There are, of course, differences in both the nature and feel of these ethnographies, but these differences are slight when measured against what might be gained from pooling our efforts. Throughout this book, then, I will speak of ethnography as a project that may help unite anthropology and sociology rather than divide them.

Some words on the argument and rationale of this monograph are now in order. By raising the question of the voice and role of the writer in the collection, rendering, and reading of ethnographic tales, I am trying to crack open the notions of culture, fieldwork, and ethnography so that new questions can be raised and perhaps revisions entertained. I do not claim to have any definitive answers to the questions I raise. If truth is at issue, all conclusions are provisional. I will argue, however, that ethnographies, as quasi-formal documents based on fieldwork, are full of persuasive, yet questionable, rhetorical appeals, and that the idea of culture is itself a most problematic one. If these appeals and representations are isolated, conventional reporting practices (and the common responses they generate from readers) may become better understood and, if need be, altered. I am conscious, however, that my own argument is also a product of conventions and ideology and is thus caught up in the same problems of which I write. This is unavoidable. I can only notify readers in advance of the self-indulgent, involuted, circular, ironic, and slightly iconoclastic (I hope) routes I follow in this monograph.

Readers should also be alert to some of the odd textual practices I adopt in this book. Each major chapter (3, 4, and 5) highlights a generic form of ethnograhic representation and provides an example or two from my own writings. These illustrations are then critiqued as the writing rolls on. There are thus realist accounts of realist writing; confessionals tucked inside and alongside other confessionals; and impressionistic interpretations of impressionistic tales. The dog doth chase his tail. And despite my concluding protest on the folly of the abstract, the astute reader will detect a degree of formalism and generalizable narrative theory supporting the entire venture. This is a representation of writing in writing. Fair warning.

Such self-criticism is not an art many of us are qualified to practice. Any effort to fully detach oneself from one's own work is bound to be quixotic. My excuse for using my own writing for lengthy genre illustrations is not because I am unduly impressed (or distressed) with its literary quality, but because I think that writing ethnography is an isolated and highly personal business and that those who discuss it in print are certain to discover that their best examples must be their own. Writers are the privileged readers of their own texts and are, within limits, the only ones who can speak with some advantage and special authority on their own intentions and textual assumptions. Readers who wish for a more general literary tour or exegesis of ethnography will have to look beyond this book.

Finally, the most conventional practice of all, the covering of one's tracks through the implication of others in what is to follow.

As always, from the trenches, my close compatriots in the Organization Studies Group of the Sloan School of Management at MIT, Lotte Bailyn and Ed Schein, provided useful commentary on drafts as they developed throughout this project, Gideon Kunda refreshed my emotional recall of fieldwork and taught me a good deal about writing in a cold sweat as he struggled through his confrontation with dissertation ethnography. Bob Gephart, Constance Perin, Steve Barley, Bob Thomas, Woody Powell, Paul Osterman, Jane Salk and Frank Dubinskas, all MIT colleagues of mine at various times, also read drafts and gave helpful advice.

Nigel Fielding, my sponsor and fieldwork confidant during a Fulbright year in the Department of Sociology at the University of Surrey, read over and suggested some much needed revision in a somewhat daft first draft of this manuscript. Maurice Punch, stalking the mixed metaphor and infinitive-split, helped correct some of my splayed thought and grammar. Marc Miller, on the phone and by letter, provided salubrious remarks while reminding me of the always running clock on this too often procrastinated final draft of the manuscript. Howard Becker, Larry Browning, Joanne Martin, Larry Levine, Jim Thomas, Bob Sutton, Clive Norris, Susan Krieger, Mike Pacanowski, Jennifer Hunt, Rosana Hertz, Carol Warren and Ken Smith also provided advice and encouragement along the way. And Peter Manning, my sometimes partner in word crime, not only critiqued my writing but also endured my usual bouts of excessive zeal and indifference with good will, high signs, and welcome advice.

To my family, however, must go the greatest appreciation for putting up with one who at this very instant still writes rather than lives. Casey, Patrick, and Nicole have learned to cut left on the big ones and drop down the expert's slope while hearing little more from their pasty, hunched-over father these past months than such endearing remarks as "put that down," "leave me alone," or the tired and always false, "just a couple more days." Their mother, kind soul, has managed to read and correct both my prose and demeanor with remarkably good cheer while maintaining a travelling heart and home. To Colleen this book belongs.

John Van Maanen
February 1987

1

Fieldwork, Culture, and Ethnography

If ethnography produces cultural interpretations through intense research experience, how is such unruly experience transformed into an authoritative written account? How, precisely, is a garrulous, overdetermined, cross-cultural encounter, shot through with power relations and personal cross purposes circumscribed as an adequate version of a more-or-less discrete "otherworld," composed by an individual author?

James Clifford

An ethnography is written representation of a culture (or selected aspects of a culture). It carries quite serious intellectual and moral responsibilities, for the images of others inscribed in writing are most assuredly not neutral. Ethnographic writings can and do inform human conduct and judgment in innumerable ways by pointing to the choices and restrictions that reside at the very heart of social life. My intention in this monograph is to organize and bring to light some often overlooked narrative conventions of ethnography so that different modes of cultural portraiture can be identified, appreciated, compared, and perhaps improved.

This is not a book, therefore, about the method of ethnography (fieldwork) or about its subject (culture). Both are vital notions, of course, because when married in an ethnography they form something of a conceptual union. To be sure, ethnography has a long history, and its techniques, goals, and representational styles mean different things, not always complementary, to its many curious readers. These matters will be covered in due course. But let us first consider what ethnography ties together—fieldwork and culture—as well as the knot itself.

1

Scribes and Tribes Together

Fieldwork is one answer—some say the best—to the question of how the understanding of others, close or distant, is achieved. Fieldwork usually means living with and living like those who are studied. In its broadest, most conventional sense, fieldwork demands the full-time involvement of a researcher over a lengthy period of time (typically unspecified) and consists mostly of ongoing interaction with the human targets of study on their home ground.[1] In print, the research is presented as occasionally boring, sometimes exciting, but virtually always self-transforming as the fieldworker comes to regard an initially strange and unfamiliar place and people in increasingly familiar and confident ways.

Fieldworkers represent themselves as "marginal natives" (Freilich, 1970) or "professional strangers" (Agar, 1980) who, as "self-reliant loners" (Lofland, 1974) or "self-denying emissaries" (Boon, 1982) bring forth a cultural account, an ethnography, from the social setting studied. While there are undoubtedly cases where fieldworkers fail to achieve a status among the studied better than "dull visitors," "meddlesome busybodies," "hopeless dummies," "social creeps," "anthrofoologists," "management spies," or "government dupes," fieldworkers themselves, by reference to the massive amounts of experience they accumulate in the field and the attention they pay to the role relations that emerge, are sure to present their stay as highly instructive.

To do fieldwork apparently requires some of the instincts of an exile, for the fieldworker typically arrives at the place of study without much of an introduction and knowing few people, if any.[2] Fieldworkers, it seems, learn to move among strangers while holding themselves in readiness for episodes of embarrassment, affection, misfortune, partial or vague revelation, deceit, confusion, isolation, warmth, adventure, fear, concealment, pleasure, surprise, insult, and always possible deportation. Accident and happenstance shapes fieldworkers' studies as much as planning or foresight; numbing routine as much as living theatre; impulse as much as rational choice; mistaken judgments as much as accurate ones. This may not be the way fieldwork is reported, but it is the way it is done.

What I mean by fieldwork is the stiff, precise, probably too visual, but nonetheless double-edged notion of participant-observation. This is less a definition for a method than it is an amorphous representation of the researcher's situation during a study.[3] Whether or not the fieldworker ever really does "get away" in a conceptual sense is becoming increasingly problematic, but physical displacement is a requirement. The method reflects a bedrock assumption held historically by fieldworkers that "experience" underlies all understanding of social life (Penniman, 1974; Rock, 1979; Georges and Jones, 1980). Fieldwork asks the researcher, as far as possible, to share firsthand the environment, problems, background, language, rituals, and social relations of a more-or-less bounded and specified group of people. The belief is that by means of such sharing, a rich, concrete, complex, and hence truthful account of the social world being studied is possible. Fieldwork is then a means to an end.

The ends of fieldwork involve the catchall idea of culture; a concept as stimulating, productive, yet fuzzy to fieldworkers and their readers as the notion of life is for biologists and their readers. Culture is akin to a black hole that allows no light to escape. The observer knows of culture's presence not by looking, but only by conjecture, inference, and a great deal of faith (Wagner, 1981; Sperber, 1974). Culture, while certainly a cosmic idea, is nonetheless expressed in some down-to-earth ways. In currently fashionable form, culture refers to the knowledge members ("natives") of a given group are thought to more or less share; knowledge of the sort that is said to inform, embed, shape, and account for the routine and not-so-routine activities of the members of the culture (Conklin, 1968; Becker, 1980; Swidler, 1986). It is necessarily a loose, slippery concept, since it is anything but unchanging. Culture is neither prison nor monolith. Nor, of course, is it tangible. A culture is expressed (or constituted) only by the actions and words of its members and must be interpreted by, not given to, a fieldworker. To portray culture requires the fieldworker to hear, to see, and, most important for our purposes, to write of what was presumably witnessed and understood during a stay in the field. Culture is not itself visible, but is made visible only through its representation.

This is what makes the study of culture so sticky. Human culture is not something to be caged for display, put on a slide for

3

inspection, read from an instrument, or hung on a wall for viewing. The fieldworker must display culture in a narrative, a written report of the fieldwork experience in self-consciously selected words. Ethnography is the result of fieldwork, but it is the written report that must represent the culture, not the fieldwork itself. Ethnography as a written product, then, has a degree of independence (how culture is portrayed) from the fieldwork on which it is based (how culture is known). Writing an ethnography is office-work or deskwork, not fieldwork (Marcus, 1980).[4]

The Limits of Ethnography

Ethnographies join culture and fieldwork. In a sense, they sit between two worlds or systems of meaning—the world of the ethnographer (and readers) and the world of cultural members (also, increasingly, readers, although not the targeted ones). Ethnographies are documents that pose questions at the margins between two cultures. They necessarily decode one culture while recoding it for another (Barthes, 1972). This is an interpretive act that occurs with the writing of texts, and as with any form of writing, certain constraints partially determine what is written. Some very general ones follow.

Ethnographies are obviously experientially driven, in that writers seek to draw directly from their fieldwork in the culture of study. Yet there are very real limits to what a particular fieldworker can and cannot learn in a given setting. Much has been written on how the personal characteristics and working habits of fieldworkers mediate the cultural scenes that unfold in their presence. Women (or men) in the field, for example, find some doors open more readily than others (Golde, 1970; Warren and Rasmussen, 1977). Rapport with certain informants may preclude it with others (Berreman, 1962). Fieldworkers in some settings are granted relatively rapid access to culturally sacred matters; in other settings they will learn nothing about them unless they devote their professional careers to such a pursuit (Clifford, 1983b). Fieldworkers may present themselves as delicately lurking, working, and getting results, but the results they achieve are always experientially contingent and highly variable by setting and by person.

Ethnographies are politically mediated, since the power of one group to represent another is always involved. Fieldworkers are typically one up on those they study (Nader, 1972). Moreover, sponsors (or lack thereof) suggest and enforce domains for "proper" ethnographic work. The practical worlds of budgets, scholarly interests, and academic politics all attach themselves to fieldwork. Insight into how to shake a grant from the Giving Tree may be far more important to understanding why one group instead of another is investigated. Most crucially, ethnography irrevocably influences the interests and lives of the people represented in them—individually and collectively, for better or worse. Writers know this, and self-imposed limits mark all ethnographies.

Ethnographies are shaped as well by the specific traditions and disciplines from which they are launched. These institutional matters affect the current theoretical position an author takes (or resists) regarding such things as the origins of culture, its characteristic forms, and its consequences (Clifford, 1983a). Such pre-text assumptions help determine what a fieldworker will find interesting and hence see, hear, and eventually write (Davis, 1971). Exotic-mongering ethnographies of a remote but romantic wind-rustling-through-the-palm-trees kind are, for instance, out of favor these disenchanted days, replaced, by and large, with more focused, technical, cold, and puzzle-solving varieties (Kuper, 1977). More general intellectual trends are also relevant to the writing of ethnography. Along these lines, the number of deconstruction workers and structural architects employed in the ethnographic trades is on the rise (Geertz, 1983; Marcus and Fischer, 1986).

The narrative and rhetorical conventions assumed by a writer also shape ethnography. Ways of personal expression, choice of metaphor, figurative allusions, semantics, decorative phrasing or plain speaking, textual organization, and so on all work to structure a cultural portrait in particular ways. Style is just as much a matter of choice when the experimentalist writes in a self-conscious, hyper-realistic, attention-grabbing dots-and-dashes fashion—where, for instance, ellipses are used to simulate (and stimulate) the effect of a . . . skipped heartbeat—as when the traditionalist falls back on the neutral, pale-beige, just-the-facts fashion of scientific reporting.[5] Some styles are, at any given time, more acceptable in ethnographic circles than others. These are the ones that most powerfully fix our understanding of what a culture is and what it is not—our own and others.

Finally, all these ethnographic conventions are historically situated and change over time. Only during the first third of this century did ethnography itself become a recognizable topical and literary genre set off from similar written products such as travel-and-adventure stories, fiction, biography, social history, journalism, statistical surveys, and cultural speculation (Clifford, 1983a; Marcus and Fischer, 1986). Shifts within ethnography occur when, for example, new faces enter the field, novel problems are put forth, funding patterns change, or, of special interest here, new narrative styles develop as older ones fade and become somehow less convincing and true.[6] These changes may be gradual and may pass without notice, or they may shock and awaken slumbering writers and readers of ethnography unprepared for the blurring or overthrow of previously uncontested ways of doing things.

My concern is primarily with the narrative and rhetorical conventions surrounding ethnography and secondarily with the historical. Whenever possible I ignore the experiential, political, personal, and institutional conventions. This is a choice that certainly restricts what I propose to say here (said, once, twice, thrice). But it is a choice that allows me a degree of tranquility in not having to gaze too far afield. More to the point perhaps, a good deal of critical analysis has been directed at other ethnographic conventions (particularly the experiential). My choice at least has some novelty on its side.[7]

What I propose to show in this monograph is simply that the joining of fieldwork and culture in an ethnography entails far more than merely writing up the results culled from making friends, staying sane and healthy, worming one's way into back regions, and taking good notes in the field. Among social scientists there is a rather persistent conviction that the problems of ethnography are merely those of access, intimacy, sharp ears and eyes, good habits of recording, and so forth. It is not a straightforward matter, however, because a culture or a cultural practice is as much created by the writing (i.e., it is intangible and can only be put into words) as it determines the writing itself (Wagner, 1981). To suggest otherwise reduces ethnography to method.

Method is, to be sure, a problem. But even when it is said to be more or less overcome, the fieldworker must still put into words what was learned of a culture so that a representation of sorts may result. An ethnography is a means of representation. Yet any claim to directly link fieldwork (and the immediacy of its experience) to the ethnography itself, unmediated or untransformed by narrative conventions, will not hold. No transparency theory can be confirmed by ethnography.[8]

Foreshadows

Most of the intellectual hopscotch that follows is about how social reality is presented, not known. Culture is not strictly speaking a scientific object, but is created, as is the reader's view of it, by the active construction of a text. While distinctive authorial voices are heard in more literary and innovative cultural accounts, all ethnographic writers make use of discernible rhetorical and narrative conventions when putting into words the presumed results of fieldwork experience. These words are the matters of my concern.

There are five chapters that carry this concern. Chapter 2 takes up, in breathless fashion, the emergence of contemporary fieldwork and considers what various readers of its written products have come to more or less expect. The following three chapters are the heart of the book. Each presents the narrative conventions that define a particular type of ethnographic tale, offers a few examples, and suggests some of the pressing problems writers of the genre face when attempting to establish their tale as accurate, authentic, and authoritative.

Chapter 3 deals with the most familiar form of ethnography— Realist Tales. These tales provide a rather direct, matter-of-fact portrait of a studied culture, unclouded by much concern for how the fieldworker produced such a portrait. Confessional Tales are addressed in chapter 4 and provide sharp contrast to their realist counterpart. As the name implies, confessional tales focus far more on the fieldworker than on the culture studied. Both of these forms are distinct from the Impressionist Tales of the field covered in chapter 5. These tales are personalized accounts of fleeting moments of fieldwork cast in dramatic form; they therefore carry elements of both realist and confessional writing.

Chapter 6 concludes the book by giving passing mention to several other kinds of ethnographic tales. These tales are grouped under four headings—Critical, Formal, Literary, and Jointly-told Tales. Put candidly, these are residual categories of ethnographic writing (quasi ethnographies) formulated largely so that my house of ethnographic classification can be ritually swept clean.

My use of the folksy term "tales" to refer to ethnographic writing may seem somewhat curious to readers. I use the term quite self-consciously to highlight the presentational or, more properly, representational qualities of all fieldwork writing. It is a term meant to draw attention to the inherent story-like character of fieldwork accounts, as well as to the inevitable choices made by an author when composing an ethnographic work. This does not, of course, imply that ethnography is mere fiction or that the whole world must be put between quotation marks. I only mean that writing is something writers do, and it stands at least one-off from what is written about. There is no direct correspondence between the world as experienced and the world as conveyed in a text, any more than there is a direct correspondence between the observer and the observed.

One final qualification. While classification can scarcely be avoided when one is faced with empirical variation, there are perennial dangers that lie in the application of any classification scheme. Always there is the uneasy feeling that the categories are too broad, too encompassing, indeed, too categorical. Here, for example, the categories of writing treated as mutually exclusive can without great difficulty be set against materials that deny classification. In this sense, the ethnographic genres covered in this book are best thought of as ways of working, of telling, of writing, of doing ethnography. They are embedded in the practices of the ethnographer and not the text (which can mix genres) or the person (who can work in several genres). Ethnographic writing is far more complex, overlapping, ambiguous, and multifaceted than it is sometimes made to appear in this book. Ethnographic tales of one sort are, for example, often nested inside tales of another sort, and shifts of narrative convention are common in many ethnographies.

All this is to suggest that my classification of ethnographic tales is a loose one. This is not a book of lists. My categories are simple and illustrated by only a few examples in the main text and a few more in chapter footnotes. The idea is to evoke a category, not exhaust it. Readers may fill up my classification scheme differently than I do, and writers may object to the slots I place them in. I can only say that I am more interested in organizing and directing thought about the ways ethnographies are written than I am in collecting categorical examples and arranging them unequivocally. Simplicity and the compressed reality that accompanies any attempt at broad classification are things the reader must endure throughout this tale of tales.

Notes

1. There is, of course, enormous variation in just how this mandate is carried out. Not all fieldwork is of the full-time or long-term sort (Foster, 1979; Adler and Adler, 1987a). Occasionally ethnographic reports appear as retrospective accounts of a distinct period in a researcher's life not marked off at the time as fieldwork (Riemer, 1977). There are also failed projects wherein the envisioned fieldwork role was, for numerous reasons, never created or, perhaps more commonly, the "write-up" never completed. The range of fieldwork plans and experiences is no doubt empirically quite wide (regarding the time spent, involvement, interaction, observation, reporting, etc.). My focus here, however, follows the myth-like versions of fieldwork given in the text, recognizing it as more of a standard toward which a good number of fieldworkers aim than as a hard-and-fast rule. See also Pelto, 1970; Pelto and Pelto, 1973.

2. I use the term "exile" self-consciously, although the bulkier phrase, "self-initiated exile" is probably more apt. Behind the term, however, lie two implications. First, fieldwork is not of an ethnographic sort when it is pursued by a team of social researchers as a sort of expedition or Foucault-like panopticon observation-and-interview project. Fieldwork of an ethnographic kind is authentic to the degree it approximates the stranger stepping into a culturally alien community to become, for a time and in an unpredictable way, an active part of the face-to-face relationships in that community. Alternative fieldwork models exist (e.g., Miles and Huberman, 1984; Douglas, 1976), but they are not in accord with the methodological values and ideology of ethnography. Second, the term "exile" implies that fieldworkers are often those who, for a variety of reasons, display some discomfort with their own culture (of origin, of profession, of work, of life-situation, of residence, etc.). Perhaps this is more of an issue when "fieldwork at forty" (or fifty, or sixty) is considered

than "fieldwork at twenty." What, for example drives the comfortably positioned, middle-aged, tenured university professor to the physical and social trials of a year or more in the field? The answer is, if frequencies are our guide, very little. Recidivist fieldworkers are notable by their exception. When such rash acts do occur, one may assume there are pushes as well as pulls. Using the adjective "marginal" to describe the men and women who do fieldwork refers to more than one culture (Freilich, 1970; Gans, 1982).

3. The book of Genesis in the fieldworker's bible is Malinowski (1922, chapter 1). Other classical descriptions of the method of participant-observation are Radcliffe-Brown, 1958; Junker, 1960; Bruyn, 1966; McCall and Simmons, 1969; Becker, 1970. As discussed later, these works stress the observational side of the definitional coin, downplaying the researcher's active participation, involvement, and interest in the life worlds studied. The ideal attitude assumed in some of the older descriptions of fieldwork is that of a cultural scientist who is empathetic with those studied but essentially detached from their concerns, a sort of "blushless Promethean observer," to use Boon's (1982:47) wonderful phrase. This view has lately come under some fire. See Johnson, 1975; Douglas, 1976; Schwartz and Jacobs, 1979; Rabinow, 1977; Clifford, 1983b; Silverman, 1985; Crapanzano, 1986; Tyler, 1986; and Adler and Adler, 1987a.

4. Not so very long ago, it seems, fieldworkers had a reputation for being humdrum, prosaic, pallid, altogether pedestrian, and not at all prone to flights of analytic fancy or angst (Sharrock and Anderson, 1980). Today, as we shall see, fieldworkers are as prone to self-doubt as anyone else and willing to say so. Much of this doubt centers on the question of just what (if anything) constitutes an adequate cultural description. In anthropology, for example, pitched battles are fought on this issue between and among members of any number of theory groups—cultural materialism (Harris, 1979); ethnoscience (Goodenough, 1971); functionalism (M. Douglas, 1966); various forms of structuralism (Sahlins, 1976; Levi-Strauss, 1966), symbolic anthropology (Leach, 1976), and so on. Similar controversies rage on across several sociologies (Giddens, 1979; Swidler, 1986). Issues revolve partly on the role the native's understanding is to play in cultural accounts and partly on how it is to be displayed. Some claim it is absolutely essential (and decry their apparent inability to be both native and non-native at the same time). Others are less convinced and prefer to take cultural theory as a point of departure (and decry the apparent lack of interest in comparative ethnography). A good treatment of some of the varieties of cultural analysis is found in Wuthnow et al., 1984.

5. Currently there is growing interest in the rhetoric of social science writing (e.g., Nelson and McCloskey, 1986; Edmondson, 1984). A nifty analysis is Gusfield's (1981:83–108) masterful and precise unpacking of the rhetoric of psychologists out to convince readers of the effects of demon rum on highway fatalities. See also Becker's (1986a:121–35) remarks on how society is represented in sociological writing. An all-purpose introduction is Mitchell's (1981) collection of essays on narrative conventions. Other helpful writings include Nisbet, 1976; Brown, 1977; and Mulkay, 1985.

6. Bruner (1986) provides a sharp example of how the implicit narrative structure surrounding ethnographies of Native American cultures shifted radically in the post–World War II years. Prior to the war, Bruner notes that the dominant story both Indians and ethnographers told was one in which the past was glorified, the present disorganized, and the future promised assimilation. After the war, this melting-pot tale rapidly lost credibility, and a new narrative emerged in which the past was viewed as exploitation and the present resistance, and the future promised ethnic resurgence. Bruner's point, beyond the fashionable character of narrative structure, is that informants and fieldworkers come to share the same stories and may, in fact, select one another on the basis of such compatibility. When both informant and fieldworker are members of the same larger society, this sharing may be amplified. See also Turner (1981) and White (1973) on how historically determined narrative structures penetrate various kinds of descriptive accounts.

7. By examining culture only as it appears in the writing of ethnographers, I obviously neglect culture as portrayed by native and student alike in photographs, films, videos, performances, pottery, theater, and documentary art. I also ignore culture as it appears in history, fiction, folklore, literary criticism, and oral history. All these forms, like mathematical models and statistical tables, I regard as distinct from ethnography. There is some slippage of late in the traditional boundaries, as Geertz's (1983:19–58) widely read essay on "blurred genres" suggests. Some of these issues are brought up again in chapters 5 and 6. The use of still photography to accompany ethnographic writings is perhaps the most common overlay. Its evocative power is seen most starkly in Agee and Evans (1960) and is used to fine effect more recently in Harper (1982). Typically, however, the curious black-and-white photos tucked into many ethnographic texts serve merely to attest to the writer's presence among the studied while disguised as visual aids. Becker (1986a: 221–317) provides a most enlightening discussion of the sociological meanings and uses of photography.

8. This point is too important to the rest of this book to let slide. It

rests on the growing recognition that we cannot represent others in any other terms but our own. Culture, from this perspective, is less a discovery than a construction within which the method and methodology are inseparable. "Being there" remains consequential to ethnographers, but it is now regarded as far more problematic than in the past. While we continue to glory in the messy, in-the-same-world, no-time-out character of fieldwork, how to translate this intimate experience into a piece of writing that is neither pat (formulistic) nor pointless (atheoretical) has become a most disturbing question for fieldworkers. Cultural description is still a worthy objective but such description, as currently argued by scholars in many disciplines, can not erase the presence of and role played by emotion, presupposition, and artistry in ethnography.

2

In Pursuit of Culture

Thou shalt not sit
With statisticians nor commit
A social science.

W. H. Auden

To write an ethnography requires at a minimum some understanding of the language, concepts, categories, practices, rules,
beliefs, and so forth, used by members of the written-about group.
These are the stuff of culture, and they are what the fieldworker
pursues. Such matters represent the ways of being and seeing for
members of the culture examined and for the fieldworker as a student of that culture. The trick of ethnography is to adequately display the culture (or, more commonly, parts of the culture) in a
way that is meaningful to readers without great distortion. The
faithful hold that this depiction must begin with intensive, intimate fieldwork during which the culture will surely be revealed.
The method and its corresponding belief system have a distinguished, perhaps glorified, history.

This history can be approached in several ways. My choice is
to handle ideas about fieldwork as they emerged in anthropology
and later in sociology as two relatively separate streams and to
merge them only at the end. This is something of a convenient
fiction, for there has always been a good deal of interaction between anthropology and sociology. The reader should recall that
many American and British universities until the 1950s linked the
two disciplines under a common administrative head (Haskell,
1977; Mitchell, 1968; Tax, 1955). More tellingly, fieldwork has
resisted the sort of codification and specialization that is characteristic of social science, and such resistence has, as we shall see,
prevented the collapse of discourse between the two disciplines. In

a very real sense, the aims, means, and problems of sociological and anthropological fieldwork remain quite similar despite spectacular differences between (and among) the cultures they study.

The Practice of Fieldwork

In anthropology, fieldwork alone sets the discipline off from other social sciences. A lengthy stay in an exotic culture (exotic, that is, to the fieldworker) is the central rite of passage serving to initiate and anoint a newcomer to the discipline. Things weren't always so clear. Many anthropologists were once stumped for an answer, in the early days of ethnographic fieldwork, as to why a promising student would bother to go squat on an island for a couple of years and gossip with the natives. There was, as it were, more important theoretical work to get on with at home. If wanderlust were the issue, better to island-hop and increase the range of one's knowledge than to remain in one place like a talkative but unproductive native (Kuper, 1977; Stocking, 1983).[1] Ethnographic fieldwork is not an idea that hatched overnight.

While records of ethnographic fieldwork are sometimes traced to the unknown sources of the Greek historian Herodotus, modern versions of fieldwork did not begin to emerge until the nineteenth century (Lowie, 1937; Harris, 1968; Penniman, 1974; Clifford, 1983a). Fieldworkers, however, were not the only strangers in the worlds they studied (Clifford, 1980). A problem faced by the early (and self-conscious) fieldworkers was how to set off their own work as different in kind from the writings of other travelers who also wrote about what they saw and heard. A member of the pioneering *Societés des Observateurs de l'Homme*, Joseph-Marie Dégerando, solved this problem in 1800 by noting: "The first fault we notice in the observations of explorers on savages is their incompleteness; it is only to be expected, given the shortness of their stay, the division of their attention, and the absence of any regular tabulation of their findings" (Dégerando, [1800] 1969:65). While the beginnings of professional enthography seem close at hand in this quote, fieldwork as the method of ethnography continued to lag behind other techniques at the ethnographer's disposal.

Taking part in large-scale scientific expeditions provided one means for acquiring cultural data. Anthropologists, along with natural scientists, cartographers, explorers, missionaries, and miscellaneous other travelers from the West, shipped out, Darwinlike, in the mid-nineteenth century to study cultural diversity face to face. The idea was, of course, to classify and compare societies like plants and animals and to note how a single culture evolved from the savage to the civilized (Stocking, 1968, 1987).[2]

A more popular method was, however, the armchair mode of cultural investigation, a form that allowed the mostly British anthropologists of the day to remain at home and conduct their studies on the basis of reading about faraway places and peoples. Reading materials were plentiful, for colonialism, military stealth, trade expansion, tourism, missionary zeal (and guilt), simple adventurism, and of course scientific expeditions provided numerous documents and reports for the anthropologist to ponder. More critically, pen pals were available for the armchair theorist who preferred the convenience of the local post and library to the headwaters of the Amazon.

Through correspondence, inquiries became focused, as homespun theories on the origins of modern life were developed and used to discipline various data-collecting efforts. Pen-pal arrangements were aided by the guidebook, *Notes and Querries in Anthropology* (first published in 1874 with the subtitle *for use of travellers and residents in uncivilized lands* and regularly revised, without the subtitle, into the mid-twentieth century). The idea behind the guide was to arm the armchair theorist's pen pal, the so-called man on the spot, with a set of questions to ask native informants (Stocking, 1983). The goal was to standardize the slabs of information gathered by the men on the spot that were sent home to be digested by real anthropologists who had the proper comparative tastes and hence higher sensibilities.

Other variants of early fieldwork were scaled-down versions of the original, big-production, scientific expeditions. These jaunts ("summertime trait surveys") were led by trained anthropologists seeking to quickly survey different cultural groups within a targeted region. A development of note was W. H. R. Rivers (1910) and his handy "concrete method" (essentially an eliciting technique for gathering genealogical data in the *Notes and Queries* fashion). This self-proclaimed breakthrough was designed to accelerate and deepen fieldwork, thus advancing the Science of

15

Culture. The advance is nicely put in perspective by Stocking (1983:88) with a period image of the Culture of Science: "(Rivers) on the deck of the Southern Cross interrogating an informant through an interpreter during one of the brief stops on its mission circuit."

By 1920 anthropologists, restless at home, were coming to the field in greater numbers—but only to the borders. Whether aboard a ship or living for a short time in a mission house or colonial outpost, the borderland ethnographers of the day sought raw, unvarnished facts of native life while maintaining a good deal of social distance from the intimacies and hassles of that life. Labeled "verandah anthropologists" by later colleagues as an insult, fieldworkers of the period collected statements from informants (usually paid) according to a logic they brought with them to the setting. Soon, however, the call would come for them to relinguish their shady salvage operation and enter into the native villages where "real life" was surely to be found (Kuper, 1977).

The point here is that ethnography as initially practiced was hardly dependent on the personal experiences of the writer going eyeball to eyeball with the Bongo-Bongo. Ethnography was either a speculative form of social history carried out by anthropologists who for the most part remained seated in their writing workshops, or it was carried out as a canonical count-and-classify social science based on a stiff form of interviewing. It was in either case shot full of imposed cultural concepts and categories, uninterested in the patterns of everyday life, and grounded almost entirely on what people said, not what they did.

The turn to personal experience or "open-air" ethnography is credited in Britain to Bronislaw Malinowski, a Polish anthropologist, who, under house arrest by the British and conveniently confined to the South Pacific for the duration of World War I, found himself tenting alongside the natives of the Trobriand Islands for several years (M. Wax, 1972; Stocking, 1983). In America, Franz Boas is credited with bringing fieldwork to ethnography and pushing the anthropologist from the university into the life worlds of those about whom they wrote (Lowie, 1937; Clifford, 1983a). The crucial contribution of both men was to urge students to stop relying on second-hand reports for the analysis of culture (native or pen-pal) and to go to the field themselves to collect their own data.[3]

By the late 1920s fieldwork and the image of the scientifically trained fieldworker stalking the wily native in his natural habitat had become the cornerstone of anthropology.[4] One current version of the goal of fieldwork is, in Geertz's (1974:30) precious but clever phrasing: "To figure out from what the native says and does, what the devil he thinks he's up to, the result being an interpretation of the way a people live which is neither imprisoned within their mental horizons, an ethnography of witchcraft written by a witch, nor systematically deaf to the distinct tonalities of their existence, the ethnography of witchcraft written by a geometer." While Geertz's interpretive blends and aims are not always acceptable to all anthropologists, his means are certainly taken for granted (to figure out from what the native says and does). The method, in short, demands the ethnographer's presence in the culture of study.[5]

Sociologists too have something of an authorized history of fieldwork.[6] Most versions begin with the late nineteenth century social reform movement in Britain and note the intense social survey and systematic observation methods used by figures such as Sidney and Beatrice (Potter) Webb to document the "unseen" conditions of London's poor (Keating, 1976; Emerson, 1983; Bulmer, 1984). In the United States, W. E. B. Dubois surfaced as an early fieldworker who, using a structured set of questions, interviewed his subjects while living among them and wrote a monograph as an assistant professor of sociology at the University of Pennsylvania called *The Philadelphia Slum* (1899). Such studies were, however, infrequent. The fieldworkers of the day lingered in the sweatshops and lodging houses of the day only as long as it took to ask a hasty question of two. It took another generation and a change of soil before what Adler and Adler (1987b) call the "flowering of fieldwork" burst forth.

The Chicago School (of urban ethnography) is usually regarded as the main force behind sociological fieldwork. What Jules Henry (1963) calls "passionate ethnography" emerged at the University of Chicago just before the Great Depression as Robert Park, W. I. Thomas, Ernest Burgess, and others pressed their students to begin exploring the city as if it were a remote and exotic setting. Students were to bring anthropology home by learning of the vigorous, dense, heterogeneous cultures located just beyond the university gates.[7] The method stressed direct participation in these cultures and the discovery of the particular. One early student at the university recalled: "(Park) made a great point of the difference between knowledge about something and acquaintance with the phenomenon. This was one of the great thrusts in Chicago, because people had to get out and if they wanted to study opium addicts, they [had to go] into the opium dens and even smoke a little opium maybe. They went out and lived with the gangs and the hobos and so on" (quoted verbatim in Downes and Rock, 1982:37).

Emerson (1983) notes that Park, like Boas, forced his students out of their classrooms and into the field. Yet the guidance from one's elders seems not to have gone much beyond that offered to the novice anthropologist of the day. In both disciplines, fieldwork was thought to be something one learned best by doing. Another student, Nels Anderson, revealed that the single instruction he ever remembered hearing from Park was simply: "Write down what you see and hear; you know, like a newspaper reporter" (quoted in Kirk and Miller, 1986:40). Presumably from such accounts of seeing and hearing sociologists, like their first cousins in anthropology, would come to know what the devil their natives were up to.

Similar to the appeal of open-air anthropology, Chicago-style sociology offered its followers an attractive alternative to the usual survey, documentary, interview, or theory-building work that then marked the discipline (and to a large extent still does). The urban ethnographers educated at Chicago took to the field not so much for scientific reasons, however, as for more quintessential American ones: Muckraking (to expose the lies and hypocricies of the Exaulted Ones in society) and Reform (to improve the lot of the Downtrodden). This may not be what kept them in the field over the years, but it is what put them there in the first place (Rock, 1979; Mullins, 1973).

Much of the early Chicago work, while not exactly scoop reporting, did carry a hard-boiled documentary thrust. Park was a former newspaper man who had great faith in the self-evident meanings of facts reported in straightforward ways. There was concern for "digging for data" so that the "real story" could be told. The representation of social reality was seen as technically unproblematic once the facts had been unearthed. Social facts consisted of the stories recorded and the events witnessed by a fieldworker, and when these words and deeds were packaged neatly by a writer, they told of individual lives that were shaped by large social forces, yet were rich in cultural and individual detail. Little need was felt to do much more than gather and arrange the materials, for they would, in Park's view, speak for themselves (G. Mitchell, 1968:154–63).

Community studies were one of the two forms of ethnography encouraged at Chicago. These projects sometimes resembled domestic versions of the expedition and survey work of early anthropologists—in which a team of social researchers descended on a town to gather as many facts as they could in the relatively short time they had available. Lead investigators might live in, but their jobs were not to hang out and gossip with the natives, but to direct the research and write up the results. The initial set of community ethnographies had a good deal in common with the verandah visions of the anthropologists (see, for example, Thomas and Znaniecki, 1918; Lynd and Lynd, 1929; Warner, 1941; and West, 1945).[8]

The second brand of homegrown ethnography was more in line with Park's dictum to get out into the city on one's own and see what was happening. The call was taken up by many students, and by the late 1930s a number of ethnographies had been written about what would become the bread and butter of sociological fieldwork—"deviant subcultures" (Rock, 1979; Bulmer, 1982). Members of the down-and-out groups in Chicago became the wily natives stalked by sociologists and inscribed in early ethnographies. The natives included Sutherland's (1937) professional thieves, Cressey's (1932) taxi dancers, Thrasher's (1927) urban gang members, and Anderson's (1923) hobos. A good part of this work was interview based (the "life history method" as the sociological equivalent of the anthropological "concrete method"). These interviews were, however, of an intensive and serial sort, accomplished in natural settings, and usually accompanied by close observation, if not participation, in the settings—pool halls, brothels, street corners, tenements, mission shelters, bars, union halls, and so on.

A transitional figure at Chicago was Everett C. Hughes, who widened the Chicago approach both by his personal example (Hughes, 1928, 1970) and by his encouraging students to look beyond the dispossessed in American society to the more comfortable and powerful (Champoulie, 1987). Dissertations bearing Hughes's stamp during the 1940s and 1950s examined, for example, the medical professions (Hall, 1944; Solomon, 1952), public school teachers (Becker, 1951), funeral directors (Habenstein, 1954), policemen (Westley, 1951), business executives (Dalton, 1951) and machinists (Roy, 1952). Investigators of these worlds approximated the archetypal anthropological fieldworker of the open-air mode by getting as close to their subjects as possible and then, more problematically, staying there.[9]

They had in this regard the blessing and protection of Hughes, who grumbled frequently about the bifurcation of anthropology and sociology, convinced that the separation of the two led to the "dehydration of sociology" (Hughes, 1960, 1974). Dehydrated or not, sociological fieldworkers managed to carve out an ethnographic niche for themselves within the discipline. Although now well dispersed, the Chicago School still represents a sort of mythical Eden to many contemporary sociologists who locate their personal pedigree and purpose in the profession by tracing back their lineage on the family tree planted in Chicago.

The niche in sociology for ethnographic fieldwork is, however, a small one. Fieldworkers trickled out of Chicago slowly, and the spread of its aims and method has been uneven and sporadic. Ethnographic fieldwork has never come close to achieving the celebrated status in sociology that it has in anthropology. Part of the reason rests in the distinctive social organizations of the two disciplines.

Sociologists have developed a status hierarchy and division of labor where the top rungs are occupied by social theorists who build broad conceptual models for others to test and modify in humble social settings. These models are supposed to predict and explain patterns of thought and action across cultural domains. But fieldworkers have trouble coming up with patterns in their own quite delimited cultural domains, and when they do, these patterns appear quite unique and specific to a setting. So field-workers represent, at best, marginal contributors to a discipline interested in grander matters (Stinchcombe, 1984; Rock, 1979). Things are not always so cut and dry, of course, for a number of fieldworkers have achieved high and honorable status within soci-ology. But as a rule status flows toward the theorists of the field, not toward the workers of the field.[10]

Anthropologists, once lured into the bush by Malinowski and Boas, never developed a similar hierarchy or division of labor. Culture remains sui generis for anthropologists, so the authori-tative interpretations of cultural matters are restricted in range and remain in the hands of the fieldworkers who write the eth-nographies. Such a state reflects, no doubt, sociological and anthropological differences regarding the kinds of substantive findings that are of interest in the field (i.e., except for kinship studies, anthropological ethnographies denote spectacular differ-ences among cultures, thus making controlled and direct com-parisons across studies unlikely, if not uninteresting; Needham, 1984), as well as the emergent theoretical commitments of the two disciplines (i.e., one to description, the other to explanation; Giddens, 1979).

The Same but Different

While I usually lump together fieldwork of the anthropological and sociological traditions in this book, the reader should not be lulled or dulled into thinking there are not disputes between and within fields as to what the method implies. The most fundamen-tal distinction is that anthropologists go elsewhere to practice their trade while sociologists stay home. Reworking the classic bon mot of Sahlins (1979): sociologists study the West, anthropologists get the rest. This brute fact has a number of implications.

Sociologists, by and large, focus their work on urban contexts that are literally close to home and where there is no alien tongue to awkwardly master. The culture of interest is at least partially known at the outset of a study. Anthropologists, despite some no-table repatriation, still do a good deal of their work in small, re-mote, semi-isolated social systems, spending long periods of time (often including lengthy revisits) in close, trusting contact with

21

the studied. Sociologists can commute to work in their Volks-
wagens, while anthropologists must arrive at and depart from
their work sites on 747s, with suitcases, not briefcases, in hand.
The former can (and do) more easily shift research sites and topics
time and time again; the latter usually remain tied to the same
general domain for a career as area specialists in a region, culture,
language, and people. History is reducing these contrasts, but to
some degree the distinctions still hold.[11]

Consider, too, the way ethnographies are received in their
respective fields. In sociology, ethnography is regarded as a low-
budget, modest, somewhat odd, but more or less respectable
product that is rather peripheral to the field and its goals. In
anthropology, ethnography is the field, its central rationale for
being. In both domains, however, fieldworkers are not much concerned with comparative matters; they are content, for the most
part, to limit their domains of interest to topics particular to the
(arguably) discrete and bounded social worlds studied (Manning,
1987). That these topics and settings have something of an ad hoc,
opportunistic, and exotic-mongering flavor to them is a charge
fieldworkers have long tolerated with only an occasional counter-
charge (e.g., J. Douglas, 1976; Marcus, 1986).[12]

Writing styles enter into these differences too. Writers often
give away their disciplinary origins by the nature and feel of the
ethnographies they produce. For instance, there remain traces in
some sociological fieldwork writings of the reporter's legacy, a kind
of naturalistic zing, zest, and zeal that goes with cultural exposé
and critique. Anthropological writings, by contrast, often offer a
less urgent and more leisurely presentation, a literary style that is
perhaps more evocative and graceful than is characteristic of
sociology.

Part of this difference stems from the topical matters taken
up by the ethnographer. It is probably easier to establish a poetic
pace and vision when writing about initiatory rites or creation
myths than when writing about assembly lines or detoxification
centers. The ethnographic realms favored by sociologists are the
secular, economic, political, public, and instrumental aspects of
daily life. Ventures into the sacred, emotional, moral, private,
and expressive areas of life are common for anthropologists,

but for sociologists they are extracurricular flings (Gusfield and Michalowicz, 1984).

Another stylistic contrast rests on the broader literary license granted to authors who presume to speak for distant, preliterate peoples, whose habits, customs, logics, and languages are unfamiliar, unrecorded, and baffling to most readers. Literal translations of cultural practices in one society for readers in another would be gibberish. Anthropologists, then, must lean heavily on ideographic approaches and telling metaphors if they are to bring their materials home. Sociological ethnographers can get away with being less conscious of their use of language and metaphor, since they share with their subjects and readers the same general linguistic and cultural landscape (Lakoff and Johnson, 1980). Moreover, sociologists, caught in their own society, must write about matters over which they are, at best, dubious authorities and therefore subject to continual challenge (in both scholarly and lay circles). Informants, research advisors, friendly and hostile peers, journal editors, libel lawyers, governmental authorities, and suspicious members of studied groups may all know a good deal about the social worlds represented by sociologists in their writing. Little wonder that many sociological fieldworkers produce texts that seem, compared to their anthropological counterparts, restricted in range, full of jargon, and stuffed with remote facts, as if to satisfy some fetish of documentation or legitimation; they exhibit little interpretive nerve.

Ethnography Today

Too much can be made of such facile comparison. Sociologists are not always so tight and timid, nor are anthropologists always so loose and bold. The same sorts of contrasts can be made equally well within each field. And with the growth of adjectival ethnography (e.g., urban, medical, legal, organizational, educational, industrial), many of the stylistic distinctions are vanishing entirely as the topical and theoretical concerns merge in pursuit of the same culture. It now seems safe to say that there is at least as much variation in ethnographic writing within sociology or anthropology as there is between them.

Correspondingly, it is also safe to say that ethnographers in both disciplines now share the same broad notion that fieldwork is their defining method. Yet despite fifty years of practice and the cheerleading of Malinowski, Boas, Park, and Hughes, the method remains, in Lofland's (1974) terms: "sprawling, diffuse, undefined, and diverse. As a research genre, it appears (relative to other domains of social science) organizationally and technologically the most personalized and primitive." Few sociologists or anthropologists would disagree.[13]

Until quite recently, such "sprawling and primitive" appearances were hardly much of an issue for fieldworkers, except perhaps when they spoke with self-appointed "real scientists" (Agar, 1980). Fieldworkers knew what they were up to and had no great difficulty in talking to each other and training the handful of dedicated apprentices willing to try their hand at this style of social research. A few, like Margaret Mead and William F. Whyte, achieved prominent and heroic images in the eyes of the general public (if not their colleagues) on the basis of their presumed adventurous, hard-won knowledge of other cultures (Sontag, 1963; Mullins, 1973; Clifford, 1983a).

Today fieldwork, along with its subject (culture) and its product (ethnography), is undergoing something of a reawakening and expansion (Spradley, 1979). The distinctive, inquisitive, intimate form of inquiry called fieldwork is becoming increasingly popular outside its traditional disciplinary and relatively insular boundaries (Van Maanen, 1983b). However embarrassing the "sprawling and primitive" characterization may be to some, it is apparently not holding people back from trying out their hands.[14] For example, ethnographies are now found in such fields as political science, law, social psychology, medicine, psychiatry, social welfare, advertising, public administration, marine studies, communications, business administration, education, computer science (i.e., "expert systems"), cognitive science, criminal justice, and policy studies.[15]

Ironically, this renewed interest in and enthusiastic embrace of fieldwork by the hoi poloi outside the temples of ethnography is occuring at the very time sharp critical questions are being raised by the high priests inside the temples. A good deal of this questioning is, as we shall see, directed not at fieldwork as an honorable method of study or at culture as a venerable object of study, but at the product itself, the ethnography, as a puzzling and sometimes profane result of experience-based study. The problems of my concern in the rest of this book are not with culture or fieldwork per se, but with the ways each are represented to readers by writers of ethnography.

Readers of Ethnography

Writing is intended as a communicative act between author and reader. Once a manuscript is released and goes public, however, the meanings writers may think they have frozen into print may melt before the eyes of active readers. Meanings are not permanently embedded by an author in the text at the moment of creation. They are woven from the symbolic capacity of a piece of writing and the social context of its reception. Most crucial, different categories of readers will display systematic differences in their perceptions and interpretations of the same writing.[16]

To produce an ethnography requires decisions about what to tell and how to tell it. These decisions are influenced by whom the writer plans to tell it to. Ethnographies are written with particular audiences in mind and reflect the presumptions carried by authors regarding the attitudes, expectations, and backgrounds of their intended readers. All texts aim at arousing the interest on the part of some more or less distinguishable flock of readers. Of course, different flocks are possible and can include any (or many) real (or imaginary) social categories such as anthropologists, sociologists, scuba divers, Presbyterians, communists, cops, Californians, effete snobs, or accursed youths.

The categories of readers an author recognizes and courts help shape the writing. In this sense, the narrative tricks the ethnographer uses to claim truth are no less sophisticated than those used by the novelist to claim fiction. Writing of either sort must not mystify or frustrate the audience an author wishes to reach. Mistakes, of course, are not unknown, as is the case when authors are puzzled by the critical reactions their books receive or, more commonly perhaps, when authors are crushed by the lack of attention, critical or otherwise, their books receive. Nonetheless, ethnographers seek to attract particular readers, and who these people are thought to be is a matter of consequence for their writing.

The kind of readers I have in mind for this book are, for example, fairly easy to identify. Clues are everywhere. The preface provides a tidy statement plus a fine list of my friends who have already read the book. Typological clues are on every page. The language and jargon I use, plus the reference-and-footnote games I play, suggest that I expect readers to be more familiar with Thomas and Thomas (1928:579) than John 3:16. Nor do I expect my readers to be lovers of textbooks, for I have tried to avoid the pseudo-objectivity and impassive compendium of well-accepted facts that mark such works.

Consider also the fullness of the empty sign. What is not in this book is as revealing as what is. There are no tables, charts, equations, pictures, inserts, underlinings, or joyless questions at the end of each chapter. This tells readers a good deal of what I think of them. The point is simply that as an archetypical author working in a fairly well specified and small field, I have a pretty good idea of just who my readers are likely to be, and this influences what I write.

So too with other writers. The broad, usually rather flattering (and self-enhancing) image authors hold of their audience helps determine what is put in and what is left out of their ethnographies. Three main, but highly generalized, readership groups can be discerned for ethnography.[17] While all three readership groups may pounce on an unusual text, few, if any, are written with such eventualities in mind.

This book, for example, is written for readers that represent the first of my three categories, Collegial Readers. They are the ones most likely to get my drift (and jokes), and it is their opinion of this work that matters most to me. Yet, danger lurks here since I write to a whole damn lot of colleagues. There are obviously finer-grained distinctions to be made here. By and large, I write for those colleagues I know and whose judgments I have come to trust. This is a small group, but one that is, I pray, representative of colleagues whom I don't know.

Writers also have images of those categories of readers to whom their work is not addressed. In my case, these are the second (Social Science Readers) and third (General Readers) categories. Both types are, of course, more than welcome to turn these pages, and I would hardly be displeased if sales reflected such an unlikely event. But the fact of the matter is that if I tried to write for either of these audiences I might well lose the attention of my collegial readers. The ethnography that makes the shelves of the mall or airport bookstore will not have been designed for colleagues, although they may well buy and enjoy it (turning green in the process). Conversely, the ethnography written for colleagues will turn up in B. Dalton's only by mistake. Consider, now, some of the ways the marketplace of readers influences the writing of ethnography.

Collegial Readers

Fieldwork literatures are no doubt followed most avidly by field-workers. As with all forms of academic publishing, academics comprise the bulk of the market. Fieldworkers are the most familiar with the ethnographic past and present and are the most concerned with its future. They are therefore the most careful and critical readers of one another's work. They are also the audience most aware of ethnographic norms within the special areas of their concern and as a result are likely to have firm ideas as to what are good and bad practices as conveyed by the text (Marcus and Cushman, 1982). Such house norms are both emergent and debatable, of course, but writers who violate them must explain in print why they did so or risk being dismissed by their colleagues familiar with the area and topics covered by the writing (Stinchcombe, 1984).

For the close collegial crowd, jargon is often an important part of an ethnographic text. Jargon works, however, in curious and sometimes paradoxical ways. Its use not only represents a writer's claim to membership in an identifiable research club, but also abbreviates matters of concern for well-versed members of that club. Examples are not difficult to come by—"grounded theory," "impression management," "social drama," "informants," "ritual order," "indexical rules," or even the seemingly perverse practice of prefacing many nouns with the phrase "the social construction of." Used carefully, these terms and phrases convey fairly stable,

27

technical, and precise meanings to knowledgeable readers and help to locate a text and, more importantly, the writer within a given tradition of ethnographic practice and interest.

Used carelessly, jargon obscured, covers up, and otherwise hides from view matters that might well be ambiguous, poorly understood, or contestable. The danger that lurks within ethnography written for an audience of specialists is that both reader and writer become overly dependent on the mercy of their mutual jargon and are therefore freed from thought. Jargon can become an exclusionary tool and can operate as an ideology as colleagues emulate one another to differentiate themselves from the rest of the crowd (Becker, 1986b:26–42). To those left out, such writing is chilly, masturbatory, restricted by design, and directed only to the already-tenured of a special-interest club.

The jargon trap is seductive. It is a way to strike a pose as a smart, well-versed, current member of a hot and influential in-group. But more than one hot and influential in-group within ethnographic circles has become over time a cold and impotent out-group, having fallen victim to its own increasingly beloved but self-deceptive wordsmithing. At present, ethnomethodologists seem as determined to write themselves out of existence with phrases like "artfully extrusive reflexivity" as did kneejerk Marxists some time ago with their signature phrases such as "bourgeois hegemony of monopoly capitalism." Such abstruse jargon repels the uninitiated, and a circle closes in on itself.

Beyond jargon, the fellow-fieldworker crowd is concerned with matters of technique, definition, coverage and scope, levels of generalization, and the informing analytic apparatus and claims that surround and comprise ethnography. Some of this may be tacit—assumed in the written document—but nevertheless such matters will surely be read into the report by this audience. Fieldworkers most familiar with a writer's subject (such as similar topical or area specialists) are most sensitive to the text. Insofar as these readers are concerned with a writer's style, it is, as Marcus and Cushman (1982) suggest, clarity and detail that matter more than literary quality or textual inventiveness. These latter refinements may even be seen as getting in the way of a presentation, as when ethnographic writers are taken to task by colleagues for being overly cute or too concerned with establishing their own style.

Substantive and theoretical frameworks are also closely attended to by readers who are also fieldworkers. Lofland (1974) develops an amusing but telling set of categories by which collegial readers are said to judge the adequacy of sociological field reports in terms of their overall perspective, novelty, use of examples, and interpretive slant. Extremes on any of these dimensions may cause disfavor in readers. For instance, examples of bad practice in Lofland's terms include the "intro-text" style of reporting, where a cliché such as "the immediate situation facing social actors affects behavior" is used to frame a set of observations; or the "moral style," where the fieldworker collects episodes of good and bad behavior on the part of the group studied and uses the list to praise or pillory the group.[18]

More generally, what Lofland emphasizes are those relatively stable community standards used by fieldworkers to assess the interest value and "contribution" of other fieldwork reports. It is no surprise that such judgments often relate to a writer's balance between abstraction and concrete example. An ethnography should be empirical enough to be credible and analytical enough to be interesting. Too little or too much of either is presumably deadly.[19] Moreover, both must be fresh to the reader rather than be set against all-too-familiar theory and turf.

Finally, when the theoretical or substantive materials in an ethnography do not in themselves excite the fieldworker-reader, the report may still be of interest for its use of language and textual organization—as contrasted to all those other reports the fieldworker-reader has already read. Here craftlike standards can be invoked in appreciating how the writer chose words to weave the reported facts into the framework or theory that is used and developed in the text. Even when the subject matter is well outside a reader's professional scope, the language of the text and its organizing structure may generate considerable interest if it offers a new style (Marcus and Cushman, 1982). Concern for the arrangement and literary quality of ethnographic reports appears to be growing among fieldworkers.

Social Science Readers

Readers from outside fieldwork traditions look to ethnographers for the information they supply on the group studied. This audience treats fieldwork as merely a method among methods, and while normally respectful of the work, this audience judges it by how well it informs their own research interests. These readers are not reading ethnography in order to be entertained, challenged, or enlightened about the nature of social science. They wish only to be informed about certain facts the fieldworker has unearthed. The raw number of facts relevant to the social scientist's area of interest will usually provide the basis for the evaluation of the work. Interpretive flights of fancy by the fieldworker-author are likely to be of little interest, and any doubts or self-questioning on the part of the writer may be grounds for dismissing the entire work (Marcus and Cushman, 1982).

But while an ethnography may be crammed with details and facts, it also conveys an argument and an informing context as to how these details and facts interweave. Ordinarily, social scientists take only the raw empirical material of an ethnography and ignore the arguments that surround and give meaning to the facts. This is irksome to fieldworkers. Becker (1986a: 130–31) notes that ethnographies are sometimes treated by sociological theorists as mere "files to be ransacked" for answers to questions the fieldworker may well deem inappropriate. Sometimes, of course, the burglars are colleagues and the infighting is fierce. Fieldworkers are probably less bothered by the out-of-town social science burglar than they are by burglars who come from their own neighborhood. Yet social scientists who dismiss ethnographies embroiled in family disputes as "invalid" often fail to note that the family squabble is less about the facts than it is about who should interpret them. The recent controversy surrounding Freeman's (1983) reinterpretation of Mead (1928) is an excellent example in this regard (see Marcus and Fischer, 1986: 158–61).

Social scientists are perhaps most uncomfortable with the broad methodological and epistemological questioning of ethnographers. While modest, marginalized, and low budget, ethnography does have an established niche—in the so-called descriptive wings of social science. Ethnographies are looked to for facts surrounding low-visibility, little-understood, deviant, or otherwise out-of-the-ordinary cultures.[20] Any controversy over what fieldwork is about or over the meaning of its findings will annoy readers who believe they already know what fieldwork does best (Clifford, 1986b). Frustration and the proverbial I-told-you-so attitude are familiar responses of these readers to any reported crisis in ethnographic circles. Moreover, any change in the form of fieldwork reporting is disturbing to social science readers, and with the reaction often comes the refrain, "it doesn't read like an ethnography."

In essence, the social scientists who sometimes turn to ethnographic literature to fill out their own studies are seen as a rather unsophisticated bunch by fieldworkers. They are occasionally regarded as dolts who want only to exploit ethnography for evidence to support (or demolish) some theoretical position well outside the fieldworker's area of interest and expertise. There is increasing sensitivity among fieldworkers about how their work is handled by others, and, as mentioned in chapter 1, such sensitivity is influencing how ethnography is being written.

But this is not a one-way street. Some social scientists are coming to appreciate ethnography in a new light, and certainly not all who read and need the literature wish to rifle the files or judge the work by older, now suspect, standards. Increasing use of qualitative methods akin to fieldwork in a number of fields has resulted in a more sophisticated social science audience than has generally been the case in the post-Malinowski era. Ironies abound as well. Fieldworkers often search the social science literatures for ideas to help fill out their own work. When they do, the originators of those ideas may feel that their ideas were used ineptly.

General Readers

Fieldwork occasionally becomes visible to a large, nonspecialist, or lay audience. Ethnographic materials can exhort, entertain, instruct, or madden a general readership looking for a message in the written word. Fieldworkers writing for such an audience become storytellers, and the allegorical nature of ethnography becomes salient (White, 1981; Clifford, 1986a). Readers look to familiar formats—the traveler's tale, the novel, the adventure story, the investigative report, and past ethnographic classics—when

31

appraising the writing. The ethnographer charged with being a novelist manqué by colleagues or other social scientists is probably the ethnographer with the largest number of readers.

The issue of good and bad writing is pertinent here because often the ethnographers with large audiences are seen by their colleagues to have moved on to something that is not quite ethnography. Writing for readers who need no special background (other than curiosity, informed or idle) reduces the weight of collegial criteria. Breaches of the house norms of cultural representation are common in ethnographies aimed at the general reader—and may, in fact, be necessary if the larger audience is to be drawn into and take pleasure from the account. Colleagues may find it difficult to honor such writing. Because certain norms have been ducked, the work is seen as "sloppy," "imprecise," "gushing," "pandering," "romantic," or, simply, "low-grade."

Collegial carping is sometimes about the breadth of the work. Ethnographies aimed at the general reader may seem wasteful and inefficient to colleagues who may already know a good deal of what is in them. Yet writers, not knowing precisely what will appeal to a diverse cross section of readers, must put more into their accounts than would be the case if they were aimed at a smaller and more predictable set of readers. They need to show cultures rather than to analyze them. Complaints about the simplified, watered-down, or shallow character of popular works are also common among colleagues. But these charges may be answered in the same way as the charges about breadth.

Attracting a general readership involves more than coverage and apparent simplification. Two other features are worthy of note. First, the ethnography must be relatively free of jargon (although a little is necessary to help establish genre typification and authorial expertise); and second, it must present materials a well-read but ethnographically unsophisticated audience would regard as interesting. The second requirement is much tougher than the first, but there are ways. One in particular stands out.

Much popular ethnography focuses on social settings and worlds that are deviant or otherwise exotic relative to (idealized) modern, Western, middle-class ones. The often-heard slogan that ethnography is "a way of learning about our own culture from examining other cultures" is applied most readily to ethnographies of a general sort. Materials that contrast sharply with the presumed background knowledge the general reader brings to the text are put forth as attention grabbers. Other cultures—at home or abroad—are presented as comparisons to the reader's own or as contrasts to what the reader may well take for granted or expect to be true of the culture studied.[21] Irony, gentle or brash, is typically the highlight for the general reader of ethnography, who learns, contrary to prejudice, of the "rational savage," the "superstitious scientist," the "emotional bureaucrat," the "moral thief," the "tribal executive," or the "faithless priest."

Such portraits, however, point to a final troubling concern. General readers are by definition in no position to judge the accuracy of these ironies by collegial standards. Among specialists of the trade there is always a nagging fear that whatever has mass appeal may also be unreliable and misleading, if not downright false and dishonest. Fieldworkers worry that literary standards such as those surrounding fiction or journalism provide no protection against conjuring and superficial work. Validity, from this perspective, can be judged only by fellow professionals, familiar with a specialized literature and following the agreed-upon standards of the day.

There is some truth here, but probably not as much as many ethnographers would like to believe. Literary standards are different, but they are not shabby or second-rate. When taken seriously they may require even more from an ethnographer than those formulated by the profession. Fidelity, coherence, generosity, wisdom, imagination, honesty, respect, and verisimilitude are standards of a high order. Moreover, they are not exclusionary ones, since those who read ethnography for pleasure and general knowledge are as able to judge whether they are achieved as those who read for professional development. Ethnographies that reach such standards in the minds of many readers are certainly far fewer than those that obtain collegial standards. They are not less worthy.

The Moving Hand . . .

In contrast to the increasing specialization and narrrower audiences of some of the social sciences, the general audience for carefully drawn but public domain ethnography seems to be growing. Powerful and influential writers such as Clifford Geertz, Claude Levi-Strauss, Mary Douglas, Erving Goffman, Kai Erickson, Edmund Leach, Victor Turner, Marshall Sahlins, and Rodney Needham, along with some prominent ancestors who had popular acclaim (e.g., Margaret Mead, Edward Sapir, Georg Simmel, Ruth Benedict, Gregory Bateson, and Everett Hughes), have achieved highly visible positions on the intellectual and literary stage. Wide latitude is allowed these authors for imaginative and poetic renderings. Good writing is characteristic of these figures, and it is of a kind that goes well beyond the competent ethnographic writing read by the more specialized audiences. Artful ethnography is evocative in addition to being factual and truthful. Since the descriptions and interpretations given by many of these authors are so vivid and convincing, attention to literary style and writing quality in general is heightened among ethnographers (Clifford, 1986a).[22]

Such attention raises the question among fieldworkers and their audiences as to whether ethnography (of any sort) is more a science, modeled on standardized techniques and reporting formats, or an art, modeled on craftlike standards and style. These are questions we will encounter more than once in this book, and they are questions that cut to the bone when ethnographic writing is considered. At this point, suffice it to say, the sacred power of observation alone has faded (i.e., fieldwork is now seen as more of an interpretive process than a simple visual or auditory one); the view that ethnography is transparent has given way to an appreciation of the narrative features of the text (i.e., all writing that tells of one thing necessarily tells of another); and truth as judged by some external, invariant standard is untenable when applied to ethnography (i.e., all truths are partial and contestable).[23] Many of the more literary writers who aim for a general audience are now providing a vision of a more subtle, stylized, complex, and in many ways open-ended ethnography than that of the past. It is a vision that is proving attractive.

Many of these shifts in ethnographic reporting are the result of an increasing interest by fieldworkers in the social philosophies of hermeneutics and phenomenology, philosophies that blur, if they do not demolish, the subject-object distinction so central to traditional ethnography.[24] It should be clear in the chapters to follow that I do not regard fieldwork as the simple observation, description, or explanatory technique that radiates from the older, objective, laws-and-causes view of human behavior. These matters are covered in various sections of the book, but for now I should note that my stance is opposed to the power of positivist thinking, since I regard the relation between the knower and the known to be a most problematic one and anything but independent in cultural studies. This is a phenomenological war whoop declaring that there is no way of seeing, hearing, or representing the world of others that is absolutely, universally valid or correct. Ethnographies of any sort are always subject to multiple interpretations. They are never beyond controversy or debate.[25]

NOTES

1. Sociological fieldworkers are still asked similar questions by contemporary colleagues, some of whom regard fieldwork as a kind of low-rent, day-labor or night-shift task compared to the high-tech analytic rigors of examining cross-classified survey data by log-linear methods. Stinchcombe (1984) suggests that part of the status gap results because the people fieldworkers study keep bewildering them by failing to act in the ways they are supposed to act according to sound sociological theory. Normal science fails in such situations, and reseach products such as dissertations take longer to write than is typical of other research products in the area. Certainly turning fieldwork experience into a sociologically acceptable problem and argument is a tortuous process that is almost sure to leave some sociological readers dissatisfied. There are broad truths here, but context modifies all generalization, for there are some sociological encampments, as Stinchcombe also observes, where to not do fieldwork brings disgrace. Although they rarely fill a department, symbolic interactionists typically carry the fieldwork load in the discipline (Blumer, 1969; Rock, 1979).

2. The idea that culture takes many forms, not just one, is a modern one, even in anthropology. Early writers on distant peoples treated culture as something some groups had lots of and the other groups had little or none. The former were "civilized" and the latter "savage." Applied anthropology in its pre-modern days sometimes meant offering savages culture in the form of European-style clothes, Christian beliefs, or monetary economies. It sometimes meant murdering savages in the name of progress, as the story of the extinction of the Tasmanians so painfully il-

lustrates (Stocking, 1987:274–283). For those attached to a singular model of culture, the convenient standards of advanced civilization almost always turn out to be their own. Vestiges of these ideas remain in contemporary discourse as well. A singular model of culture, for instance, allows us to separate the high arts from the low. Crude biblical or evolutionary justifications are rarely heard these days but, rest assured, our in-house savants of high culture are unlikely to grant much respect to such cultural products as Andrew Wyeth paintings, romance novels, or nude mud wrestling. If they are noticed at all, they will be treated as debased and vulgar cultural forms, valued only by those who do not know better (the "uncultured"). All cultures, of course, have specialists who seek to define what is proper, just, and good. Social scientists seem just as drawn to these salubrious roles in this culture as drama critics, sportswriters, or personal advice columnists.

    3. This is not to say that either Boas or Malinowski was an exemplar of modern fieldwork practice. Boas, who went to the field earlier than his British counterparts, stubbornly refused to interpret or much analyze the voluminous data he gathered over a lifetime and on his death left a massive collection of virtually uninterpretable data. And tireless as he was, he rarely spent more than a short time ("flying visits") in most of the cultural settings he visited (Rohner, 1969; Stocking, 1968:195–233; Stocking, 1974:88–128). Malinowski, as his scandalous diary (1967) suggests, brought some very strong opinions to bear on some rather flimsy evidence. Nor did he apparently much like or respect the Trobriand Islanders he studied. M. Wax (1972) makes the point that Malinowski ("Mistah Kurtz") never much practiced the method his worshipful students went to the field to emulate. Stocking (1983:107) notes, for example, that it takes a very keen reading of *Argonauts of the Western Pacific* (1922) to realize that this "man of songs" to islanders always remained sitting on the beach when the Kula expeditions ventured forth. A good deal of what he wrote about he never witnessed. There are important nuances to the stories of both Boas and Malinowski—both personal and historical. Nor should we be too harsh on these founders of modern fieldwork. Not only did they leave work of lasting value, but they compelled their students to take their good advice, not follow their example. From Malinowski came the advice: The fieldworker must spend at least a year in the field, use the local vernacular, live apart from his own kind, and above all make the psychological transference whereby "they" becomes "we." (See Kuper, 1977:1–36; Stocking, 1983:70–121). From Boas came the advice: The fieldworker must collect the traditional materials (folktales, myths, etc.) from informants in a face-to-face situation and record it in their native tongue. Such "texts" will reveal with special

clarity the culture of a people and eliminate the unavoidable distortions any visitor brings to cultural description (Stocking, 1974:85–86).

4. The male pronoun is used purposely here. With some notable exceptions, most ethnographic writing was created by male fieldworkers concerned mostly with the comings and goings of male natives (Roberts, 1981; R. Wax, 1979; Weiner, 1976; Colde, 1970). Of late, some revealing methodological work in sociology is surfacing that is explicitly concerned with how gender roles are negotiated in the field and with the influence such roles have on the researcher's experience in the field (e.g., Hunt, 1984; Thorne, 1983; Horowitz, 1983; Easterday et al., 1977; and Warren, forthcoming). One result of the growth of feminist scholarship is the realization that there are many tales of the field to be told (see Atkinson, 1982; M. Rosaldo, 1980; and M. Rosaldo and Lamphere, 1974).

5. This section carries what is mostly the well-documented story of British anthropology. In America the pre-Boasian anthropology was marked by similar sorts of expeditionary, pen-pal, and survey forms of fieldwork (Stocking, 1968, 1974; Diamond, 1980; Lowie, 1937). The "savages" of interest were, of course, what were left of the Native Americans after the West was won. This gave a greater sense of urgency perhaps to American fieldworkers, who for a time put great store in the salvage and preservation aspects of their work. Hinsley's (1983) account of Cushing and Fewkes among the Zuni in the late nineteenth century is instructive in this regard. The most famous salvage and preservation project of early American anthropology was probably the documentation and display of "living ethnography" that followed the so-called discovery of Ishi in 1911 (Kroeber, 1961). There is also an object or specimen-oriented version of early anthropology that emerged in France long after the short-lived *Sociétés des Observateurs de l'Homme* of Citizen Dégerando in 1800. A number of rather parasitic fieldwork expeditions to Africa mark the late nineteenth and early twentieth century period. The image is provided by Marcel Griaule, a sort of Indiana Jones character, whose aim in going to the field was to bring back the goods, not the stories or the kinship charts, belonging to the people studied. The museums of the period in Paris wanted artifacts, and the French adventures in fieldwork were organized with such collections in mind (Clifford, 1983b). The history of anthropology is a swiftly developing field. Interested readers should consult Stocking's important annual volumes beginning in 1983, as well as his recent *Victorian Anthropology* (1987).

6. My treatment of anthropological and sociological fieldwork, if read by professional historians, might be dismissed as Whiggish; a contemptuous label applied to narratives that judge the past in terms of the present and embody the idea of history as a tale of progress. Whiggish

histories are common in science writing where the standard myth of science, called "textbook cardboard" by Gould (1987:5), suggests that the past is ever more inadequate the further back we go. Textbook cardboard versions of fieldwork history ignore context in favor of a sort of Great Leader perspective in which certain fieldworkers win acclaim on the basis of personal daring, hard reason, and the use of techniques that overcome the fact-generating flaws and faults of their forebears. Predecessors are often viewed as overly timid, biased, and remote; informed by antiquated speculation, not sound data. The fieldwork history put forth in this section has something of a Whiggish slant. But, as will become apparent in later chapters, this history is not meant to suggest that those fieldworkers treated well here are in any way the White Knights of truth and enlightenment. Each figure is a purveyor of a particular view of fieldwork that is rooted in social time and space. All, by rhetoric, equate their views with rationality and rectitude. Most of those mentioned found their views accepted—at least until the new generation laid them low. Yet it must be said that none of these perspectives came about as a direct result of simple induction from unambiguous fact. Their views are based as much on vision and vanity as on actual practice and product. While historians have long recognized the false, misleading, self-serving, and mythologized character of the villains-followed-by-heros view of science, their message has been slow to seep through to fieldworkers and their students.

7. Sociologists had considerable help in this regard from their anthropologists cousins at the university who included, at various times, such figures as Robert Redfield, Ralph Linton, Edward Sapir, W. Lloyd Warner (eventually to become a born-again sociologist) and, from across the ocean, Radcliffe-Brown. In many respects, the Chicago School was an interdisciplinary affair and must be regarded as one of the most productive joint ventures in the history of anthropology and sociology. Good histories of the Chicago School (largely from the sociological perspective) include Anderson, 1983; Blumer, 1984; Caven, 1983; Matthews, 1977; Platt, 1983; Carey, 1975; and Faris, 1967. Anthropologists have been silent on these collaborative endeavors at Chicago.

8. The Lynds' (1929) study of Middletown (Muncie, Indiana) is a good example of some of the difficulties sociologists encounter when borrowing anthropological visions of communities as islandlike, functional wholes. Soon after the Lynds' original monograph appeared, Middletown began to prosper as the country emerged from the Depression. When the Lynds returned ten years later, they found a very different community whose internal dynamics were "no longer" isolated from the surrounding society (Lynd and Lynd, 1937). Malinowski late in his ca-

reer came to regard his failure to examine the European influence in the Trobriands as his greatest professional shortcoming (Kuper, 1977:34). So did many of his students. The refusal of communities to remain motionless before and after their portraits are sketched is a problem that has continued to plague fieldworkers.

9. Hughes's advice to fieldworkers was not much different from Park's. Roy (1970:49) recalls: "Hughes taught us to sally forth with pencil and paper and notebooks, like newspaper reporters, to observe and question." Ironically, the masterpiece of sociological fieldwork was not produced in Chicago, but in Boston by William F. Whyte while he was a fellow at Harvard (although carrying Chicago credentials). *Street Corner Society* (1955) is in many ways the sociological equivalent of *Argonauts of the Western Pacific* (1922), and several generations of students in sociology have emulated Whyte's work by adopting his intimate, live-in, reportorial fieldwork style in a variety of community settings. There have been many successes (e.g., Liebow, 1967; Suttles, 1968; Gans, 1962, 1967; Berger, 1968; Hannerz, 1969; and recently Halle, 1984).

10. Another aspect of this matter depends on the stature of the groups and institutions studied. Most sociologists would not object to being regarded by colleagues as the cultural specialists of the Congress, the judiciary, the stock market, or even the Boston Celtics. These same sociologists, however, would probably cut their wrists before wanting to be known as the cultural specialists of refuse collection, housework, transvestism, soap operas, or professional bowling. There are apparently few ways to escape what Harrison Trice (personal communication) calls the "courtesy stigma" that attaches to fieldworkers operating in socially polluted domains. "You are what you study" seems to hold here, and it has a degree of contaminating power for sociologists. Such stigmatization is less likely among anthropologists—although many outsiders still regard the anthropological fieldworker as an exotic-mongering romantic who seeks only to don a loincloth and dance by the fire with savages to the beat of the Tom-Tom.

11. I rely on Manning's (1987) breezy but helpful review of fieldwork norms. He would no doubt add to my list of differences the rather inflexible roles available to anthropologists in the field (as obvious outsiders), versus the more flexible roles available to sociologists (who can if they choose conduct their studies under a variety of covers, some covert). He also notes that the Chicago School mentors encouraged students to do research on cultures with which they were already familiar—as current or former members. This latter feature of early sociological fieldwork has become something of an anathema to anthropologists and sociologists alike, who now regard previous experience in the group under study as

potentially tainting and distorting, since the domain of interest is, to an unknown degree, preanalyzed (Spradley, 1979). Malinowski (1922:1–25) also scorned such an approach.

12. Marcus (1986) claims it was anthropology's long fascination with the exotic that led to its marginalization as a discipline within the social sciences. Others suggest that it was precisely this focus that led to its prominence in the first place (Clifford, 1980, 1981). Perhaps with the demise of the exotic native as found in the wilds of the Columbian jungles, and the rise of the exotic native as found in Times Square, the coast of California, the fern bars of Washington, DC, or among the dynastic rich of Grosse Point, anthropology can finally come home. Repatriation seems to be picking up these days. See, for example, Schneider, 1968; Wolcott, 1973; Jacobs, 1974; Edgerton, 1979; Spradley, 1970; Perin, 1977; Spradley and Mann, 1975; Latour and Woolgar, 1979; Gamst, 1980; Myerhoff, 1980; Mars, 1982; Agar, 1973, 1985; Mars and Nicod, 1984; and Konner, 1987). Marcus and Fischer (1986:111–36) provide an interesting account of some of the troubles at-home anthropologists face.

13. This is not to say that fieldwork practices have remained fixed since Malinowski or Park. There have been modest changes in emphasis and style, and some of these are covered later in the book. In general, the trends in fieldwork style have been toward increasing intimacy and participation in the studied culture. For example, existential elements are now attached to Chicago School traditions (Douglas, 1976; Douglas and Johnson, 1977). Rather than being asked to keep their intellectual wits about them and maintain a reserved stance toward members of the culture studied, fieldworkers are being asked by some to become, in Adler and Adler's (1987) phrase, "fully participating members," in order to grasp experientially the meanings and emotions that go with membership. Manning (1987:chap. 1) provides a useful review of some of the changes that have occurred in American sociological fieldwork circles.

14. One of my favorite theoreticians, Yogi Berra, provides a line that partially describes the current situation. "It's so crowded," said Yogi of a New York restaurant, "no one goes there anymore." In the context of current fieldwork practice, the present wave of self-trained and self-styled ethnographers (such as myself) may be somewhat disturbing to keepers of the disciplinary faith who may worry that the new barbarians of fieldwork will destroy a precious method and ruin a reputation that has taken decades to construct. There are probably some grounds for this concern. But like Yogi's theory, such concern also smacks of more than a little elitism. In unvarnished form it suggests that only those who have suffered the rigors of the right training should be allowed to write the sacred texts

on priest-approved topics. Backyard ethnography has not often had the approval of priests, although changes are now afoot.

15. More disconcertingly, the recent sprouting of adjectival ethnography also reflects the bad times that have befallen anthropology and sociology as disciplines within the university. Shrinking enrollments, budgets, faculties, and programs drive fieldworkers and their students (both current and prospective) into safer and more rewarding harbors. There is, in other words, push as well as pull, and fieldworkers are now offering their skills within a tight job market. This is said with some shame, but no guilt, by one who currently practices his trade in the management school at MIT—an institution whose anthropology department numbers six faculty and whose sociology department is missing. Whether or not the disciplinary downslide and displacement of ethnography will eventually bottom out and reverse itself is anyone's guess. I'd rather not guess just now and I interpret the current enthusiasm for backyard ethnography in as optimistic a light as possible. See again Marcus and Fischer (1986:111–36).

16. This section touches briefly on reader response or reader receptivity theory. Iser (1978) and Fish (1980) provide good introductions to this broad field and provide lucid accounts of why some literary critics are shifting their focus from writers and their polished texts to readers and their loosely coupled "interpretive communities." This is a most promising development for it suggests that the meaning of a given object only emerges from the interaction of the symbolic properties of that object and the cognitive categories of those who experience the object. Thus, the meanings of such things as books, plays, cars, clothes, and legal tender vary not only by the objects themselves but by the cultural understandings carried by the groups that encounter and use such objects. A neat example of this approach in sociology is Griswald's (1987) analysis of the critical reaction in different countries to the novels of West Indian author George Lamming. Her findings argue that lasting works of fiction are marked by a divergence of opinion as to the meaning of the tale but leave little doubt among readers as to what actually occurs in the tale itself. This perspective is similar to Levine's (1985) notion of the "irresolvable ambiguity" associated with coherent social theory. I assume throughout this book that meaning is indeed fabricated by the interaction of reader and text, and I will argue in the closing chapters that good ethnography always allows for open and multiple interpretations across readers. But, I hasten to add, this is a book about writing, not reading, and I therefore pass quickly over the issues of reader receptivity.

17. I draw here on the sixfold classification of readers of ethnography put forth by Marcus and Cushman (1982). Since I wish to include a

41

broader audience, not simply anthropologists, my categories are more general than theirs.

18. Bad behavior is certainly less fashionable in ethnographies than good behavior. Indeed, collegial expectations hold that fieldworkers should come to appreciate, if not admire, the thoughts and actions of their informants. Displays of sympathetic understanding are quite common in fieldwork reports. The house norm seems to be one in which the fieldworker not only represents, but also takes the side of the studied and thus becomes something of an official voice for their aims, ambitions, and general perspective on the world (Becker, 1967). Rather than discrediting the ethnography, advocacy often adds to its believability. When actions that readers might regard as atrocious are presented in an ethnography, the writer is normally careful to provide a good-people-caught-in-a-bad-situation account of such conduct, or, perhaps more frequently, the writer quickly makes relative whatever standards the reader might be bringing to the text by arguing the logic of such conduct from the native's point of view.

19. Lofland (1974), presumably with tongue in cheek, suggests the proper balance for the adequate field report to be between 30–40 percent theory and general discussion and 60–70 percent data and presentation of examples. Such a standard has its appeal, although what it might mean to achieve such a balance is a matter very much context and topic specific. One can imagine, for example, an ethnography in which the ideas seem too diffuse or lacking in structure, yet the way to right the balance may have less to do with adding empirical examples to the narrative than with further development of a cogent argument and an informing theoretical perspective.

20. Sociological fieldworkers have long been considered by their social science colleagues as students of "nuts, sluts, and perverts" (zootsuit sociology). Anthropologists, while treated somewhat more charitably, have also been characterized as students of "witch doctors, savages, and wild tribes" (pith-helmet anthropology). Neither view has much truth to it, since both fields are remarkably specialized and cover a great variety of theoretical, methodological, and substantive interests. This is an image problem that apparently won't go away. It is, however, a problem that helps to keep fieldwork in its place and out of the mainstream of social science (Marcus, 1986; Rock, 1979).

21. A problem with many of these striking contrasts is that the comparative work on which they should logically rest is nonexistent. The domestic culture that serves to set off the "exotic" practice of a faraway people is known only in loose, informal, commonsensical ways based largely on the writer's knowledge of his own culture. There are perhaps

some general middle-class American values, beliefs, and practices, but these are never studied very carefully by the writer who draws on them to make certain points. Margaret Mead's (1928) work is instructive, since the sexual liberties apparently enjoyed by the young Samoan women she studied were thought to be in sharp contrast to the repression facing their American counterparts of the time. Marcus and Fischer (1986:158–60) suggest that had Mead paid as much attention to what young women in America were up to as she did to her Samoan informants the implied contrast might well have collapsed. Similarly, when sociological field-workers point out, for example, the aggressive, violent, and materialistic culture shared by some ace gang members in an urban ghetto, they imply that the rest of us don't belong to that culture. Yet the rest of us are known in only the most general, taken-for-granted ways. The contrast rests on cultural conceits and secondary sources, not firsthand fieldwork. The same is true when sociologists allow more explicit normative criteria to serve as a backdrop for an ethnography, as when officials are taken to task for not accomplishing the objectives for which they are formally responsible. One response of readers to such indignation is "so what else is new?" Indeed, what may be lacking in sociological studies is one careful ethnography where people actually do what they say they do and official goals are met. Without such studies, to know what is normal (or even obtainable, much less desirable) seems most troublesome. Problems such as these may be more apparent in mass-appeal ethnography but they are certainly not unknown in the professional literature.

22. By powerful ethnographies I mean those that attract and stick in the minds of general readers. These works typically strain collegial criteria, play with semi-sacred social science categories, and challenge but do not baffle general readers. Compared to other branches of social science, I think ethnography harbors a disproportionate number of fine writers who possess uncanny abilities to formulate and develop arguments, find appropriate analogies and metaphors for their support, are felicitous in their choice of words, and allow for multiple interpretations of their writings while somehow retaining a coherent story line. Part of this distinctive prose style may be due to a sort of practice-makes-perfect experience because ethnographers must sit daily before their writing desks slavishly developing fieldnotes before tackling their ethnographies. If only for self-amusement perhaps their writings grow self-conscious and innovative. Another part may be due to the model of science followed by most ethnographers, a model that does not glorify simple, general systems subject to experiment, prediction, and quantification. Ethnographers usually prefer a model of complex, unique systems subject to situational logic, interpretation, and narration. Since most ethnographers have no holy

rite called the Scientific Method to defend or have not made a fetish of quantification, their writing is often more accessible to general readers since they apply nonspecialized, universal tools of intellect to the analysis of their distinctive materials.

23. Close studies also reveal the discourse-based, partial, and contested nature of truth in the natural and physical sciences. In our post-Kuhnian world, facts seem bloody difficult to come by. See Latour and Woolgar (1979), Knorr-Cetina (1981) and Lynch (1985) for some hard facts about real science.

24. To get into matters of social philosophy would take us too far afield. It must suffice to call the roll: Dilthy, Gadamer, Habermas, Husserl, Schutz, Rorty. Readers interested in the emergence of what some call the "interpretive turn" in social thought, particularly as it influences what fieldworkers think and do, can consult Clifford and Marcus, 1986; Agar, 1986; Clifford, 1983a; Dreyfus and Rabinow, 1982; Rabinow and Sullivan, 1979; and the call to arms, Geertz, 1973.

25. To be fair, the interpretive approach and the accompanying rejection of positivism proclaimed in this polemic passage arise out of more than the philosophical heads of some heavy-duty European thinkers. The switch in the social science from behavior to cognition as the center of attention has not passed unnoticed by ethnographers (Geertz, 1983: 73–93). Of equal importance, perhaps, is the growing sense within anthropology and sociology that much of the ethnography now produced is dull and irrelevant: ethnography as reduced to the steady accumulation of standard monographs on standard topics and the saying of similar things about increasingly similar groups (D'Andrade, 1986:25). Another complaint is aimed not so much at the cognitive bent or Tayloristic procedures and formats but at the "New Columbus Theorizing" that sometimes is used to give an ethnography its punch and mandate. Lofland (1987) uses this delicious phrase to label those explanatory frameworks fieldworkers sometimes dream up to encase a routine ethnography of a much-studied group. His point is a good one and suggests that once a previously unknown world has been mapped out, fieldworkers who then journey to this world face a different set of intellectual tasks and problems that those who went first. Namely, they must correct, specify, and elaborate on what is already known rather than simply stuff what is already known into a novel framework (i.e., old wine in new bottles). All of these matters are interconnected. Chapter 3 examines some of the discontent surrounding classical ethnography, a form of representation I call "realist tales of the field."

3

Realist Tales

You observe a lot watching.
 Yogi Berra

By far the most prominent, familiar, prevalent, popular, and recognized form of ethnographic writing is the realist account of a
culture—be it a society, an occupation, a community, an ethnic
enclave, an organization, or a small group with common interests.[1] Published as a set of volumes, a scholarly monograph, an
article, or even a subsection of an article (or book), a single author typically narrates the realist tale in a dispassionate, third-
person voice. On display are the comings and goings of members
of the culture, theoretical coverage of certain features of the culture, and usually a hesitant account of why the work was undertaken in the first place. The result is an author-proclaimed description and something of an explanation for certain specific,
bounded, observed (or nearly observed) cultural practices. Of all
the ethnographic forms discussed in this book, realist tales push
most firmly for the authenticity of the cultural representations
conveyed by the text.

There are at least four conventions that mark a tale as realist
and set off the work as a distinct product, different from, say, traveler's tales, fiction, journalism, or most critically, other forms of
ethnographic reporting. These writing or representational conventions are, of course, social ones, the result of the lengthy and
often contentious struggle to put ethnography on the intellectual
and literary map, as discussed in chapter 2. Moreover, each convention is currently undergoing slight-to-massive revision. In essence, the criteria for what counts as a good cultural account do
not stay the same over time any more than the cultures represented by these writings stay the same over time. Neither convention nor culture can, therefore, be settled once and for all.

Experiential Author(ity)

Perhaps the most striking characteristic of ethnographic realism is the almost complete absence of the author from most segments of the finished text.[2] Only what members of the studied culture say and do and, presumably, think are visible in the text. The fieldworker, having finished the job of collecting data, simply vanishes behind a steady descriptive narrative justified largely by the respectable image and ideology of ethnographic practice. A good-faith assumption surrounds realist tales (Stoddart, 1985). At root this assumption of good faith permits readers to hold the attitude that whatever the fieldworker saw and heard during a stay in the studied culture is more-or-less what any similarly well-placed and well-trained participant-observer would see and hear. Ironically, by taking the "I" (the observer) out of the ethnographic report, the narrator's authority is apparently enhanced, and audience worries over personal subjectivity become moot.

Credentials are important for the writer since ethnography is increasingly a professionalized craft. Fieldworkers writing in the realist style take on something of an institutional voice. They are identified not as natives, of course, but as scholars with graduate training, academic affiliations, and impersonal disciplinary interests that legitimate access and inquiry within the target culture. In realist tales, fieldworkers are content to let their background as a trained and properly motivated fieldworker stand as a given and allow the relevant audience to judge the adequacy of the ethnography along contemporary, largely implicit, but, nonetheless normative lines.[3]

This suggests that a good deal of what is by and large the unproblematic quality of fieldwork authority rests on the background expectancies of an audience of believers. These expectancies rely, in turn, on the rather exemplary status of the fieldworker as a scholar or scientist, trained in the latest analytic techniques, allergic to the imprecise, and able to get to the heart of a culture faster, with greater sensitivity, than rank amateurs.[4] As Clifford (1983a) points out, however, this claim and its acceptance is no simple matter, since the status took some energetic and zealous fieldworkers many decades to achieve. The legacy of such culture heros as Boas, Malinowski, Firth, Evans-Pritchard, Margaret

Mead, Park, Whyte, Hughes, and Becker, among others, falls to current fieldworkers and gives their work a respectable and reasonable cast, provided their work looks relatively similar to what has gone before. Basically, the narrator of realist tales poses as an impersonal conduit who, unlike missionaries, administrators, journalists, or unabashed members of the culture themselves, passes on more-or-less objective data in a measured intellectual style that is uncontaminated by personal bias, political goals, or moral judgments. A studied neutrality characterizes the realist tale.

There have, of course, been changes in realist tales over time. In early ethnographic writings fieldworkers often went to some pains to document that they were, in fact, doing science, albeit adventurous and chaotic science, by using field data to both derive and test social theory.[5] Thus matters of the reliability and validity of the data assumed some importance. More recently, with the failure or, at least, the demise of positivist social theory and the increased importance of the problem of meaning, fieldworkers are more likely to cover their claims of realism on the more commonsensical grounds of naturalism and interpretive expertise; meaning essentially that only one who has actually "been there" in the field talking to and living it up (or down) with the natives could possibly understand what the natives are about and presume to interpret it for those who have not been there. In both cases, doing science or soaking up member meanings, the convention is to allow the fieldworker's unexplicated but assumed experience in the culture to stand as the basis for textual authority.[6]

So conventionalized has experience become as the ineffable grounds of ethnography that fieldworkers rarely say very much about precisely what experience in the field consists of, letting the representation stand for itself (i.e., "The X do this," not "I saw the X do this"). Thus realist tales swallow up the fieldworker, and by convention the text focuses almost solely on the sayings, doings, and supposed thinkings of the people studied. Materials are organized according to topics and problems relevant to the fieldworker's conceptual and disciplinary interests. The presence of the author is relegated to very limited accounts of the conditions of fieldwork (its location, length, research strategies, entrance procedures, etc.). This information is given in prefatory remarks, brief methodological segments clearly set off from the report, or the subtext commentary in footnotes. In short, the diary is effaced from the account. The body of the ethnography reads as statements about the people studied rather than what the ethnographer saw or heard (or thought) about the people studied.

Typical Forms

The second convention associated with realist tales is a documentary style focused on minute, sometimes precious, but thoroughly mundane details of everyday life among the people studied. The power of observation is often useful here because from the apparent attention to detail come organizing precepts presented as containers for such detail—rites, habits, practices, beliefs, and, generally, ways of life. More often than not, however, the precepts come not from the field but from the academic speciality from which the hearty fieldworker hails.[7]

Part of the flat, dry and sometimes unbearably dull tone of elaborate realist ethnographies is a result of this explicit focus on the regular and often-observed activities of the group under study. Observations of the mundane are plugged into more-or-less standard categories thought necessary within a subfield for cultural description (e.g., family life, work life, social networks, authority relations, kinship patterns, status systems, interaction orders, etc.). Occasional glimpses of the dramatic are allowed, but largely in the form of exceptions or contrasts to the commonplace. They drive home the overwhelming presence of domesticated patterns of thought and action among the people studied. Aside from the representative anecdote tossed out from time to time, little is told about the particular experiences of the people studied, but much about the categories or institutions that are said to order their lives.

Details are not randomly arranged in a realist tale. They accumulate systematically and redundantly to demonstrate some point the fieldworker feels is important. Details are in a sense precoded in a realist ethnography to serve as instances of something important, usually a structural or procedural unit (i.e., precept) the fieldworker has "discovered" in the field (or, more recently, developed by way of "readings" taken in the field).[8]

Realist tales also decry the abstract and celebrate the concrete reference. A vagrant in a realist tale is not simply a stock, unwashed character, but a "shabby, foul-smelling sort who is wearing a dirty torn overcoat exposing white hands that tremble noticeably." Or similarly, a dog is not simply a dog, but a "large, brown-and-white dog who jumps on people and answers to the name of Blue." Details suggest intimacy and establish presence (who else could know such things?). They are often used to try to draw the audience into the world of the people studied. The ghost of Charles Dickens enjoys the realist tale.

Immediacy and evocative readings are at stake when realist accounts are provided. The particularistic and ordinary details not only make denial of the fieldworker's authority difficult, but also, when piled on top of one another, present the "real life" of the observed. By focusing on the everyday and, presumably, for members of the studied culture, taken-for-granted and common activities, the ethnographer places a structure on the materials so that a typical vagrant, a typical dog, a typical marriage, a typical divorce, or, more to the point, a typical member of the culture can appear as a logical, if inferential, construct (Manning, 1982). Fieldworkers display the daily concerns of what Marcus and Cushman (1982) call "common denominator people." The actions and words of singular persons are minimized in realist tales in favor of what typical natives typically do, say, and think.

The Native's Point of View

Unlike a traveler's tale or an investigative report, an ethnography must present accounts and explanations by members of the culture of the events in their lives—particularly, if not exclusively, the routine events. This is a touchy business and one I will continue to consider throughout this monograph. For now it is enough to note that realist ethnographers are at pains to produce the native's point of view. Extensive, closely edited quotations characterize realist tales, conveying to readers that the views put forward are not those of the fieldworker but are rather authentic and representative remarks transcribed straight from the horse's mouth.[9] This is particularly true of current work.

A good deal of typographical play, stage-setting ploys, and contextual framing goes into presenting the native's point of view. More importantly, there are epistemological stunts to be performed on the ethnographic highwire. Such fancy footwork is rarely discussed by fieldworkers constructing realist tales. But as Geertz (1974) so persuasively argues, it is no longer adequate for a fieldworker to tell us what the native does day in and day out. We must now know what the native makes of all this as well. This is something of a Gordian knot for fieldworkers, but, nonetheless, realist tales are increasingly making room for more displays of members' thoughts, theories, and world views than in times past.

To do ethnography in the realist mode these days is to offer the perspective as well as practices of the member of the culture. Unlike the first two conventions, however, techniques for doing this follow a number of contested formats. Doing descriptions by orchestrating the voices of members of the culture is perhaps the most common form, along with the extensive use of cultural slogans, clichés, and commonly heard, setting-specific terms. Formal techniques have also been developed to help shape the native's point of view into something reportable. Ethnoscience is one popular method (Tyler, 1969; Spradley, 1979). Ethnomethodological enactments of sense-making practices of members of a culture is another (Garfinkel, 1965; Leiter, 1980; Lynch, 1985). Both are controversial.

The Boasian tradition of realist ethnography offers the native's point of view by means of translating the stories and myths of the members of the culture. When single informants tell their own stories, however, a degree of suspense and improvisation sneaks into the realist tale through the tales of others. Rosaldo (1986b) notes that by avoiding the composite accounts, retelling informant stories allow highly personalized and unique experiences to enter into the realist tale. This is, of course, a breach of realist conventions, and such breaches are typically few and far between, introduced perhaps to keep readers awake and the realist tale alive.

What, precisely, might be called the native's point of view is indeed subject to much debate in fieldwork circles. But rest assured, realist ethnographies all claim to have located it and tamed it sufficiently so that it can be represented in the fieldwork report. Whether this is done by simply allowing some natives to have their say (through the author's pen) or by various formal elicitation techniques, indigenous meaning systems have claimed a place in realist tales. In a sense the debate concerning the native's point of view now turns on how such a perspective is to be rendered in a text rather than on whether or not it belongs in one. Observation in this sense has given way to interpretation.

Interpretive Omnipotence

The final convention characterizing realist tales to be discussed here deals with the no-nonsense ways in which fieldworkers present their representations and accounts. In brief, the ethnographer has the final word on how the culture is to be interpreted and presented. The matter is put candidly by Malinowski, who, reflecting in his diaries on his feelings of ownership over the Trobrianders, wrote, "It is I who will describe them or create them" (quoted in Stocking, 1983:101).

Such a godlike pose toward those one studies is now fortunately rare, but equally rare are ethnographers who question aloud (or in print) whether they got it right, or whether there might be yet another, equally useful way to study, characterize, display, read, or otherwise understand the accumulated field materials. In fact a distinguishing mark of ethnographies outside the realist mode is the troublesome worries the ethnographers themselves make public regarding the accuracy, breadth, typicality, or generality of their own cultural representations and interpretations. Self-reflection and doubt are hardly central matters in realist tales.

The convention of interpretive omnipotence works in several ways. Sometimes a cultural description is tied to a theoretical problem of interest to the fieldworker's disciplinary community (or increasingly, subcommunity). Field data, in such cases, are put forth as facts marshaled in accordance with the light they may shed on the generic topic of interest and the fieldworker's stand on the matter. What Clarke (1975) calls "didactic deadpan" is the style that prevails in these ethnographies, in which the interpretations of the author are made compelling by the use of a string of abstract definitions, axioms, and theorems that work logically to provide explanation. Each element of the theory is carefully illustrated by empirical field data. The form is aseptic and impersonal, but it is convincing insofar as an audience is willing to grant power to the theory.[10]

Such power is enhanced, of course, if the theoretical system stems from honored and respectable figures and intellectual traditions—if it is an example of Marxian, Durkheimian, Freudian, Weberian, or Saussurean thought and their intricate, if unfathomable, connections. Selective packaging of field data to exemplify generalized constructs is a standard practice, even though the precise empirical situations in which the field data are developed are perhaps far less coherent or obvious than the concepts they serve to illustrate. The dividing up of a society or an organization into its functional, systemic, symbolic, dramatic, or other analytically required elements, as dictated by an acclaimed theory, allows the humble fieldworker to stand on the shoulders of giants (and see farther) by using well-received constructs as receptacles for field data.

Another fashionable device useful for establishing interpretive credibility works in almost the opposite fashion. Rather than relying on tall theoretical ancestors, the fieldworker rests his case on the members themselves. The situations that comprise the field data are presented conventionally as the events of everyday life. These situations, along with generalized renditions of the native's point of view, are collapsed into explanatory constructs, so that the fieldworker's analysis overlaps with, if it does not become identical to, the terms and constructs used to describe the events.

A final device is suggested by Geertz (1973), who argued for the jettisoning of "experience-distant" concepts in favor of those that are "experience-near." This signals something of a recent trend in realist tales: working with theoretical frameworks drawn from phenomenology, face-to-face interaction, discourse analysis, symbolic interactionism, semiotics, and other "theory of meaning" approaches. Grand theory, concerned with collective behavior, cultural function, social structure, or historical change, gives way to a communicative-interpretive theory, concerned with how people achieve common understandings. These theories are presumably much closer to the fieldworker's reach (and no less general) than the social system theories that held the interest of a previous generation of fieldworkers.

The point, however, turns not so much on the exact basis for claiming interpretive authority as on the mere fact that it is claimed. Realist tales are not multivocal texts where an event is given meaning first in one way, than another, and then still another. Rather a realist tale offers one reading and culls its facts carefully to support that reading. Little can be discovered in such texts that has not been put there by the fieldworker as a way of supporting a particular interpretation.

Marcus and Cushman (1982) suggest that these rhetorical features of ethnographic writing are exaggerated in the short monograph and article forms in which so much ethnography appears today. There simply is not space (or perhaps interest) for the underanalyzed or problematic. Only enough data are allowed in to support the analysis. Early ethnographies often appeared as multivolume texts worked up to account for the entirety of a given culture (partly as a way of demonstrating and building authority, displaying vast knowledge of a previously unknown culture, and in keeping with the scholarly fashions of the day). Because of their length and leisurely style, a massive amount of material could be included in them. Malinowski (1935), for example, put forth a good deal of material he must have regarded as beyond even his ken since he never even tried to interpret its significance. Boas (1973) was even more of an ethnographic nudist, preferring to display, not analyze, his collections of cultural materials.[11]

Current ethnographies are most frequently constructed by fieldworkers who make comparatively short visits to the field, confine themselves to highly selected aspects of the culture studied, and make tightly focused interpretations of definitionally-specific topics. This is partly a way of meeting the demands of contemporary academic careers, studying a relatively "thin" culture—as is often the case when the target group is organized at a level well below that of a society—or contributing to small, ever-splintering subdisciplines and applied specialities in the social sciences. Indeed, in much recent work, as Tyler (1986) suggests, a reader may find it hard to avoid getting the impression that an ambitious fieldworker is imposing a rather narrow and crude portrait on a reasonably subtle people.

Finally I should note that rarely is interpretive omnipotence candidly or overtly claimed in realist tales. It is simply a matter of closing off or nailing down an interpretation without allowing alternative views to creep into view. The narrator speaks for the group studied as a passive observer who roams imperialistically across the setting to tell of events that happen in this way or that.

For example, my own writings show "the police" doing, saying, and thinking things. Rarely do identifiable individual natives speak of such things except in notoriously supportive quotes. Footnotes and theoretical asides are orchestrated to support a particular interpretation, and when other views are presented they are given short shrift; they are merely foils representing mistaken and foolish perspectives. Realism in ethnography is a singularly splendid thing.

Producing Realist Tales

It is important not to judge realist tales too harshly. I am concerned here with writing conventions, not with substantive or (necessarily) theoretical ones. Realist ethnography has a long and by-and-large worthy pedigree. Writers in this tradition have created masterpieces that have lived very long lives. To subject the writing to scrutiny is not to say it is false or wrong. In fact the durability of some realist work indicates that despite the invisibility, high-science stance, or interpretive omnipotence of the author, the tale is fundamentally sound. When one considers the rapid promotion and demotion of theoretical works (and their authors) in the social sciences, many a realist tale appears as a rock of Gibraltar in an otherwise stormy sea. Consider, for example, the realist tales of Malinowski (1922), Evans-Pritchard (1940), Firth (1936), Whyte (1955), Leach (1954), Gouldner (1954), Dalton (1959), or Becker et al. (1961). While some of these works may seem a bit clumsy today, their authors have nonetheless produced powerful work which remains, decades later, engaging, vivid, stimulating, and somehow still true. [12]

Let me now provide some examples of realist tales from my own work as a way of showing how the conventions discussed above work in cold print. Unlike the masters just mentioned, I can make no claims about my examples being insightful, convincing, or particularly well conceived snatches of realist work. I do claim, however, they are representative of the realist style— particularly as it is employed by sociologists of a symbolic interactionist slant. My excuse for presenting these examples here is that since self-criticism and doubt mark the ethnographic tales discussed in the following chapters, it makes good sense to begin with some immodest realist examples of my own on which to later reflect.[13]

I begin with several excerpts on method and go on to a substantive tale dealing with sergeants in an American police agency. The ramblings on method are included not only as necessary background materials, but more importantly, as rather ordinary illustrations of how ethnographers represent their own activities in the field and carefully segregate these representations from the realist account itself.

(The) analysis that follows was based on the observation of novice policemen *in situ*. The study was conducted in Union City (a pseudonym) over a nine-month period in 1969–70. Approximately three months of this time were spent as a fully participating member of one Union City Recruit Class. Following the formal training phase of the initiation process, my fully participating role was modified. As a civilian, I spent six months riding in patrol units operated by a recruit and his FTO (Field Training Officer, charged with imputing "street sense" into the neophyte) as a backseat observer. From the outset, my role as researcher-qua-researcher was made explicit. To masquerade as a regular police recruit would not only have been problematic but would have raised a number of ethical questions as well. . . . The conversational data [are] drawn primarily from naturally occurring encounters with persons in the police domain. . . . While formal interviews were conducted with some, the bulk of the data contained here arose from far less structured situations. (Van Maanen, 1973)

Several realist conventions are at play here and are worthy of note. First, there is the already-mentioned severing of the method description from the ethnographic materials that follow in the text. The excerpt appeared in small print, clearly set off from the rest of the article under the title "Methods." Second, whatever existential features of the research world that surround the fieldworker in the setting are banished from its representation. The fieldworker is required by realist conventions to stand before what Punch (1986) calls the "bar of disciplinary standards" as a sober, civil, legal, dry, serious, dedicated, straightforward transcriber of the world studied. Finally, since fieldworkers regard their presence and techniques as potentially tainting the "natural state" of the studied scene, they must take care to invoke the widely approved means of neutralizing such threats. Participation in routine activies, time in the field, attention to spontaneous, overheard, ordinary, natural conversation are all used in the excerpt to suggest that the fieldworker's visibility eroded and whatever reactive effects the method provoked simply vanished over the time spent in the field. The thrust of this excerpt is that whatever is to be reported about the Union City police is completely independent of the fieldworker who is cast as a transparent looking-and-hearing machine. [14]

In a later publication, I amended the previous method note to include this:

Following my initial encounters in the field, I have been back to Union City on numerous occasions. Formal periods of study included six weeks in 1973 and ten weeks in 1978. Again, my methods of study were largely those of the cultural anthropologist, emphasizing direct, sustained, participant-observation and the repeated interviewing of key informants. Most of the data reported here stem from informal interaction with members of the police world as they attended to their ordinary work activities. Since I rarely used a tape recorder, the conversational data are only as accurate as memory and ear allow. (Van Maanen, 1983a)

Again realist conventions hold, although there are some additional cryptic remarks that expand the method. Notably, ancestors (cultural anthropologists) are now invoked to provide further legitimacy and a mandate for the fieldwork. A few more-or-less technical terms also appear, such as "participant-observation" and "key informants," thus embedding the fieldwork within a presumably common set of assumptions (held by both readers and author) as to its good form. Consider too that the informal and hence possibly inaccurate recounting of the conversational data to be featured in the report are casually mentioned as something of an afterthought. Ironically, the passing mention of a fallibility or two may help to establish the fieldworker's credibility given the enormous pretentions of the realist enterprise. Without some slight defect the fieldworker might appear too perfect and thus strain the reader's good faith.

As a final method note, consider the following Johnny-jump-up footnote tacked onto the station house sergeant materials to follow.

In this section, I draw on my own participant-observation work in a large, urban police agency (for methodological details, see Van Maanen, 1978b). I consider the agency a rather ordinary, unspectacular police department within which such general organizational practices can be easily investigated. I should note however that while I believe participant-observation produces some of the most interesting and evocative accounts of organizational life to be found in the literature, it also suffers from several significant flaws. In particular, the absence, in many works, of any consistent analytic framework has guaranteed much participant-observation work marginal status within organization theory. For all the Chandleresque prose and for all the authenticity and close detail, participant-observation is but a method in need of supplemental procedures. In the example of the text, I give testimony to the dangers of participant-observation by omitting any depiction of the larger social, political, and economic context within which police work is conducted. (Van Maanen, 1981a)

While stretching the boundaries of realist presentations, this example, like the two preceding ones, still indexes fieldwork practice in highly conventional ways (i.e., referring to separate method discussions outside the text, use of in-group fieldwork terms, and framing the work topically in terms of a search for particular instances of the general). Where it departs from tradition is when readers are asked to refrain from making too much of the forthcoming description. Presumably other perspectives count in matters described beyond those of the police as put forth by the author. As we shall later see, when the genre itself is questioned or ethnography itself becomes part of a larger canvas, realist conventions have slightly slipped from view and we may then be dealing with other forms of the ethnographic tale.

The last exhibit of realist work I present here is of a substantive sort. The excerpt is an unpublished one, although it closely corresponds to the lengthier published versions of the same materials (see Van Maanen, 1982, 1983a). My excuse for using the unpublished version is merely that it is short and relatively self-contained, and thus spares the reader some of the more punishing displays of realist writing, such as run-on details, too-clever phrasings, pretentious associations with grand ideas, and various stage-setting devices intended to perk the interests of fellow field-workers in the police studies crowd.

Hats-on Harry, Off-at-Seven George, Handle-It-Yourself Fred, and The-Eternal-Flame Edward Who-Never-Goes-Out

Among first-level supervisors in American police agencies are patrol sergeants. These men (and they are overwhelmingly men) differentiate their position from those of patrolmen on the assumptive grounds that they are "responsible for the activities of patrolmen" whereas patrolmen are "responsible for the activities taking place on their beats." This seemingly clear-cut contrast is pregnant with operational difficulty, for it is apparent to anyone spending more than a trivial amount of time within large police departments that "being responsible for the men" can be demonstrated in a variety of ways, under a bewildering set of circumstances. It is by no means clear what it is that can properly be called supervision, leadership, management, or direction within these organizations. Yet tasks do get performed, calls answered, budgets drawn up and expended, reports written, and, in fact, all members of the organization would give ready testimony that the three stripes worn on a sergeant's sleeve are indeed significant.

This is simply to say that chaos does not permeate police agencies—although, on occasion, such a beast does enter into the picture. Since there is not chaos, then, some sort of order does sustain a precarious existence. One way in which such order can be described is to examine the more-or-less routine activities of a set of differentiated members of the organization and note how they maintain relations with others who contrast with them in rank, status, or any other organizationally relevant way. Space does not permit lengthy analysis, but in bare detail I will explore some activities associated with the organizational role I have labeled the "Station House Sergeant." This will be a brief exploration. My intent is mainly to highlight the role rather than to exhaust it.

The main preoccupation of the station house sergeant is to avoid entanglements in the incident-specific world of policing. From a carefully built-up perspective on work-a-day duties, the station-house sergeant believes this job is to "efficiently run groups" rather than to "effectively police a given district." In the words of one such sergeant, "my job is to coordinate what the troops are up to because legally I can't tell 'em what to do." What this veteran sergeant alludes to in this remark is an arrived-at interpretation for his official activities. He is signaling a style of supervision characterized by its relative unconcern for the always situationally defined police task. The style has more in common with styles of the nonpatrol supervisory and administrative ranks in the agency than with those of other patrol sergeants or, more critically, patrolmen. Whatever opportunities exist for the station house sergeant to become involved in particular police-citizen matters are studiously avoided. It is, in short, an administrative role that is sought, and it is by and large an administrative role that is played.

This, of course, begs the question of what activities could be said to satisfy the administrative tastes of the station house sergeant. Consider the following activities as examples of the sergeants' use of space inside and outside the station house.

As the label implies, station house sergeants can be located most readily in the station house. The amount of time the sergeants spend on the streets largely depends on what the sergeants deem proper reasons for being on the street. These reasons are few. They respond to the so-called "hot" or "trouble" calls as dispatched from central communications. Such calls provide occaions not only to observe their charges in action and be aware of any peculiar occurrences relevant to squad activity, but also to exercise supervisory prerogatives such as assigning paperwork to patrolmen on the scene, calling in investigatory personnel, advising the responding officers as to search or interview protocol, and, perhaps most frequently, encouraging patrolmen to disband from the scene and get back to work.

Other occasions for street activity include "meets" with patrolmen arranged through the dispatcher at patrol officer requests so that reports can get signed and delivered; "cruising" the district in an apparent effort to be "on the air" and, symbolically at least, to be a part of the action; breaking in a new man assigned to a district by accompanying him on portions of his early tours of duty in the district (mostly for an inexperienced or rookie officer); checking out men assigned fixed posts on special duty, such as parades, civic celebrations, and sporting events; and so on. What is distinctive and striking about all the actions of the station house sergeant when he is not in the station house is, however, not these activities per se. What is distinctive is his apparent unwillingness to become involved in any of the specific police incidents encountered on the street.

Station house sergeants are careful to avoid being first on the scene for any call; the general rule of the police is, with few exceptions, "first car in owns the call (and takes the paper)." Station house sergeants are respectful and even watchful of the autonomy granted patrolmen to handle calls in the way the responding patrolmen themselves feel appropriate. They are eager to dispel any notion that they are themselves "in on the action" and justify any unusual street presence by reference to supervisory responsibility as dictated by departmental procedures. If asked about what legal or quasi-legal action an officer should take, the sergeants will of course respond, but will virtually always qualify their response with a shrugged reminder to the questioning officer that it is "his call" and he should do what he thinks correct.

What station house sergeants consider their real work takes place in police buildings—central headquarters or precinct stations. Here station house sergeants are most comfortable and at home. Here they listen to the "radio," knowingly and skeptically monitoring selected details of the reported activities of their men. Here station house sergeants make themselves available to the "troops," to sign various documents of their concern—arrest reports, overtime statements, equipment releases, and so forth. Here roll call is held at the beginning of each shift, during which station house sergeants lecture a captive audience of bored, restless patrolmen, often bulging out of cramped student-sized desks or sitting uncomfortably on hard metal chairs. The lectures are about the importance of their public appearance (haircuts, weight, upkeep of uniforms, clean patrol vehicles, and avoiding general sloth), their repeated sins of laziness and displays of bad attitudes, the delinquent behavior of some, always unnamed, patrolmen (their long lunches, choice of on-duty beverage, or improper use of police authority), or their failure to master correct grammatical forms and spelling on submitted reports.

Station house sergeants also lay territorial claim on the station house itself. Unless patrolmen are involved in interrogating suspects, ushering prisoners around police territories, questioning witnesses, writing reports, or attending to other narrowly defined police work, they have no business, between roll call and booking off, being in the station. Frequent or lengthy visits to the station house by partolmen without obvious police work to conduct are seen as time-wasting peccadillos, and such patrolmen are shooed back to the streets.

In essence, station house sergeants sidestep, whenever possible, any practical or operational involvement in the incidents that constitute police business. By being unwilling to attend to routine police calls, by scrupulously avoiding having to make legally responsible police decisions, by turning over virtually all accountability for police-citizen encounters to patrolmen, these sergeants construct a readily recognized role within the organization. More to the point, it is a role they can support and rationalize easily. To use the imagery of a bureaucratic and sometimes paramilitary organization, station house sergeants have a valuable resource at hand to justify their actions (or better, their inactions). To such supervisors, organizations are systems in which the practices and relations of the membership are intended to closely mirror the rules which define the division of responsibility (and competence) between the ranks (and among the specialities). By refusing to grant any validity to the claim that the formal rules are situationally specific, vague, and rarely obvious, station house sergeants limit their commitment to and involvement in the field. If an incident arises calling for some judgment as to whether or not to investigate further a citizen's allegation of, say, a residential buglary, station house sergeants are quick to call in the detectives to make such choices. That the matter could be an investigatory or patrol concern is not seen as negotiable, since the station house sergeant will invoke an official statement of purpose and function, thus defining the matter as "out of his hands."

The response of patrolmen to this style of supervision is in large part derision. As the nicknames for station house sergeants suggest—Duck-out Dick, By-the-book Brubaker, All-fears Malloy—patrolmen regard the style as something of an art form that serves to protect a sergeant from the necessity of making operational and responsible decisions. It is seen as a kind of buck passing, of running away from one's duties, of "concentrating on the bullshit." For this reason, station house sergeants are often characterized as cowardly—although not (ordinarily) for a lack of physical courage. They are seen as afraid to become involved in specific incidents because they fear making a wrong decision and therefore blurring their image of competence with superior officers with whom they are seen by patrolmen as being cozy.

For patrolmen to make such judgments, certain assumptions are required. Most critical is the widespread belief that one wins acclaim or favor from the higher-ups in police organizations by playing by the rules and, as is frequently heard, "keeping one's nose clean." Such an assumption mediates whatever personal irritation a patrolman may feel toward his boss, since it offers an explanation grounded on a decipherable motive. "Bookmen" such as Hats-on Harry or Off-at-Seven George can be tolerated, if not approved, by subordinates.

I must note finally that station house sergeants would not exist as a recognizable type were it not for their counterparts, the street sergeants, some of whom are known by such names as Radio Free Lebanon, Stick-it-to-em Dick and High-Beams

Bobby. Briefly, whatever a station house sergeant is, a street sergeant is not. Street sergeants view themselves first and foremost as practical policemen, uninterested in managerial affairs. For a street sergeant, the significance of the stripes he wears is a troublesome matter, since it is unclear to him what being a sergeant means and entails. Street sergeants, for reasons too numerous to discuss here, find little difference between police work as a patrolman and police work as a sergeant. One experienced sergeant of the street put the matter this way: "I suppose some of my men go bofo on me (book on fuck off), but I care more about getting out there myself and doing the job the city pays me to do, which, when it comes down to it, means putting the bad guys where they belong. It don't mean I won't say nothing to those guys if I find out they've been fucking around, but I don't go looking for them like I'm their keeper."

The irony of a street sergeant's elevated rank lies in his sense of being an odd man out. Despite his professed attraction to street-level work, he believes he can intervene only in certain kinds of police matters and even then only with difficulty. No longer dispatched directly to calls, street sergeants live in a shadowy occupational world where charges of "poaching," "oversupervision," "snooping," "sticking their noses into another's business," "neglecting their duties," "not following up on their paperwork," and, alas, "undersupervision" are ever present. Although such charges are clearly negotiable, the number of charges is to be minimized. If the charges become widespread, the officers under the sergeant's command and over him can make his daily life most uncomfortable.[15]

Underpinning this view is what Bittner (1970:27) regards as a key to understanding police behavior on the street: the virtually unlimited granting of "reciprocal tolerance" by members of an organization toward one another. The legal mandate of the police in American society (as interpreted by the police) is important here, as are other sources of justification for such tolerance. Perhaps of most importance, however, is the deeply held notion in police circles that to become involved in another's incident is to invite trouble. Though subject to less public ridicule and private slander, street sergeants walk a very thin line in maintaining the respect (and obedience) of their men.

Realist Tales in Perspective

This tale reveals, among other things, a fieldworker-author who more or less disappears into the described world after a brief, perfunctory, but mandatory appearance in a method footnote tucked away from the text. The only other glimpse of the ostrich-like writer is a brief walk-on or cameo role in which he puts into place the analytic framework. The voice assumed throughout the tale is that of a third-party scribe reporting directly on the life of the observed. The tone suggests anonymity, a characteristic of science writing, where the fieldworker is self-cast as a busy but unseen little fellow who is confident that the world as represented in the writing is the real one. Authority rests largely on the unexplicated experience of the author in the setting and the "feel" he has apparently developed for the time, place, and people.

Such a feel is expressed by the author's apparent mastery and savvy within the studied scene as repeatedly displayed by localized, detailed accounts of routine activities and the tossing around of the natives' vernacular. Folk terms appear throughout the tale, giving the impression that the author is fully able to whistle native tunes. The ungrammatical and profane phrases heighten the claim that the words flow from the members, not the author. Quotes are redundant, staged, and of course closely edited to embellish the fieldworker's methodical observations and analytical categories with native jargon. The result is that the interested interpretations of the members themselves seem to overlap and comprise the analysis itself—"It's not my perspective," says the author, "but theirs." The native's point of view is thus put forward.

The focus of the tale is nonetheless a restricted one, tied to a particular problem (paradox) posed in the opening paragraph of the text and more or less resolved by the conclusion. This is a conventional realist practice of textual organization, especially in short-burst ethnographies published in article form. By framing the representation in such a fashion, closure of the materials can be claimed. Closure is itself an argument for certain knowledge. Leaving matters indeterminant, up in the air, ambiguous, or otherwise uncertain might be disturbing to readers and might undermine the authority of the text.

Styles of other realist tales are similar. For example, closure can be obtained by pigeonholing materials into well-regarded functionalist or social system concepts (although these are less well regarded today); moving through the constituent parts of a single activity, performance, ritual, or role (any one of which can be presented as emblematic of the culture); or by following a group through a day, a week, or an annual cycle (Marcus and Cushman, 1982). These organizing schemes all work largely by synecdoche, where a part is allowed to stand for the whole (e.g., a few sergeants for police management and culture). In my illustration the laconic reference to Bittner's (1970) notion of "reciprocal tolerance" is invoked at the end to explicitly suggest such a cover. Since culture is ordinarily defined in far-reaching and encompassing ways, synecdoches are invariably prominent metaphors in realist tales (Manning, 1979). How they work, however, rarely concerns the writer (although it may puzzle the reader).[16]

Presenting an account that a reader will regard as certain may also require the use of the ethnographic present. In my tale, the station house sergeant is represented not as a character of some particular historically situated organizational and occupational world existing at the time of the study. He is presented rather as a timeless feature of the police world and is frozen as a composite creation. The work world is presented in the active voice (They do this now) that collapses any sense of change or movement in that world. To do otherwise would bleed doubt into the story and indicate that things are not quite so vivid, total, and obvious as they are made to seem (Clifford, 1983b).[17]

Of note, too, is the realist convention of suppressing the individual in the tale in favor of programmatically constructing an entity to serve as a kind of cultural prototype. The station house sergeant of my story is nothing less than a normative role model for an undefined, uncounted, and vague collection of individuals. This is an ideal type, of course, to which no single sergeant precisely corresponds. But interestingly, while I hesitate to attribute motives or other psychological states to the few recognizable people who populate the scene, I have little trouble doing so for the groups created. To wit, station house sergeants are "respectful" of patrolmen's autonomy, "at home" in the precincts and headquarters, "suspicious" of patrolmen who, in equally composite fashion, are sometimes "bored," "restless," and "derisive" in response to the antics of their superiors. How such matters are known is not touched on in the ethnography but rests fundamentally on a reader's good faith and willingness to trust the fieldworker's experience as valid.

There is also a sort of metatheory that runs through ethnographic tales (of all sorts) and that bears mention. Such metatheory is tuned to the intellectual fashions of the day, and authors may be only dimly aware of its influence on their writing. For example, the imagery of my tale suggests that the police world is gamelike and full of social drama. The imagery is not of a squeeky machine, an ill-tilled garden, or faulty plumbing. The metaphors are those of gaming, of poses, of performances, of roles, of hide-and-seek, of strategic moves, of sidewalk scenes. These are the informing tropes (Manning, 1979). They are perhaps more familiar to dramatists or military tacticians than they are to engineers, farmers, or plumbers. Yet were this tale twenty years older, I suspect things would have been different (with the machine, garden, or pumping station replacing the game and drama). The point here is that no ethnography, despite claims to the contrary, is written in a social and historical vacuum where the informing social theory emerges only on some mythical match to the data. Fieldworkers are notorious analytic bricoleurs, sniffing out and sifting through current theory for leads as to how fieldwork materials might be conceptualized. Times change, theory is revised, and the realist metaphors and reporting styles change too.[18]

In sum, a number of the more prominent conventions of realist tales can be read into my station house sergeant material. The narrator's authority, based on unarticulated experience, invisibly glides through the text. Everyday details about the police life are continually inserted and both justify the method and certify the Johnny-on-the-spot or I-was-there claim on which my authority rests. The native's point of view is asserted and shaped-up to serve as the analytic framework for the story. The interpretation comes not out of my mouth (or pen), but presumably from the natives themselves. And while there are no particularly evocative or stylistic features of note in the tale, part of its effect no doubt turns on the flow, tempo, and form of the writing which edits and twists member phrases and terms alongside my own. With this quasi-literary critique in mind, what is one to make of such conventions in ethnography?

Embarrassment with such realist conventions is one response in some fieldwork communities. When viewed as literary creations, realist tales may not seem so very real at all. At times they seem like cheeky appropriations that rest on mystified technique. The next chapter takes up this reaction with a vengeance by considering another form of ethnographic writing, the confessional tale. This form takes as its mission the explication of how fieldwork is accomplished. As such, it is sensitive and sometimes sharply critical of some of the realist devices portrayed in this chapter. As another form of fieldwork representation, it is apologetic about some sins of commission, but mostly those of omission, in realist tales.

NOTES

1. The title of chapter 3 derives from Clifford (1983a) and Marcus and Cushman (1982), who do a superb job of defining the genre for anthropological work and illustrating its conventions. It is a genre that makes sense only in terms of its contrasts. Historically, realism takes shape against the older ethnological and survey-based tales (Malinowsky, 1922:1–25) and against the newer self-conscious and personalized tales (Nash and Weintraub, 1972). Another useful source for ethnographic writing is Stoddart (1985), who takes his inspiration from the ethnomethodological studies of everyday practices. "Doing realism" might be Stoddart's label for the writing conventions I discuss in this chapter. See also Bittner's (1973) critique of social realism.

2. Authorial voice is not, of course, entirely banished from realist tales. It is manifest in the style of certain willful and writerly ethnographers (Clifford, 1986a). Margaret Mead, for example, has a distinctive accent, as does Clifford Geertz. Both possess rich literary styles that make it abundantly clear that they are always present, even in the most realist of their tales. My point is that realist conventions restrict the intermingling of the author's voice with the presented reality. The author's essential subjectivity is kept from view. Except for those extraordinarily stylish, the author that comes through in most realist tales is the Distant One; something of a pallid little troll who provides a smooth voiceover in the bland style of a National Geographic special or a BBC documentary. Certainly banned from realist tales are moments of fieldwork error, pleasure, distaste, or puzzlement. Also lost from realism as transformed into speciality

writings are the colorful, vivid, lush, and sometimes humorous visions of Malinowsky (1922), who had originally planned to give *Argonauts of the Western Pacific* the title *Kula: A Tale of Native Enterprise and Adventure in New Guinea* (Stocking, 1983:106).

3. Such matters are sure to be revealed, however, on the title page or in the publisher's blurb about the author on the book's dust jacket. Typically authors manage to smuggle their institutional credentials into the preface and assure their readers that they are the right sort of person to be writing the book. My own ironic self-portrait in the preface to this book serves as a good example of how such character infiltration and polishing occurs in ethnographic writings. In the text itself, language, jargon, referencing, punning, footnoting, and many other tactics are available to establish the credibility and identity of the unseen author of the realist tale. The late Erving Goffman in virtually all his work was the absolute master of such practices. Despite minimal self-referencing, one can never forget while reading his work that these are the Tales of Goffman.

4. Here culture theory enters the realist equation since the authority also derives from working in recognized analytic traditions. For example, facts arranged according to the gospels of Radcliffe-Brown, Max Gluckman, Victor Turner, Erving Goffman, or Mary Douglas may carry added punch. Such arrangements can vary, of course, from the free-flowing, seemingly haphazard models of Malinowski (1922), Mead (1928), or Whyte (1955) to the precise, steel-trap models of Cicourel (1968) or Spradley (1970). Essentially, routinization and specialization moved in on realist writing, and the sprawling, undisciplined tales of the past have given way to short, sharp ones. Authority by association and authority by theory are matters I take up again in this chapter when I discuss the "interpretive omnipotence" of realist tales.

5. There is now a fairly large literature that attempts, in Goffmanesque, to "normify" fieldwork practices along the lines of an observational (i.e., natural) science. This literature provides something of a defense for those fieldworkers who wish to deny accusations of subjectivity. To some degree, natural science methodologies offer shelters which, however bunker-like they may have become, still shield fieldworkers from those dreaded charges that their work is merely "opinion, not fact," "taste, not logic," or (shudder) "art, not science." Good statements of model fieldwork within this tradition include: Palmer, 1928; Radcliffe-Brown, 1958; Junker, 1960; Glaser and Strauss, 1967; Schatzman and Strauss, 1973; Pelto and Pelto, 1978; Kirk and Miller, 1986. Strictly speaking, these fieldwork texts border on the confessional genre discussed in the following chapter, since the focus is on the fieldworker, often the author(s), not the culture.

6. Method writing concerned with the newer modes of "soaking up member meanings" include: Bruyn, 1966; Denzin, 1970; Lofland, 1976; Schwartz and Jacobs, 1979; Ruby, 1982; Burgess, 1982; Douglas, 1985; Agar, 1986; and Adler and Adler, 1987a. Large chunks of all these texts fall squarely in the confessional genre as discussed in chapter 4. Moreover, as we shall see, these texts offer methods that welcome and praise subjectivity, treating it as a central and essential tool of the ethnographic trade rather than as a potential source of error or unwanted variance to be foreclosed.

7. An interesting set of issues in anthropology has recently arisen over this very matter. It is put in focus by R. Rosaldo (1980), who tells of posing standard fieldwork queries to Ilongo tribesmen about ritual, kinship, myth, and so forth, but getting virtually no response from them except puzzlement. By the standards of the discipline, it appeared he stumbled on a group with no culture whatsoever. The problem was solved in the end, but if nothing else, Rosaldo's cautionary tale poses some difficult questions for fieldworkers heavily dependent on received cultural theory and its categories. See also, Sass (1986) for a popular account of some of the current shifts in anthropological theory and practice.

8. An image of the mail system in an old-fashioned post office comes to mind when one thinks of how some realist tales are constructed. Writing it up, following this analogy, requires, first, that the fieldworker label all bits and pieces of written ("inscribed") field notes or data as instances of this or that cultural category. Second, the fieldworker stands back, mail-clerk style, and sorts all the bits and pieces into their respective slots. Third, the write-up is arranged on the basis of the slots with the most mail. Almost-empty slots can be ignored. Fourth, the text is written to illustrate the categories and go through the mail bit by bit as a way of representing category existence and content. This image appears to be close to what computer jocks have in mind for ethnography: Research events or experiences become notes, notes are coded, codes are amassed as entities are stripped of context, and the situational and conversational aspects of fieldwork are banished from the final analysis and text. Promoters of ethnoscience run some of these risks, although they also regard them as part of the cost of doing such business and therefore consider them manageable (Werner and Schoepfle, 1986; Agar, 1982).

9. Followers of various technical forms of conversational analysis are no doubt less impressed by the authenticity of the quotes that find their way into ethnographic texts than are other readers. They would criticize a quote pulled out of a stream of discourse. They would also fuss when the pauses, ahems, coughs, stutters, fractured syntax, asides, skipped pho-

nemes, hiccups, and other speaker twitches are edited out of native quotes. Such editing is necesary (arguably) to make a readable manuscript. But as we know from close studies of communicative interaction, the difference between what was said and what was heard or meant can often be very great (Goffman, 1981). More generally, by cleaning up and sanitizing native remarks for publication, ethnographers have made informants rather mannerly, pleasant, rational, and down-to-earth chaps who speak the King's English remarkably well. What readers might regard as uncouth, alien, or disgusting was edited out. For many years sociologists self-censored their ethnographies by removing profanity and correcting the grammar of informants' talk put on public display. Conventions have changed, and "real talk" is no longer taboo. About fucking time, too, since (burp) "real ta-ta-talk" is apparently a mark of authenticity.

10. A superb example in this regard is Rappaport's (1968) use of system theory to make comprehensible and convincing his representation of the meaning and use of pigs in a New Guinea tribal village. His account comes close to the didactic deadpan with its rigorous conceptualizations, but still maintains something of a narrative thrust. Stripped of the narrative, however, the conceptualizations standing alone come close to representing a society locked in functional equilibrium with all its parts moving in sweet harmony.

11. Such work, while confusing, does serve to bring home the documentary presence and experiential authority of the author to the reader. Its hard and bare appearance speaks of its objectivity untouched by the soft subjectivity of one who feels compelled to interpret it all. Classics of this sweeping ethnography, full of materials that overflow a single volume, include Malinowski's *Coral Gardens and Their Magic* (1935, 2 vols.) and Thomas and Znaniecki, *The Polish Peasant in America* (1918–21, 5 vols.). Multitext ethnographic projects are still occasionally pursued, although lately they are rarely of the realist sort (see, for example, Manning, 1977, 1980, forthcoming; and Dumont, 1976, 1978).

12. As I will note later, one problem with these works is that we can't do much more than admire the awesome skills of their authors. How such masterworks were created remains problematic. Evans-Pritchard's (1940) study of the Nuer is astonishing in this regard. The author spent only eleven months in the field, not all of it in close proximity to the cattle-raising people he studied. He did not speak the language with any fluency until the last few months of his stay. Moreover, he was constantly troubled by colonial authorities intent on controlling the Nuer, 200,000 people spread across 30,000 square miles. Yet an ethnographic classic was created. It is also worth noting that the work represents something of a turning point from the sprawling and undisciplined realist tale to a

sharply focused one where little is put in the tale that does not serve an explicit purpose. Kuper (1977:93–97) regards *The Nuer* as more of an argument than an ethnography. Clifford (1983a), Marcus and Cushman (1982) and Rosaldo (1986a) provide some intriguing recovery work on this study.

13. This should in no way suggest that realist tales of recent vintage are difficult to locate. While sensitive to the charge that realism withers as it becomes commonplace and routinized, contemporary ethnography offers, nonetheless, numerous examples of the genre. A few of my favorites include Caven, 1966; Polsky, 1967; Scott, 1968; Young and Willmott, 1962; Jacobs, 1974; Rubenstein, 1973; Ditton, 1977; Dreher, 1982; and Halle, 1984. These works, mostly in urban ethnography, focus on emblematic cultural performances and key institutional processes that presumably set off the studied group as distinctive. Each follows something of the standard realist format, with the setting laid out in the beginning and the world view or ideology portrayed at the end. The middle is filled with accounts of various aspects of daily life—family, friendship, work and leisure patterns, status orders, rituals, social exchanges, negotiation over norms, and so on. Realism is very much alive even though its conventions are under a good deal of fire. Perhaps it is most appealing when used to illuminate close-to-home settings that have previously avoided the ethnographic klieg lights and camera. Miner (1956) provides the satirical classic of homegrown realism, but consider also the work of Wolcott (1973), Sudnow (1967), Mars (1982), and Richman (1983) as solid realist tales on some very familiar subjects.

14. Realist tales are definitely not the ethnographic equivalent of cinema vérité, in which the camera is used to provoke the scenes it records. Any hint that the presence of the fieldworker as a curious onlooker might have something to do with what is witnessed in the research setting (or what is hidden) is tactfully played down or avoided altogether in realist writing (Stoddart, 1985). An interesting treatment of ethnographic films that raises this issue is found in Heider, 1976.

15. In a similar study conducted in England during the early 1970s, Chatterton (1975) makes a like distinction among the first-line supervisors he studied. Chatterton's "administrators" are my "station-house sergeants," and his "practical coppers" are my "street sergeants" who, rather than seeing themselves as the "odd men out," refer to themselves as "spare parts." (Footnote in original.)

16. Required reading here is Hayden White (1978). Organizing schemes and popular synecdoches are not mere inventions of a writer. Most stem from what is fashionable among colleagues at the time of the writing and therefore reflect the ethnographer's own culture as much as

71

the one studied. Thus, early anthropologists gave prominence in their writing to matters of fascination at the turn of the century, notably, sex, marriage, and war. Their successors emphasized other matters such as work, social life, child raising, and mental health (Diamond, 1980). Sociological fieldworkers fare no better, since they did not even "discover" the middle classes until the 1940s and it took another twenty years (and a Goffman) before they began to include everyday behavior in their work. Nonetheless, as fieldworker texts so often suggest, some ethnographers still hope to achieve something akin to a Frederick Taylor model of ethnography whereby fieldworker-writers are made interchangeable through proper training, and quality control is ensured by prescribing the relevant parts and assembly orders for each product. In such a world, ethnographers could settle back for a long run of normal science based on solid empirical, theoretical, and institutional grounds. This is, of course, a pipe dream if only because the interests of one generation are sure to be challenged by those of the next.

17. The widespread use of the ethnographic present reflects what is apparently a strong belief among fieldworkers that it is possible to analyze groups from an ahistorical perspective. The history that counts is, according to this view, embedded in the daily practices and symbolic life of the group studied and hence will be taken into account naturally. More to the point, however, the question driving ethnographic work is not the historical one (How did this come to be?) but rather a logically prior question of definition (What is this?). History is seeping back into ethnography as another "blurred genre," and native histories—as retellings or reconstructions—are being represented (e.g., R. Rosaldo, 1980; Sahlins, 1981; Wallace, 1978). With history comes more problems, of course, since it is harder to finesse the issues of the relative power of the group studied (and its isolation as an analytic unit) if its ebb and flow are explicitly examined (Marcus and Fischer, 1986:95–108).

18. My use of the term metahistory derives from White (1973) and his analysis of metahistory. White notes that much nineteenth century social history was written to overcome the rationalist traditions associated with the enlightenment. In this effort, the metaphors of romance, tragedy, farce, comedy were used as rhetorical devices. In a similar way, social theorists may be reacting to what are regarded by many interpretive theorists a overly deterministic versions of the world by using the game and social drama imagery. See also Canary and Kozicki (1978).

Confessional Tales

If you want to understand what a science is you should look in
the first instance not at its theories or its findings, and certainly
not what its apologists say about it; you should look at what the
practitioners of it do.

Clifford Geertz

Chapter 3 suggested that ethnographic writing is anything but
a straightforward, unproblematic descriptive or interpretive task
based on an assumed Doctrine of Immaculate Perception. Rather,
ethnographic writing of any kind is a complex matter, dependent
on an uncountable number of strategic choices and active constructions (e.g., what details to include or omit; how to summarize and present data; what voice to select; what quotations to
use). In this chapter I explore another representational form of
ethnographic writing, the fieldwork confessional. It is an increasingly popular genre that contrasts sharply in a number of ways to
the realist tale. The distinguishing characteristics of confessional
tales are their highly personalized styles and their self-absorbed
mandates.[1]

The confessional tale is often a response to some of the realist
conventions that have proved most embarrassing. In some instances, the confessional tale stems from the notorious sensitivity
of many fieldworkers to aspersions cast on the scientific status of
their undertakings. The result, then, is an attempt to explicitly
demystify fieldwork or participant-observation by showing how the
technique is practiced in the field.[2] Stories of infiltration, fables
of fieldwork rapport, minimelodramas of hardships endured (and
overcome), and accounts of what fieldwork did to the fieldworker
are prominent features of confessions.

In other instances (perhaps more important), the confession is a response to the growing importance and penetration of European social thought in American social science.[3] In various ways, some mentioned in chapters 1 and 2, the implications of phenomenology, hermeneutics, semiotics, and other intrepretive procedures are being felt in the empirical trenches. By and large, American fieldworkers have been, until fairly recently, at ease and comfortable with their seat-of-the-pants, homespun methods, and have been unreasonably proud of their outward-bound, lonewolf, muddy-boots image. Given the lofty issues of human meanings treated in ethnographies, many a fieldworker-author fits Boon's (1982:5) ideal type of "Icarus with dirty feet."

Such pride apparently goeth before a fall, because in the confessional form of ethnographic writing, fieldworkers now show themselves to be somewhat nervous about the looseness and open-ended nature of their work. Considerable worry is expressed about the obvious lack of a theory of description that might help legitimize an enterprise premised on the delicate good-faith assumption, the assumed self-evident value of exploring little-known social worlds, and the presumptive use of natural science notions concerning the power of observation. Such discomfort surfaces in confessions as writers try to show that ethnography is not merely old-fashioned social science in its geriatric decay. These writers attempt to demonstrate that an ethnographic report is more than a personal document; that it is something disciplined by proper fieldwork habits, including the attention an ethnographer pays to the epistemological problems characteristic of social science. Most confessionals have at their core some hope of making fieldwork, if not fully safe for science, at least respectable in terms of upholding some community standards and disciplining the undisciplined of fieldwork. As with realist writings, there are conventions at work in the confessional tale. A discussion of three such conventions follows and serves to set up an example.

Personalized Author(ity)

Author-fieldworkers are always close at hand in confessional tales. Their writings are intended to show how particular works came into being, and this demands personalized authority. No longer is the ubiquitous, disembodied voice of the culture to be heard (e.g., The police do X). In its place is a person (e.g., I saw the police do X). There is an intimacy to be established with readers, a personal character to develop, trials to portray, and, as with realist tales, a world to be represented within which the intrepid fieldworker will roam. With this last feature, the aims of fieldwork confessionals and realist accounts may overlap, even though the textual means of supporting the resulting cultural portraits are quite different.

Confessionals do not usually replace realist accounts. They typically stand beside them, elaborating extensively on the formal snippets of method description that decorate realist tales. They occasionally appear in separate texts and provide self-explanatory and self-sealing accounts of how the author conducted a piece of research reported elsewhere. Confessions also appear, with increasing frequency, as separate articles, chapters of books devoted to fieldwork practice, or lengthy appendixes attached to realist monographs. All are distinct, however, from the ethnography itself. The confessional writings concern how the fieldworker's life was lived upriver among the natives. They are concerned primarily with how the fieldwork odyssey was accomplished by the researcher. There is then a clear break between the representation of the research work itself and the resulting ethnography (which appears elsewhere in the text or in another text altogether). Normally only the former is of concern in a confessional tale.

Much confessional work is done to convince the audience of the human qualities of the fieldworker. Often the ethnographer mentions personal biases, character flaws, or bad habits as a way of building an ironic self-portrait with which the readers can identify (See, I'm just like you, full of human foibles). The omnipotent tone of realism gives way to the modest, unassuming style of one struggling to piece together something reasonably coherent out of displays of initial disorder, doubt, and difficulty.

According to Clifford (1983a), there are two conventional ways for ethnographers to orient themselves for the confessional audience. One is to cast oneself as a simple student of the observed group, an apprentice of sorts, who comes to learn of the culture much as any child or newcomer to that culture might (Van Maanen and Kolb, 1985). Learning from living in the culture is the predominant theme. The other way, possibly more fashionable these days, is to cast oneself as a translator or interpreter of indigenous texts that are available to the ethnographer in the field (Geertz, 1973). The major problem with this tactic is convincing the audience that such texts are in fact authentic, natural, useful for analytic purposes, and more or less untainted by the field-worker's touch. Fieldworkers, unlike literary critics, historians, or linguists, face the problem that their texts (on behavior, belief, ritual, etc.) taken from the field must first be constructed, since they do not come prepackaged. The first orientation lends itself nicely to a cognitive, rule-based and behaviorally focused ethnographic display; the second to a more reflexive, language-based, interpretive one.

The details that matter in confessional tales are those that constitute the field experience of the author. This human bundle of exposed nerve-endings stands alone in the culture supposedly perceiving and registering the various happenings around him. Emotional reactions, new ways of seeing things, new things to see, and various mundane but unexpected occurrences that spark insight are all conventional confessional materials that suggest how the fieldworker came to understand a studied scene. Moreover, confessional writings rarely portray the author as a passive, unremarkable character who simply stands around waiting for something to happen or for the arrival of the white flash of discovery. Who could trust such an unadventurous and timid soul? The narrator of the confessional is often a foxy character aware that others may be, intentionally or unintentionally, out to deceive him or withhold important information. The ethnographer as the visible actor in the confessional tale is often something of a trickster or fixer, wise to the ways of the world, appreciative of human vanity, necessarily wary, and therefore inventive at getting by and winning little victories over the hassles of life in the research setting (e.g., Berreman, 1962; Powdermaker, 1966; Gans, 1982; J. Douglas, 1976).[4] Nor is the fieldworker who writes most confessions brimming over with correctional zeal or tied to hard-and-fast ethical principles. Indeed, some of the most unflattering portraits of ethnographic practice arise, as the label implies, in fieldwork confessions where it seems apparent that the researcher has less patience and good will than his subjects (e.g., Turnbull, 1972; Malinowski, 1967).

The Fieldworker's Point of View

As autobiographical details mount in confessional tales, it becomes apparent that the point of view being represented is that of the fieldworker. Typically, the concern for the fieldworker's perspective is told as something of a character-building conversion tale in which the fieldworker, who saw things one way at the outset of the study, comes to see them in an entirely different way by the conclusion of the study. The new way of seeing the world is normally claimed to be similar to the native's point of view. But careful attention is given to insuring that the fieldworker does not appear to be fully altered, the proverbial cultural dupe or convert. The attitude conveyed is one of tacking back and forth between an insider's passionate perspective and an outsider's dispassionate one. Perhaps no other confessional convention is as difficult for the writer as maintaining in print this paradoxical, if not schizophrenic, attitude toward the group observed. A delightful dance of words often ensues as fieldworkers present themselves as both vessels and vehicles of knowledge.

In much confessional writing, a sort of tentative "surrender" is used by the fieldworker as a temporary resolution to the daily problems of fieldwork. But, going native can hardly be presented with terminal glee. The mere presence of the confessional suggests that the fieldworker is now seriously back among his peers, ready to tell of the adventures in the field. This is perhaps why some find Carlos Castaneda, the flying nun of anthropology, such a silly character, for if he were fully committed and converted why would he bother with us?

A reader often learns of the ethnographer's shifting point of view during a period of fieldwork in a confessional. Common features of research confessions are episodes of fieldworker shock and surprise. Subjects include the blunders of fieldworkers, the social gaffes they commit or secrets they unearth in unlikely places and ways. Such accounts are frequent and indicate perhaps that despite the different theoretical languages and attitudes taken into the field by ethnographers, the significance of inserting the self into the daily affairs of others is, at least on the experiential plane, similar for everyone.[5] The unplanned, almost random, happenstance is dramatically set forth in confessional tales with the universal message attached that fieldwork is as much a matter of luck and being in the right place at the right time as it is a matter of good training. Given this advice, time in the field and close, involved contact with the group studied (allowing for a greater opportunity for lightning to strike) provide the normative guidelines (the more the better).[6]

There is, however, a line to be drawn, for the fieldworker cannot stay in the field forever and still be considered a fieldworker. Conventions grow up around what is to be considered an adequate field experience, and various communities (and subcommunities) of fieldworkers adopt different standards. The more targeted or limited the ethnography is to a particular and well-defined cultural problem, the less time in the field is thought necessary in order for revelation to strike.

Much of the confessional genre is familiar to readers of method texts where the various pros and cons of intense involvement or participation in the culture of interest are discussed. Within confessional ethnography, however, the writers seem less sanguine about the presumed wide range of role options available to fieldworkers. There is, in fact, something of a they-made-me-do-it character to many confessionals in which certain non-negotiable demands are made by the natives, the refusal of which would mean instant exile. These demands may be tied to biographical particulars (e.g., young women must behave appropriately) or to situational particulars (e.g., "don't do that now"), but such demands are represented as being made on the fieldworker in no uncertain terms. In confessional tales, then, cultural knowledge may rest securely on the testimony of personal experience and can be presented to readers in the form of explicit behavioral norms or interpretive standards the ethnographer learned to follow in the field in order to stay in the field.

Naturalness

The last convention of the confessional tale I want to exhibit is also the broadest and perhaps the most inconsistently treated one. It concerns the way fieldworkers argue that their materials are reasonably uncontaminated and pure despite all the bothersome problems exposed in the confession. Fieldwork confessions nearly always end up supporting whatever realist writing the author may have done and displayed elsewhere (in or out of the text in which the confessional tale appears). The linguistic footwork required is considerable, but it often boils down to the simple assertion that even though there are flaws and problems in one's work, when all is said and done it still remains adequate. Though confessional writers are forthcoming with accounts of errors, misgivings, limiting research roles, and even misperceptions, they are unlikely to come to the conclusion that they have been misled dramatically, that they got it wrong, or that they have otherwise presented falsehoods to their trusting audience. The implied story line of many a confessional tale is that of a fieldworker and a culture finding each other and, despite some initial spats and misunderstandings, in the end, making a match.[7]

No doubt part of this is due to the screening policies of the professional communities at which fieldwork accounts are aimed, as well as the self-screening work of the authors, so that the only ethnographies in print are the more-or-less successful ones about which the author (and at least some reviewers) are fairly confident that the work is up to snuff. We rarely read of unsuccessful field projects where the research was presumably so personally disastrous to the fieldworker that the study was dropped or failed ever to find its way to publication. While there may be some nervous indications that things are not so certain as they appear in print or that future voyagers into similar research worlds may see things in different ways, confessional tales usually end on an upbeat, positive, if not fully self-congratulatory, note.

Stoddart (1985) provides a happy list of conventional practices of confessionalists by which some intractable fieldwork dilemmas can be said to be overcome (for all practical purposes). One practice, readily apparent, is the way authors normalize their presence coming on the scene, in the scene, and leaving the scene. Adequate ethnographic practice in the confessional requires fieldworkers to tidy up their roles and tell how they think they were received and viewed by others in the field. The good guy presentation is one familiar role, as is the just-like-anyone-else role, where the fieldworker claims to more-or-less melt into the research setting by virtue of being ever present and hence, disattended to by all.

Sometimes member tests for fieldworkers are represented as ways of displaying the acceptance and competence of the ethnographer. The confessional becomes, in part, a special kind of etiquette book in which fieldworkers show how they learned to comport themselves according to the proper standards of behavior in the culture of interest. The writer becomes a Miss Manners of fieldwork, a Dear Abby of the studied scene. Typically lessons are said to be learned through breaches of local propriety. Thus the experiences of the bumbling, awkward fieldworker, painfully figuring things out, provide a good deal of the substance of the confessional tale. The result is a guide to how to get along and live with grace and honor among fierce warriors of the Gitchi-Gumi, shy hunters of the frozen north, or laid-back winos of Peachtree Plaza.

Another way of showing that one has the right stuff to get to the heart of a culture is through displays of empathy and involvement. Under most conditions, fieldworkers are expected by readers, if their accounts are to be trusted, to like and respect those they study (and vice versa).[8] They are also expected not to withdraw from the passing cultural scene but to become as involved and fully engrossed in the daily affairs of the people studies as possible. Empathy and involvement are, however, tricky matters. Writers of confessionals are therefore quick to point out that they liked some people more than others, and that there were certain periods during the study that were dull, uncomfortable, and perhaps distasteful. Moderation becomes the key which normalizes the setting and conveys to readers the sense that fieldwork is not very different from other kinds of work. The exotic is downplayed, the theatrical is understated, intense feelings are left out, and few of the absurdities of minding other people's business are allowed into the confessional tale.

Finally, consider how natives, as informants of the fieldworker, are handled in confessional writings. An often-stated platitude (however infrequently it is treated as such) notes that fieldworkers are only as good as their informants. Fieldwork novices are sternly reminded of such things in confessional accounts in which ethnographers must reveal (or claim to reveal) how they came to know what they know. In Back's (1956) words, the "well-informed informant" is one answer to this problem, and fieldworkers are often under some obligation to trot out these legendary figures when daring to bare all. Such figures must be said to know the culture well. They are represented therefore as "experienced," "veteran," "revered," "respected," "senior," and "central" informants. The question here is how much knowledge the fieldworkers should attribute to their having squatted at the feet of their informants during their field trips.

Confessional ethnographies are ordinarily vague on such matters, for being precise may raise anxious questions for the reader about who is doing all the ethnographic work, anyway? Too little reliance on entitled informants may suggest that too many imaginative liberties are being taken in the realist claims of the ethnographer. Too much reliance on informants also raises anxious questions about the representativeness of the fieldwork materials and may lead readers to worry about the identity of the real author of the realist tale. Either over- or underappreciating informants provokes concern in readers.

Producing Confessional Tales

These three conventions provide a short guide to how confessional tales are constructed. The genre is now a fairly large one. While the quality of confessionals varies tremendously in terms of both the self-reflection of an author and the sophistication with which an author faces the epistemological issues involved in fieldwork, the necessity of providing a confessional to supplement substantive (realist) reports of fieldwork is now more or less institutionalized in both anthropology and sociology. It is pro forma these days to append a confessional to a fieldwork dissertation or to include one in a separate chapter of the thesis under the "methods" label. Most confessions, like most dissertations, never see publication. Those that are published, however, normally issue from authors who have first published notable, attention-getting tales in the realist tradition. The confessional is apparently interesting only insofar as there is something of note to confess as well as something of note to situate the confession.[9] It is apparently more difficult to achieve the latter than the former. Authors of unknown studies, while they surely have much to confess, will rarely find an audience who cares to read their confessions.

Collections of autobiographical reflections on past projects represent the most common outlet for confessional tales of the field. In anthropology, Casagrande (1960) is a standard setter, focusing on work with informants. Other, more general-purpose collections include Epstein, 1967; Kimball and Watson, 1972; Freilich, 1970; Spindler, 1970; Ben-David and Clark, 1977; Naroll and Cohen, 1970; and, in a reorienting mission, Hymes, 1972. In sociology, Emerson's (1983) recent collection includes a good number of confessionals. Others include Shaffir et al., 1980; Bell and Newby, 1977; J. Douglas, 1972; Habenstein, 1970; Filstead, 1970; and Vidich et al., 1964. Also, since the confessional tale is ordinarily tied to giving the craft norms, a reader can find confessions—although they may be abstracted as missteps to be avoided—in fieldwork method primers, where authors in search of examples (extraordinary or dull) reach back to their own field experiences for guidelines for the novice. Examples include Agar, 1980; Burgess, 1983; Douglas, 1985, 1976; Loflanda, 1971; Schatzman and Strauss, 1973; Pelto and Pelto, 1973; Powdermaker, 1966; R. Wax, 1971; Glaser and Strauss, 1967; and Schwartz and Jacobs, 1979.

Let me now provide a reasonably elaborate example of the confessional tale. Again, it is my own work that serves as the exhibit. The excerpt is called "Johnny gets his gun." The materials were originally published under the more somber and serious title, "Notes on the production of ethnographic data in an American police agency," in 1981. The piece is drawn from a collection of confessionals written by fieldworkers interested in the sociology and anthropology of law. Unlike the previous example of a realist tale, which was reasonably self-contained, this illustration is only a small part of a fairly lengthy, normal-form confessional.[10] It is edited here in rather herky-jerky fashion to explicitly highlight a few of the more rampant and obvious conventions of the genre.

Johnny Gets His Gun

In 1969, I wrote in my thesis proposal: "The police are quite possibly the most vital of our human service agencies. Certainly they are the most visible and active institution of social control, representing the technological and organizational answer to the Hobbesian question of social order, the *deus ex machina*. Through their exclusive mandate to intervene directly in the lives of the citizenry, the police are crucial actors in both our everyday and ceremonial affairs, and, as such, deserve intensive and continual study for their role and function in society is far too important to be taken for granted or, worse, ignored."

Such high sounding sentiments provide, I am sure, the sort of doctrinal or ideological canopy which covers virtually all police studies. Yet, speaking sociologically, such statements are inadequate explanations for why such studies are undertaken in at least two ways. First, questions about the place of police study within the social sciences are glossed over neatly when a researcher points only to the "peculiar and significant" aspects of a specific research location. Second, research, especially research conducted in the fieldwork tradition, is both a social and a personal act, and, as such, is subject to the same sorts of biographically and situationally specific understandings through which any individual act can be understood.

Social scientists generally adhere to something of a hierarchy of professional values in which personal motives rank low and scientific motives high. At the apex of such a hierarchy are usually the formal theoretical concerns—what is it that is to be explained by the research? In my case, I was interested in questions surrounding adult socialization and the formation of occupational identities. As such, I searched about for a work world that might compel new entrants to accept, if not seek, a good deal of change in their personal identity and style of life in the process of becoming fully accepted members of an occupation and organization. From this analytic (and somewhat remote) standpoint, the police seemed to be a logical, and downright dramatic, choice. Yet, alternative possibilities were most certainly available—doctors, lawyers, crooks, priests, accountants, professors, architects, railroad workers, and so on. At this point, then, more gritty matters concerning why a specific researcher chooses to study a specific social world must be raised. Of course, to establish a motive, even one's own, is a tricky business. . . .

Three rather personal and perhaps pivotal factors seem best to explain my particular choice to study the police. First, when I began thinking seriously of the police as a topic for research in the late sixties, the police were prominently fixed in the imagery of the day. Whether damned or praised, they were both participants and subjects in the dramatic and searing issues of public debate. Indeed, the police were visible reminders that the American society was bitterly divided. Second, however, not much seemed to be known about the police. While everyone I knew had cop stories to tell, there remained in all these tales something of a mystery as to why the police acted as they did. I discovered rather quickly that the police-related literature was at the time relatively thin, particularly when it came to describing the actual activities of policemen. Third, the available literature did not seem to square with my own random observations and run-ins with the police. Certainly, with few exceptions, the arid portraits which represented a good portion of the social science literature of the day (circa 1968) did not match my own visceral beliefs. As a young man growing up in a Los Angeles suburb, I had many times been subject to police attention. As a teenager driving a series of unusually shabby but stylized automobiles, it seemed as if I could never undertake a journey of any length without being stopped by the police for some reason or another. I had been arrested several times for minor misdeeds such as underage drinking, curfew violations, petty theft, and fighting. And, of more immediate experience, the cordons of grim, often antagonistic, policemen that demarked the boundaries of every political demonstration I attended could not be easily forgotten. In many ways, I both feared and loathed the police. . . .

My access (into the Union City Police Department) was, to put it bluntly, the result of good fortune. While good fortune does not lend itself well to analytic discussion, a few events in my entry process should be noted primarily to provide context for my discussion of working roles in the field.

Most critical to the entry process was a contact I developed at the University of California, Irvine, while in the midst of seeking a "representative" American police department (i.e., large and urban) within which to conduct my work. After six frustrating months of attempting to gain access, I discovered, almost by chance, a faculty member in the Graduate School of Administration, my school, who had once run a series of encounter group sessions with upper echelon police officers in Union City. I sought out this professor, told him of my general plans and interests, and asked for any assistance he might be willing to provide. I also told him of the great difficulties I was having getting into a police agency. At the time we talked, I had been denied access to fourteen departments on various and sundry grounds, the most popular of which seemed to be the legal complications that administrators claimed my presence in their particular department would create. At any rate, this faculty member agreed to help and, using the rapport that perhaps only a sensitivity trainer can achieve, was able to persuade the command in Union City of the merits of my planned study and approach.

The rest of the negotiations followed in a rather hurried and *pro forma* fashion. Within a week, I flew to Union City, met with the Chief of Police and several of his aides. After an afternoon of meetings with these men, I was granted access to the department on what could only be called open terms. In the following two weeks, I had a number of telephone conversations to work out some administrative details of my study with the Captain of the Training Division, who was to be my official guide and sponsor in the organization during the period of my residency. The next week I began my work in Union City with a reserve commission (which neatly solved whatever legal complications there were—at least from the police perspective), a slot in the upcoming recruit training class, tentative approval, subject to my graduation from the police academy, for several months of study in the patrol division (which I was able to stretch to almost six months and then renew several times, years later). . . . No editorial control was asked for nor was there any direct discussion of what the police themselves hoped to get out of this initial research bargain. . . .

To penetrate the back regions of police organizations requires a researcher, like any newcomer to the setting, to undergo a lengthy process of examination. As I have described in some detail elsewhere, the novice in police organizations must cross several work boundaries, pass a series of social tests designed to discover something about the prudence, inclinations, and character of the person, and, of course, carve out a few intimate relationships with members of the organization upon whom the newcomer can depend (Van Maanen, 1973, 1974, 1978a).

Furthermore, the student of the police, again like any rookie patrolman, must also come to terms with some rather concrete

85

and pervasive emotional issues. In short, there are personal qualms about one's own safety to quiet. Indeed, much of the occupational talk of the police carries the tune of violence. Danger, whether real or imagined, is a constant companion to the police. And, fear is consequently an emotion every researcher who spends time in the field with the police must face.

Fear, to an observer of the police, stems from several sources. Certainly, by associating closely with the police, it may come from the ever present danger existing in city streets. I can recall feeling as if I had a bull's eye painted on the side of my head the first few times I rode in the front seat of a patrol car. Fear may also arise from the police themselves. I once witnessed a bar fight between two officers, each believing the other had embarrassed him in the eyes of a Captain. The police, of necessity perhaps, are not gentle, impassionate sorts who can easily tolerate a deviant in their midst. The working style of an ethnographer is sure to reflect this. Of course, one cannot know until the moment arises how he will handle these fears. But, the police will certainly be watching closely to determine, on the one hand, whether or not they can "depend" on the researcher, and, on the other hand, whether or not they can "take the researcher out" without adverse consequences arising should the need arise.

At another level, the police adhere to an organized format in going about some of their daily tasks. This format is rigid in some cases, such as the police academy, and relatively loose in other cases, such as roll calls and street work in the patrol division. A researcher, in either context, is conspicuous to the degree he does or does not fit the format. In the academy, for example, a researcher who did not participate in the program would have been so conspicuous as to preclude him from asking questions that might uncover the attitudes recruits might be forming toward each other, the staff, the department, or the work itself. On the street, however, there is considerably more leeway for a fieldworker to fashion a research role for himself without following a rigid format.

In my study, I entered the police academy as a self-acknowledged researcher who, I wanted made known, would stay with the class through graduation and spend some time working with the recruits after they had left the academy. During training, I consciously avoided establishing obvious links with the academy staff.

When asked, I turned down offers to sit with staff members at lunch, visit their offices on breaks, or go drinking with them after work. I felt this appropriate since a very strict formality normally obtains between recruits and staff members. Similar to the industrial workers studied a generation ago, police recruits (and patrolmen in general) were particularly sensitive to the possible connections a researcher might have with their bosses. On several occasions, when I had chanced to have an extended conversation in the hall with a staff officer, I was immediately quizzed on my return to the recruit areas as to what the conversation had been about. Early in the training program I was asked on a few occasions to plead a special case on behalf of a particular recruit to our academic superiors. I replied on those occasions that as far as the staff were concerned I carried no more weight than they themselves (which may or may not have been true)—although I usually said after my disclaimer that if they felt my talking to the Sergeant in charge of our particular class would do some good, I would do so. When it became apparent to the men that my nominal interventions were of little or no assistance to them, I was not asked for more special favors.

The police academy, with its strict discipline, prescribed calendar, and enforced lines of authority, was an environment clearly at odds with the patrol division. Yet, without doubt, my 13-week stint as an academy recruit helped immensely when it came to building an observational role among working patrolmen. During my first six weeks in the patrol division. I always worked with a recruit I had known in the academy and his assigned veteran partner, called, in Union City, the Field Training Officer (FTO). On virtually every occasion, I was introduced by my recruit colleague to his FTO with a tag line that went something like, "This is John Van Maanen, he's OK, he went through the academy with me."

Following the initial period in the patrol division, I decided to begin to focus my fieldwork in two sectors and, in particular, with two squads, thus, confining my work to one shift (7 PM–3 AM). Several reasons were behind this choice. First, the shift I chose was the most active in terms of dispatched calls. Second, the sectors I selected were thought to produce the most "police work." One sector took in the skid row and downtown business district and the other sector included a large part of the black ghetto in Union

City. Third, several of the men with whom I had developed the closest ties in the academy were assigned to the squads I picked and a disproportionate number of men from my academy class worked in the same sectors on overlapping shifts. Finally, by restricting my range, I hoped to be able to build firmer, more trusting relationships with the officers, both rookies and veterans, of the two squads. Although I sometimes worked outside of these two squads, I spent at least four of the five working shifts each week with these two squads.

A critical point needs to be made in this regard. By allowing myself to be closely identified with the patrolmen, I was purposely making a choice about the data I would gather. My self-imposed isolation from the managers of the organization and the other enclaves of special police interest very clearly biased my study toward the perspectives of those at the street level. In the police system, as perhaps in any social system, those of the lower caste (in this case, the patrolmen) are thought to be subservient and differential to those of the higher caste (in this case, from sergeants on up), who, in turn, balance the system, theoretically at least, by showing a paternalistic regard for the lower caste. In the police world, the power of the higher caste holds the system relatively stable, but there is a good deal of tension and conflict existing not far below the surface. To a field worker, this usually means that the members of the lower caste will make better informants (reveal more). Not only do they have less to lose objectively, but they are under less strain to appear faultless to either their internal or external audiences. . . .

My appearance while on patrol was tailored after the plainclothes officers in the department. My hair was closely cropped, I wore loose fitting sport jackets that did not make conspicuous the bulge of my service revolver. I wore hard-toed and heavy shoes, slit or clip-on ties, and carried with me a flashlight, chemical mace, rosewood nightstick, handcuffs, various keys, and sometimes a two-way portable radio. Several patrolmen, at various times during the study, gave me (for no doubt mixed reasons) fist loads, sap gloves, and an assortment of jacks to carry with me on patrol. And I did carry a few of these tools of the police trade although departmental regulations prohibited their use. One officer insisted I carry a second gun, a "two incher," in my coat pocket in the unlikely event, he explained, we were to be disarmed. This too violated departmental regulations. Even my 357 magnum revolver was against departmental regulations. This was a gift from my academy classmates, given to me formally during the graduation exercise in front of the police command, members of recruits' families, and local television news cameras. Even the ammunition I received through regular departmental channels was officially taboo. While I was something of a walking talking rule violation, so, too, were my colleagues. . . .

On the street, I encountered little overt hostility from patrolmen, although a few veteran officers refused to allow me to work with them. One instance bears mention because it sheds light on the research process itself. I was working the "last out" shift (11 PM–7 AM) with an academy classmate when we received an assignment to check on a possible "break" in a warehouse closed for the evening. We were some distance away and when we arrived at the call, several other units were already on the scene. In fact, a few officers were already inside the warehouse, flashlights in hand. As we got out of the car to enter the building, another officer came over and, after asking who the hell I was, told my partner to clear the call as unfounded, there were no burglars on hand, just an open door. If anything had been taken, the manager of the warehouse would make a report in the morning. We did as we were told, stayed on the scene for a short time, but left before the other officers departed. During the next hour or so, my partner enlightened me about what might have been occurring in the warehouse when we arrived. "Those fucking mopes," he said, "trying to make off with as much as they can get and on my call yet! You can't trust anybody in this outfit." . . .

[In summary] To some officers with whom I worked, I was a sort of "acceptable incompetent," capable perhaps of shortening the long hours on patrol through talk but incapable of doing anything remotely connected to the job itself. To most officers, I was more the reserve officer, a "friendly helper" sort who could, when called on, handle some light paper work, the radio, conduct an interview at, say, the scene of a fender-bender traffic accident, but, nonetheless, required continual supervision and could not be assumed to know what to do should an occasion arise in the field that called for "real police work." To a very few officers, two or three at most, I was more or less a "working partner," albeit a temporary one.

As an acceptable incompetent, I sat in the backseat of a two-man unit, taking no part in the decision being reached in the front seat, save those decisions about where and when to eat or take a break. On these shifts, I rarely spoke with anyone but my police guides. I did no police work other than to occasionally keep a personally protective eye on a prisoner who might happen to share the backseat with me.

As a friendly helper, my time was split somewhat evenly between one-man and two-man units. In this role, I was delegated tasks such as keeping the log or calling radio for a license plate check on a vehicle that just might turn out to be stolen. Other times, I would be asked to post myself at the corners of buildings when checking out a potential burglary or prowler call. In this role, I was also expected to physically or otherwise assist and back up an officer if any altercation arose during the tour.

Finally, as a working patrolman, I was put in the role of what Union City police called the shotgun partner. I played this part only with officers working solo beats and during these tours I was responsible for radio communications, paperwork (often signing my name to the log, arrest reports, field invesigation slips, etc.), back-up responsibility on traffic stops (positioning myself just outside the passenger door on the patrol car), and for the shotgun carried in most police cars should its use be required (hence, the Union City tag for the role, "you're shotgun tonight, I'll drive"). On calls such as the various sorts of disturbance calls, I would help separate the quarreling parties, restrain them if need be, and usually take a share in the decision about what, if any, police action was to be taken. On no occasion, however, did I drive a vehicle on routine patrol. This was probably for the same reason few rookies do much driving of prowl cars—veteran officers do not trust the novice driver who, first, does not know the district, and, second, is unaccustomed to the unpredictable ways other motorists react when spying the police black-and-whites.

What comes through as a result of this cursory overview of these three somewhat distinct roles played by one fieldworker is the inconsistency associated with the ethnographic research role. At times, I frisked suspects, put handcuffs on prisoners, wrote assault reports, while at other times I simply stood in the shadows and watched the police go about their tasks or, less frequently, but more discretely, "did a train" and slipped from view entirely. . . . In the academy, I helped cover for tardy classmates by concocting what I thought to be reasonable tales to tell superior officers. Several times I cheated on exams by passing my answer sheet around the back of the room (as I too looked at others' answers sheets). These mostly mundane matters would hardly be worth mentioning were it not for the fact that they point to the difficulty, if not impossibility, of maintaining a clear cut and recognizable observational *or* participatory research role. At least in the police world, the variation existing in the environment as well as that among the people studied, requires a situational and very flexible set of guidelines not easily categorized—even when writing with the luxury of hindsight.

Confessional Tales in Perspective

The confessional tale has become, as I argued earlier, an institutionalized and popular form of fieldwork writing. The confessional attempts to represent the fieldworker's participative presence in the studied scene, the fieldworker's rapport and sensitive contact with others in the world described, and something of the concrete cultural particulars that baffle the fieldworker while he learns to live in the setting. It is necessarily a blurred account, combining a partial description of the culture alongside an equally partial description of the fieldwork experience itself. Since the authors are writing of their own sightings, hearings, and interpretations, the soft subjectivity of the fieldwork experience begins to slip into fieldwork confessions in a way it does not in realist versions of a culture. Missing data, incompleteness, blind spots, and various other obscurities are admitted into the account. The avowed purpose, of course, is to lift the veil of public secrecy surrounding fieldwork.

Unmasking fieldwork is a relatively recent phenomenon. A generation (perhaps two) of fieldworkers, in both anthropology and sociology, apparently felt no great urge to enlighten their readers as to what canny tricks of the trade carried them through their respective research projects. For the most part, they were willing to simply state something to the effect, "This study is based on two years of fieldwork" and leave it at that; allowing readers to judge the adequacy of the method by the final result. No more. Several reasons can be generated for the current popularity of the fieldwork confession.

First, much of the traditional authority claimed for fieldwork by its early promoters and justified by them on the basis of their establishing ethnography as a human and behavioral science, akin to the observing natural sciences, has worn thin. Some confessions are therefore an attempt to shore up the fieldwork craft as a still scientifically valid one. They attempt to show how a reader might work back from a display of the conditions under which the fieldwork was accomplished to some assessment of how reliable and valid the realist ethnography itself might be. Presumably the claims, anecdotes, and personal jitters contained in my confessional tale might inform the reader who worries about the trustworthiness of my stationhouse sergeant depiction. Because realist accounts are methodologically silent, because they adopt the conceit that data must be cleanly separated from the fieldworker (implying, no doubt, that virtually anyone would see, hear, and think the same things were they in the fieldworker's shoes), and because they offer only the fieldworker's tightly packaged account of the culture studied, confessions are necessary.

Second, some confessional writers are not at all interested in reestablishing and confirming orthodox views on the scientific charter of fieldwork. In fact, some confessional tales are written explicitly to question the very basis of ethnographic authority and to transform ethnography, insofar as possible, into a more philosophical, artistic, phenomenological, or political craft; a craft sensitive to matters thought by these writers to be more relevant and important than what ethnography provided to readers in the past.[11] In skilled hands, the personal voice can be a gift to readers and the confessional becomes a self-reflective meditation on the nature of ethnographic understanding; the reader comes away with a deeper sense of the problems posed by the enterprise itself. In unskilled hands, a wild and woolly involuted tract is produced that seems to suck its author (and reader) into a black hole of introspection; the confessional is obsessed with method, not subject, and drifts toward a single-minded, abstract representation of fieldwork. Yet however involuted some confessional accounts may appear, the reader who wonders why the confessional writers don't do their perverse, self-centered, anxiety work in private and simply come forward with an ethnographic fact or two are, quite frankly, missing the point.

A good deal of recent confessional work rests on what many (myself included) take to be a fundamental turning point in American social thought. No longer is the social world, as mentioned in chapter 1, to be taken for granted as merely out there full of neutral, objective, observable facts. Nor are native points of view to be considered plums hanging from trees, needing only to be plucked by fieldworkers and passed on to consumers. Rather, social facts, including native points of view, are human fabrications, themselves subject to social inquiry as to their origins. Fieldwork constructs now are seen by many to emerge from a hermeneutic process; fieldwork is an interpretive act, not an observational or descriptive one (Agar, 1986). This process begins with the explicit examination of one's own preconceptions, biases, and motives, moving forward in a dialectic fashion toward understanding by way of a continuous dialogue between the interpreter and interpreted (see Rabinow and Sullivan, 1979).

Some confessionals suggest that the acute self-consciousness brought on by working through such a process can lead to something of a paralysis (e.g., Jules-Rosette, 1976; Thorne, 1983; Krieger, 1983; Tyler, 1986). There is obviously a need for balance between introspection and objectification. When only the former is involved, a sort of "vanity ethnography" results, in which only the private muses and demons of the fieldworker are of concern. Conventions of confessionals offer some aid, if not comfort, for fieldworkers trying to grasp occurrences in the field empathetically, but to stand away to situate them in other contexts, both social and personal. The textual organization of the standard confessional tale may be of some help for fieldworkers who regard participant-observation as a metaphor best reformulated in hermeneutic terms: a dialectic between experience and interpretation.

There is, as exemplified in my confessional, something of a norm about what constitutes a minimally acceptable table of contents for an account of fieldwork. Authors must discuss their pre-understandings of the studied scene as well as their own interests

Chapter Four

in that scene; their modes of entry, sustained participation or presence, and exit procedures; the responses of others on the scene to their presence (and vice versa); the nature of their relationship with various categories of informants; and their modes of data collection, storage, retrieval, and analysis. To work through such matters deeply forces on the fieldworker a private encounter with some very basic hermeneutic issues, an encounter which may become public. As fieldworkers consider and report their practices, confessional tales grow more complex and sophisticated.[12]

In this vein, when I consider my own confession I find it now a rather flat, traditional, and unremarkable one.[13] All the conventions discussed in the introductory section of this chapter are present. The authority is highly personalized. It is certainly the case that it is my own point of view that is at issue in the tale and not that of the police. The naturalness of the data is implied by the various ways I document my acceptance into police circles as a quasi member in good standing. On this matter, the unsaid but unavoidable implication of the writing is that these world-weary policemen ignored me as a researcher and paid attention to me only as an awkward novice or easy friend who was seen as reliably on their side; they went about their mostly unmerry way in much the same fashion as they would had I not been there. Certainly this is the message I wished to convey at the time I wrote the confessional, and in a sense it is my hope that it still represents at least a partial truth.

But I must admit I am far less certain or confident now about the veracity and faithfulness of either my confessional or my realist tales than I have been in the past. Both kinds of writing are highly conventionalized in both a representational and a stylistic sense. Both, as I know only too well, leave more of my knowledge out of the accounts than they put in. Both close off too early (and too casually) what remain rather open matters. Fiddlesticks. I am, in short, still very much in the process of coming to understand my materials—which continue to develop each time I revisit Union City, talk to my friends there, read the newspapers, review articles and books by others relevant to my materials, or sit and consider old writings or notes of my own.

I am also troubled by my rather strait-laced and straight-faced handling of informants for whom I unproblematically claim to speak in my tales. I know full well that the understanding I have of their talk and action is not only incomplete, but rests fundamentally on the contextual matters that surround my coming together with particular people, at particular times, for particular purposes, in particular places, and so on. Thus I put forward the meaning of such talk and action untruthfully in my writing without also considering (and representing) the various contexts within which it occurs. In what is rapidly becoming something of an in-group term in fieldwork circles, both informants and fieldworkers are "interlocutors" in cultural studies and are therefore jointly engaged in making sense of the enterprise (Clifford and Marcus, 1986). The line between what informants and fieldworkers make of the world is not an easy one to locate (Van Maanen, 1979, 1981b).

At issue is the fact that there are always many ways to interpret cultural data. Each interpretation can be disputed on many grounds. The data fieldworkers come to hold are not like dollar bills found on the sidewalk and stealthily tucked away in our pockets for later use. Field data are constructed from talk and action. They are then interpretations of other interpretations and are mediated many times over—by the fieldworker's own standards of relevance for what is of interest; by the historically situated queries put to informants; by the norms current in the fieldworker's professional community for what is proper work; by the self-reflection demanded of both the fieldworker and the informant; by the intentional and unintentional ways a fieldworker or informant is misled; and by the fieldworker's mere presence on the scene as an observer and participant.

Fieldworkers are increasingly conscious that the so-called data they produce and carry away from the field have already been thoroughly worked over. "Textualization" is Ricoeur's (1973) term for the process by which unwritten behavior, beliefs, values, rituals, oral traditions, and so forth, become fixed, atomized, and classified as data of a certain sort. Only in textualized form do data yield to analysis. The process of analysis is not dependent on the events themselves, but on a second-order, textualized, fieldworker-dependent version of the events. The problem here is how to crack open the textualization process itself. As we shall see, several possibilities are being entertained in the more experimental forms of ethnographic writing.

Nonetheless, despite growing discomfort among many fieldworkers with these apparently intractable dilemmas facing their craft, if they are to write at all about their research, they must get on with it or retire from the sport entirely. Two forms of practical resolution have been discussed thus far. In gross form, realist writings take what the authors know (or at least think they know) as their subject matter and, by and large, ignore how such things came to be known. In equally crude fashion, confessional writers take the author or knower as subject matter and by and large bypass what it is that the author knows as a result of fieldwork. Each treats the other as supplemental.

In chapter 5 another class of fieldwork tales are examined. I call these "impressionist tales" and argue that they are an attempt to explicitly bring knower and known together in representational form. Currently, impressionist tales of the published sort are often buried within realist or confessional ones and are thus something of a subgenre and a marginal type of ethnographic writing. More frequently, however, impressionist tales are told to little gatherings of friends, colleagues, students, and other interested groups. While they rarely make it into print, impressionist tales are the backstage talk of fieldwork. Telling them is a familiar enough occurrence in fieldwork circles to warrant closer inspection. There are, of course, important differences between the spoken and written tales. I've chosen, however, to join the two in chapter 5, with only a ritual nod given now and then to the distinction between them.

NOTES

1. Until the 1960s, fieldwork was with few exceptions simply done and not much written about or analyzed. Critics of ethnography delighted in pointing this out. To some, fieldwork became known, with a certain condescension, as the "anthropological method;" by others it was thought of as preparatory to the main business of social research and was hence called a "pilot" or "exploratory" study; and to the most vehement fieldwork was merely "pseudoscience" (Hughes, 1960). Early confes-

sional tales attempted to set their critics straight by demonstrating the sanctity and worth of their "timeless way of knowledge." These legitimizing works were celebratory in tone (sanctification by grace), and while exposing some of the warts of the activity, fieldwork came off splendidly in the text, as might be expected since the fieldworker was doing the writing (e.g., Casagrande, 1960; Adams and Preiss, 1960; Maybury-Lewis, 1965; Vidich, Bensman and Stein, 1964; McCall and Simmons, 1969; Spindler, 1970). These forms have now hardened into the genre presented in this chapter. As I suggest, however, confessional tales, like realist ones, are being modified now as the power of observation slips away as the unique ethnographic strength. Marcus and Fischer (1986:33–44) discuss the direction such changes are taking under the label "interpretive anthropology."

2. I have in mind such examples as Junker, 1960; Freilich, 1970; R. Wax, 1971; Kimball and Watson, 1972; Bogdan and Taylor, 1975; Lofland, 1976; and many of the essays in Van Maanen, 1983b. This list is, however, a drop in the bucket. Apparently the quip attributed to Evans-Pritchard (quoted in Clarke, 1975): "Anybody who is not a complete idiot can do fieldwork," seriously underestimates the felt need of fieldworkers for more explicit guidance.

3. Examples here would include Agar, 1986; Emerson, 1983; Hammersley and Atkinson, 1983; Ruby, 1982; Schwartz and Jacobs, 1979; Rabinow and Sullivan, 1979; and Douglas, 1976. This literature continues to grow.

4. Confessional tales do not always praise the trickster image. In some, fieldwork is presented as a moral trial having anguish and ambivalence as the felt result. In my own work, for example, I was once thanked by some of my police acquaintances for coming to the funeral of one of their mates. I still feel like a hypocrite recalling the incident, since I was at the funeral to unravel a cultural rite and not to pay my respects. Hypocrisy is always at issue in fieldwork, and these (and other) inner experiences mark the confessional tale (e.g., Powdermaker, 1966; Henry and Saberwal, 1969; Gans, 1982; Habenstein, 1970; Thorne, 1980; Punch, 1986; R. Rosaldo, 1986a).

5. From this standpoint, theory would seem to have most relevance at the second moment of ethnographic production, the writing phase, where an author's selection and choice of ethnographic facts and arrangement of them create the text. Theory matters in the field only insofar as similar kinds of fieldwork experience for very different fieldworkers are given contrasting readings and weight. The same informant's account or activity can be seen as an example of false consciousness or as situationally appropriate and creative behavior. Theory doesn't determine

fieldwork experience, but it may provide the dictionary with which it is read. See Feyerabend (1972) for a useful, though polemic, treatment of this matter.

6. As noted earlier, a relatively new school of fieldwork practice is emerging in sociology under the existentialist banner. This group argues cogently for more intimate involvement ("become the phenomena") in order to personally experience emotion and meaning in the life world studied. Fieldworkers within this school regard both discourse and observation as inadequate devices for getting past the fronts, duplicity, and secrecy that often surround certain settings (e.g., nude beaches, message parlors, drug dealing, adult bookstores). See J. Douglas (1976, 1985) for a statement of aims and theory and Adler and Adler (1987) for a useful review of some of the ways the existentialist desperadoes of fieldwork are putting their views (and feelings) into practice.

7. This matchmaking sense of ethnography resembles Gidden's (1976) idea that different cultural realities are, insofar as they are aware of one another, frames of meaning always in the process of mediation. Thus, fieldworker and native frames of meaning meet in an ethnography which presents the results of a mediation process. These results could, of course, represent the triumph of rationality, delusion, or coercion in fieldwork. Readers have only the final product on which to reflect and surmise.

8. Things are somewhat more in flux here than the text suggests. A part of the confessional literature also debunks the previously unquestioned (and charming) myth of fieldwork rapport. Malinowski (1967) was again path breaking in this regard (posthumously). More recently, it has become fashionable in some circles to speak of a confrontational form of fieldwork where from the outset of the study little faith is placed in the innocent attainment of rapport as the necessary precondition to unlocking cultural knowledge. Clifford (1983b) points out that there is always a certain amount of violence involved in fieldwork if only because the fieldworker's presence is manifestly an intrusion. Confrontational fieldworkers no longer avoid mention of such violence, so they attack the assumption of rapport and with it the dream of an unobtrusive ethnography. In the hands of some sociologists confessions read like debriefings after a battle in the social combat zone with accounts of how informants were bullied, how tactics of coercive persuasion were employed, and how the weaknesses, disunity, and confusion of the natives were exploited (e.g., J. Douglas, 1976, 1985; Humphreys, 1970: 185–92; Bulmer, 1982; Punch, 1986).

9. In this light, to publish a confessional tale is often something of a reward given the fieldworker for having first presented a realist account

deemed interesting enough by one's colleagues to warrant another account of how such sterling work was apparently done. Much confessional writing helps to establish the respectability of the ethnographic work that preceded it, either by showing how the traditional canons of practice were followed in the field, or, conversely, by showing why traditional canons were inadequate to produce the worthy tale the confession indexes.

10. I should also note that while confession was partly on my mind when I wrote this article, so, too, was a rather blatant attempt to smuggle in some of my police material that I found more difficult to represent in the realist tradition. This secondary objective is hardly atypical of confession, and, as I noted earlier, some ethnographers (and their readers) find the confessional format perfectly tuned to their own theoretical, philosophical, and personal commitments. It therefore serves them as a favored form of fieldwork reporting.

11. The fieldworkers of interest here are likely to consider ethnography more an art form than a science (see Geertz, 1983; Marcus and Fischer, 1986; Rabinow and Sullivan, 1979). They often chastise their more scientifically oriented colleagues for what they regard as failed prophecies, trivial research, and little progress toward any iron laws of behavior despite the constant whine for more research on a given topic. Not only do the critics of traditional ethnographic aims draw on interpretive theories for inspiration, but this bolting from the fold occurs, as Clifford (1983a) suggests, at a time when colonial authority has vanished and most liberal democracies are said to be in a crisis of conscience (partly as a result of the social upheavals of the 1960s and 1970s). In this climate, the institutional role of fieldwork has been attacked, sometimes savagely, for being but a special branch of the queen's secret service, serving mainly to inform the crown during those long, hot summers when the natives are restless. A new form of ethnography is therefore required on moral grounds—one with a more dispersed form of authority and less claim to possess the correct interpretive stance. Strong statements urging a more active and politically savvy role for ethnography are found in Hymes, 1972; Dwyer, 1977; and Thomas, 1983b.

12. While complexity and sophistication may indeed grow, there are limits to the genre as well. Confessions, endlessly replayed, begin to lose their novelty and power to inform. In the extreme, they also lose their way altogether by tacitly suggesting that fieldwork is a better method for learning about the fieldworker than it is for learning about the culture the fieldworker went to study. It may be that standard-form confessional tales have exhausted the possibilities for improving what remains a necessarily uncertain and risky task. New ways of understanding fieldwork may be required in order to look more closely and critically at the prestudy as-

sumptions and practices that govern the production and dissemination of ethnography. Both history and literary criticism are models for the kind of work that is needed. Movement along these fronts is visible (e.g., Rock, 1979:178–217; Gusfield, 1981:83–108; Stocking, 1983; Geertz, 1983; Clifford, 1983a, 1983b; Bulmer, 1984; Clifford and Marcus, 1986; Marcus and Fischer, 1986; and Becker, 1986a, 121–25.

13. A striking example of this is the fact that I made no mention in this confession of my simple desire to do fieldwork. This seems a curious oversight in retrospect, because I was very much committed to getting beyond the university and trying my hand at what I was beginning to regard as "real research." At the time, my only exposure to what the craft entailed were two hurried observational projects, one in a commercial bank, the other in several local city halls. I had, however, read enough about fieldwork to prefer my image of it to other thesis prospects of mine, such as standing over an IBM machine in the computer center running data or hanging out in the library talking to myself. A very real motive behind my commitment to fieldwork was (and I suppose still is) that it seemed like fun. A good part of my imagery came, of course, from the lively confessionals I was then reading. The irony of all this is that, as mentioned in the Preface, when all was said and done, my thesis, despite the lengthy fieldwork, still put me in front of the IBM machine cranking out survey results and running back and forth to the library to develop some comparative framework for my numbers. I was not yet confident, nor had I learned to write it up. Writing, not fieldwork, turned out to be my problem. Becker (1986b) provides some much needed advice and insight on the most practical problems of deskwork in sociology.

5

Impressionist Tales

To recognize the poetic dimension of ethnography does not require one gives up facts and accurate accounting for the supposed
freeplay of poetry. Poetry is not limited to romantic or modern-
ist subjectivism; it can be historical, precise, objective.

James Clifford

The label I use for the tales considered in this chapter is drawn
from art historians who regard impressionist painting as a novel
representational form emerging in the West during the late nineteenth and early twentieth centuries.[1] Impressionist painting sets
out to capture a worldly scene in a special instant or moment of
time. The work is figurative, although it conveys a highly personalized perspective. What a painter sees, given an apparent position in time and space, is what the viewer sees.

Renoir, Van Gogh, Seurat, and Monet are classic examples of
impressionist painters. The movement itself took shape as artists
moved away from idealized landscapes and formal portraits painted
in the studio toward more familiar, common, everyday scenes
done in situ. Roses and vases gave way to tangled wheat fields. An
aristocrat and his horse gave way to a dreary night cafe. Impressionist painting is often marked by earthy group scenes of an un-
posed character (e.g., dance, tavern life, public gardens, family
meals, street vendors, common vistas, plain rooms). The attempt
is to evoke an open, participatory sense in the viewer and as with
all revisionist forms of art, to startle complacent viewers accustomed to and comfortable with older forms. For my purposes, it is
the impressionists' self-conscious and, for their time, innovative
use of their materials—color, form, light, stroke, hatching, overlay, frame—that provides the associative link to fieldwork writing.

The impressionists of ethnography are also out to startle their
audience. But striking stories, not luminous paintings, are their

stock-in-trade. Their materials are words, metaphors, phrasings, imagery, and most critically, the expansive recall of fieldwork experience. When these are put together and told in the first person as a tightly focused, vibrant, exact, but necessarily imaginative rendering of fieldwork, an impressionist tale of the field results.[2] Such tales comprise a series of remembered events in the field in which the author was usually a participant. They are bundled together in such a way that they alter, in the end, whatever state or situation was said to obtain at the beginning of the tale. What makes the story worth telling is its presumably out of the ordinary or unique character. Impressionist tales are not about what usually happens but about what rarely happens. These are the tales that presumably mark and make memorable the fieldwork experience.[3]

Impressionist tales present the doing of fieldwork rather than simply the doer or the done. They reconstruct in dramatic form those periods the author regards as especially notable and hence reportable. Tales often initiate an analysis of the nature of cultural understanding and the fieldworker's role as a student. Reflective, meditative themes may develop from the story and spin off in a number of fieldworker-determined directions. The story itself, the impressionist's tale, is a representational means of cracking open the culture and the fieldworker's way of knowing it so that both can be jointly examined. Impressionist writing tries to keep both subject and object in constant view. The epistemological aim is then to braid the knower with the known.

To explore the analytic treatment of fieldwork epistemology is, as noted, well beyond the scope of this monograph, which is concerned primarily with clarifying and illustrating the various forms of ethnographic expression. Suffice it to say, the interpretive turn (discussed briefly in previous chapters) has been taken by many fieldworkers, thus making the impressionist tale a representation itself subject to many forms of critical analysis (e.g., phenomenological, semiotic, symbolic, linguistic, semantic, literary, textual, philosophical, hermeneutic). Here I restrict my focus to the tales fieldworkers tell of their work and not what they make of the tales. I recognize that tales are often told strategically as a way of getting to matters more dear to the writer's heart. Nonetheless, the story itself is the object of my interest and affection in the remainder of this chapter. Some conventions follow.

Textual Identity

The form of an impressionist tale is dramatic recall. Events are recounted roughly in the order in which they are said to have occurred and carry with them all the odds and ends that are associated with the remembered events. The idea is to draw an audience into an unfamiliar story world and allow it, as far as possible, to see, hear, and feel as the fieldworker saw, heard, and felt. Such tales seek to imaginatively place the audience in the fieldwork situation—seated ringside as witness to a tribal ceremony of consequence, tasting the low life with the Hell's Angels in some sleazy beer bar, or shooting the falls in a barrel at Niagara.

Impressionist tales can stand alone with or without elaborate framing devices or extensive commentary. There are in the telling of tales many opportunities, of course, for the fieldworker-author to slip out of the story and make an analytic point or two. These interruptions are not unnoticed by an audience, nor are they always welcomed. Tellers of impressionist tales, once they begin, must keep the narrative rolling or risk losing continuity and with it their audience. The power of a story to spark interest and involvement is as much a function of staying close to the sequential, immediate, and tightly linked flow of events as it is a function of the substance of the tale itself. The point here is that the audience knows very well what is a part of the story and what is not.

By holding back on interpretation and sticking to the story, impressionists are saying, in effect, "here is this world, make of it what you will." Transparency and concreteness give the impressionist tale an absorbing character, as does the use of a maximally evocative language. Moans, cackles, and epithets, for example, are used to suggest the emotional involvement of the fieldworker in the tale and to intensify the events. The audience is asked to relive the tale with the fieldworker, not interpret or analyze it. The intention is not to tell readers what to think of an experience but to show them the experience from beginning to end and thus draw them immediately into the story to work out its problems and puzzles as they unfold.

Fragmented Knowledge

Readers of impressionist accounts are often puzzled by their novelistic character. "It doesn't read like ethnography." This is, of course, precisely the point and is what distinguishes the impressionist tale from other forms of ethnographic reporting. Because the impressionist tale unfolds event by event, matters of disciplinary or methodological concern to the audience are met, if at all, in irregular and unexpected ways. Certain sensibilities are jarred as the author is seemingly swept away by a series of recalled events that have uncertain meanings to an audience unsure of where it is being taken and why. A look here, a voice there, a glance at some half-hidden object, all characterize the well-told, suspenseful tale. How will it all turn out? Cultural knowledge is slipped to an audience in fragmented, disjointed ways.

In short, a learning process is suggested by the impressionist tale. Certain unremarkable features of the beginnings of a tale become crucial by its end. Or similarly, certain features seemingly vital in the beginnings of the tale prove unimportant to the eventual turn of events. The audience cannot know in advance what matters will prove instructive, and thus by trying to hang on to the little details of the tale, they experience something akin to what the fieldworker might have experienced during the narrated events.

Characterization

Fieldworkers are certainly not indifferent to their own images in their tales of the field. We can be certain that they wish to be judged as charitably by their audience as they judge themselves. Individuality is expressed by such poses as befuddlement, mixed emotions, moral anguish, heightened sensitivity, compassion, enchantment, skepticism, or an apparent eager-beaver spirit of inquiry. A stance must be chosen to help shape the lead character's action simply as a way of making the tale easier to tell and, at least to the fieldworker, attractive. Like the writers of confessions, fieldworkers, as impressionists, take some pride in demonstrating that they were anything but simple scribes, absorbent sponges, or academic ciphers in their research worlds. Such disinterested characters would hardly make engaging narrators for an impressionist tale.

So, too, the supporting players in an impressionist's tale. Common-denominator people do not make good stories. To say "the police sometimes kill people for mistaken reasons" is, flatly, not a story. To say "Officer Allen shot Officer Roberts while both men were on a drug stakeout" is a story. The narrator of a tale can not converse in a story with "types" of people. Characters in impressionist tales must be given names, faces, motives, and things to do if a story is to be told about them. More important, when a story is at stake, these supporting players must be given lines to speak. The fieldworker must then give individual voices to the natives displayed in an impressionist tale.

Dramatic Control

Both confessional and realist accounts often suggest the not-so-gentle irony that members (or at least most of them) know their culture less well than the fieldworker. Irony of this kind is less likely to baldly surface in an impressionist tale, since an impressionist tale is about events that supposedly preceded the creation of such a wise and imperial character. Impressionist tales move their authors back in time to events that might have later given rise to understanding (or confusion). But in the storyworld, it is the fieldworker's reading of those events at the time they occurred that matters.

Organizing such an illusion requires skill. Recall is sometimes put in the present tense to give the tale a "you-are-there" feel. The author must not give away the ending before it is time. A degree of tension must be allowed to build and then be released. Contextual descriptions must be condensed yet rich enough to carry the reader along. Artistic nerve is required of the teller. Literary standards are of more interest to the impressionist than scientific ones. A general audience unfamiliar with the studied scene can judge the tale only on the basis of its plausibility or believability, not on the basis of accuracy or representativeness. In telling a tale, narrative rationality is of more concern than an argumentative kind. The audience cannot be concerned with the story's correctness, since they were not there and cannot know if it is correct. The standards are largely those of interest (does it attract?), coherence (does it hang together?), and fidelity (does it seem true?).[4]

105

Finally, since the standards are not disciplinary but literary ones, the main obligation of the impressionist is to keep the audience alert and interested. Unusual phrasings, fresh allusions, rich language, cognitive and emotional stimulation, puns, and quick jolts to the imagination are all characteristic of the good tale. Whatever allegory the fieldworker may have in mind for the story will not catch a sleepy audience. It is no surprise that some of the best ethnographic writing is done when impressionist tales are told.

Producing Impressionist Tales

Impressionist tales, as noted, remain very much a subgenre of ethnographic writing. They are typically enclosed within realist, or perhaps more frequently, confessional tales. When impressionist tales dominate a text something notable has been attempted, and these texts are often much discussed. Two very striking examples are, in fact, fiction (Bowen, 1954; Lurie, 1969). In a similar vein, nonfiction work in the impressionist style operates by converting the temporal nature of a fieldwork experience into the spatial organization for the text—fieldworkers display their own day-by-day experiences in the field in the order in which they occurred. In anthropology, outstanding examples are Chagnon, 1968; Briggs, 1970; Rabinow, 1977; and Dumont, 1978. In sociology good examples of book-length impressionist tales are Reinharz, 1979; Krieger, 1983; and Beynon, 1973.

Worthy of note, too, is Johnson's (1975) confessional, because of the author's concern for reducing, if not obliterating, the researcher-researched distinction. The book is topically arranged—nominally a method text—but a number of highly personal tales are told in each section. The stories keep the text moving as the reader strains to learn what author Johnson, stumbling around in a large welfare agency, will eventually learn in the setting. Also Hayano's (1982) intensive look at California poker palaces and players deserves note. Hayano develops the notion of "auto-ethnography," a wet term signaling the cultural study of one's own people. Here Hayano's full participation, active membership, and identification with a loose network of nocturnal poker devotees provide the means for an impressionist work of considerable appeal (see also Hayano, 1979).

Most frequently perhaps, impressionist tales appear in essay form. In paradigmatic form, the impressionist tale provokes multiple, often contrasting, interpretations, each of which the author, in due leisurely course, addresses and assesses. Perhaps the most famous is Clifford Geertz's (1973) "Deep Play," which exhibits all the conventions mentioned here plus some of his own. In this tale of Balinese cockfighting as a cultural form, Geertz dashes off a number of clever, erotic puns embedded in a lush narrative landscape while he pursues his own thick description. The essay is made especially memorable when Geertz begins it with a lengthy and amusing tale involving a police raid on a local cockfight where he and his wife are in attendance.[5]

Other notable examples of impressionist tales, all drawn from segments of more conventional ethnographic work, include William Whyte (1955) stuffing the ballot box in a Cornerville election; Melville Dalton (1964) turning the tables on his industrial employers by converting his closely observed managerial role into an ethnographic one; Evans-Pritchard (1936) attempting to run his own household according to Zande beliefs; or more recently, Peter Manning (1980) wandering around in the dark trying to make sense of a police narcotics raid; Renato Rosaldo (1980) trying to steer Ilongot tribesmen toward a discussion of some high-church anthropological topics; Brad Shore (1982) hot on the trail of cultural signifiers in the midst of a Samoan murder mystery; or Charles Savage trying to stay clear of the "doctores" in a Columbian pottery plant so he can win the workers' respect (Savage and Lombard, 1985).

All of these published and to many classic fieldwork stories display considerable textual self-consciousness. Book-length versions are particularly effective, since they embody theoretical and topical digressions in the realist and confessional modes while maintaining the coherence of storytelling. While all are good to read and enjoy, they are slightly off-putting to the rest of us who do not write like Geertz or his literary-kin. Certainly writing an evocative tale is no easy matter. There are no doubt more failed, unpublished storytellers among fieldworkers than published ones.

Yet when it comes to the oral telling of tales, a quite different situation prevails. Indeed, fieldworkers without stories to tell about their adventures are unimaginable, and if found out they would surely be banished from their respective tribes. Impressionist tales may be infrequent in print, but they are certainly familiar among fieldworkers at the podium, hanging around airports with cronies, in the classroom, at the local saloon, holding forth at a party, or loafing on the beach drinking wine from screw-top bottles with friends.[6]

There is, I think, a great disparity between the way fieldwork is written about and the way it is talked about. Impressionist tales do not easily fit into realist or confessional writings because of the highly specific character of the events and people that fill them out. The tales take time to tell properly, and the details important to a story may be peripheral to the other aims of a writer. There is also, even among ethnographers, something of a scholarly neurosis affecting many writers: fear of the particular and unusual (Geertz, 1983). Stories are not made from common and routine occurrences. Impressionist tales suggest that we learn more from the exceptional than from the topical. In some quarters this is heresy.

Impressionist tales when told in the flesh possess something of the provocative, sweet, secretive glitter of conspiracy. They are told to selected audiences in selected ways. When, where, and how stories are told reveal patterns of intimacy. Like gossip, the telling of impressionist tales implies closeness. Stories must be told in certain ways, however, if the audience is not to be put off but drawn in to the tale. The fieldworker must tell the tale in a way that hints at an informal, down-to-earth, modest, accessible demeanor. Qualifiers, endearments, sotto voce tone, colloquialisms, irreverences, sarcasm, down-home argot, all mark story time for fieldworkers.[7]

Impressionist tales, because they can stand alone and need not masquerade as anything other than stories, allow fieldworkers who are characters in them to exaggerate to make a point to omit tedious documentation, to entertain, to be uncharacteristically kind (or unkind), to use crude figures of speech typically forbidden, to intensify the relived experience, and otherwise to say things that under different circumstances could not be said. The impressionist, in Goffman's (1981) view, relies on the ability of the audience to absorb the spirit of the tale and not just the literal words that comprise it. Of course behind any story is the tacit claim that there is something being said worth saying. This is allegory and it is always associated with impressionist tales.

Let me now provide an example of an impressionist tale. It is something of a reckless story I've been working on and telling for some time. It dates back to a sequence of events that occurred on a summer night in 1978. In written form, it is a bloodless telling and a sham of a talking tale, for the tonal shifts, gestural dances, passion, two-finger dangles, twinkling of eyes, and opportunities for audience participation, challenge, revenge, or revision are all absent. I tell it here as I might say it, but the attentive reader will know what is missing.[8]

One with a Gun, One with a Dog, and One with the Shivers

This is a story about an incident in Union City. It happened during my third bit of fieldwork, a time when I really thought I had things well put together. I was working the Northend, in Charlie Three, with a good friend named David Sea. It was a Sunday night shift and not much was going on. We'd written a couple of movers, traffic citations, and handled a few radio calls: a domestic, a possible B-and-E that turned to shit, and a fender-bender down by the lake. Typical stuff, nothing very glamorous.

By midnight it got so quiet we went over to David's place for a while just to get out of the car. We had a couple of beers and sat around talking about his ex-wife, the pennant race, our kids, guns, and so on. After an hour or so, we got a call on the portable to take a family disturbance over at the projects, about a fifteen-minute drive from the apartment.

On the way to the call, another unit, Charlie Two, comes on the air to say they're already at the projects on a smash-n-grab and when they finish up they'll take our family beef for us. "Fine," says David, and we're off the hook for the call. Only a couple of hours are left on the shift. I'm tired and a little drowsy and consider asking David to drop me off at home rather than slog it out on this uneventful night. But perhaps as a response to his earlier hospitality, I decide to stick it out.

We drive around with no particular place to go and then David figures he'll show me where the new precinct substation is to be built in the fall. As we start moving in that direction, a call comes in from dispatch. It's about a car that refuses to stop, a possible roll'n stolen "heading east on 17th, just passing Park." It's the time of the sign, for a chase is now in progress.

The chase is real police work. The chase is action. It's the symbolic enactment of your basic war-on-crime mythology involving search, pursuit, capture; the holy trinity for cops. In contrast to the mundane reality of aimless patrol duties and endless public order work, the chase is excitement extraordinaire and something of an acid test of one's courage and commitment.

David motions for me to buckle up and heads the cruiser toward Interstate 13, where he thinks our culprit will head trying to get out of town. We make the interstate and are soon hitting speeds close to a hundred with lights flashing and siren ringing.

David once told me that good cops look relaxed when the tension is on, while bad cops always show the strain. Well, David doesn't look exactly like he's on a Sunday drive, but compared to me he's cool, with one steady hand on the wheel and the other flitting across the instrument panel attending to the lights, siren, and radio. My knuckles are pale from gripping the shotgun jiggling in its cradle before me and hanging on to the handhold of the door. I can barely manage the appearance of even limited self-control. Blood is throbbing in my ears. My powers of speech have vanished. I am scared.

After a couple of minutes of this mad rush to nowhere, David pulls off on the 51st Street exit, brakes, and flips the lights and siren off. We find ourselves suddenly and slowly climbing a hill in a quiet residential neighborhood. David has no idea why he took this particular exit, although later he is to claim "instinct." My adrenalin flow subsides (presumably David's too) and I am now able to show enough self-command to take part in a small exchange on how much fun these chases are but what pigs these police cruisers seem to be. I hope I'm not leaking too much anxiety (or relief), although I still feel flushed.

The next coherent (to me) message from the radio is that there is now a suspect, a young, black male driving a late-model Mercedes 450 SL convertible, dark brown or maroon, and believed to be stolen. Contained in this same message is word from radio that the other units have lost the car and the chase is no longer hot.

"Fuck a duck," says David, "no chance of picking it up now. It's a blind chase. The asshole's probably dumped the sucker by now."

These words are no more out of his mouth when over the crest of the hill comes a dark brown Mercedes 450 SL convertible. The driver is barely visible behind the wheel, but the car is bearing down on us and bearing down hard.

"Christ, that's the goddamn car!"

In a flash David hits the lights and siren. The Mercedes goes out of control. It bounces off one car parked on the narrow street, jumps the curb, and comes to a halt by slashing through a garden wall and slamming into a tree on someone's lawn no more than ten feet away.

The driver is indeed a young, black male; a kid, perhaps as young as twelve or thirteen. The kid crawls quickly across the front seat, pops out the door on the passenger's side, and runs full tilt up the driveway just to the right of the house.

David in one motion throws me the mike and unsnaps his safety belt. As he flies from the car, he tells me to give radio our location. Fumbling with the transmitter, a device I haven't used in at least five years, I somehow manage to get on the air the message of where we are and what we're up to. I then run up the driveway and around a garage until I spot David peering around a garden shed into some bushes.

He's got his service revolver out and is closely watching the bushes which grow tall and dense around a chain-link fence with wire barbs on top. Behind the fence are more bushes and, David thinks, an alleyway.

"Come outta there, you little fuckhead."

At a glance from David, I pull out my own revolver tucked away in a shoulder holster. The gun is on loan. I haven't fired a weapon in years, and despite good training and some familiarity, I am rather skittish and slightly fearful of guns.

My benefactor in the arms business was an ex-academy mate of mine who figured that if I were to spend time riding patrol, I shouldn't do so unarmed. Presumably this meant I was now dangerous, although it was not precisely clear to me to whom this danger attached: myself, my police colleagues, or this slippery car thief we were closing in on.

"You fucking creepo," I hear myself say in echo of David, "come on outta there or I'll blow your good-for-nothing ass away."

Despite our gentle invitations, no surrender is forthcoming. We both hear movement in the brush but can't see a thing. David now realizes he'd left his flashlight on the front seat of the patrol car.

"John, go get the goddamn light in the car. If we can see him, he'll come out."

I run toward the car to get the sturdy multicell flashlight, a copper's tool that gets more service as an effective truncheon than as a source of light. At the car, bumblebee policing—swarming—is in full glory. There are five patrol units plus the K-9 (canine) unit, whose driver arrives saying breathlessly, "not bad time, eh?"

I point the men in the general direction of where I'd left David and scramble around in the car to find the flashlight. I find it under the front seat and run back up the driveway to find a half-dozen cops stomping through the bushes, all with guns drawn. I'm standing in civie garb, trembling, and thinking, "Don't shoot the fieldworker."

David's gone. I'm told by a vaguely familiar officer that David bummed a radio and a light and is apparently now in hot pursuit of what this officer calls "your legendary flying asshole." A moment later, the K-9 officer and his pal Rex are off on the chase.

Along with the remaining officers, I wander back to the front of the house and find still more policemen arriving on the scene. The flag is being shown. Some of the new arrivals are searching the Mercedes for whatever information or goods it might yield. The section sergeant has also arrived and is sitting behind the wheel of the posh car, a "Benzo" in police slang, admiring our suspect's good taste. A few patrolmen are wandering around the immediate area on foot while others comb the rest of the neighborhood in prowl cars. There is a portable perched on the roof of the Mercedes and I can follow the progress of the chase.

The K-9 officer reports a good track. Officer Pinefield reports that the suspect is under a house. David reports that the suspect is up on the roof of the library. After asking for the police chopper to be sent in, he goes up to check. Another officer reports that he's spotted the suspect running across the Interstate. Most of the on-duty personnel of the Union City Police Department seem now to be fully involved and thoroughly enjoying the chase. Police are everywhere. They are cheerful. The radio is babbling. The K-9 officer reports that Rex had taken him down to the Interstate.

As all this is occurring, another story develops. Snooping around the area, a veteran but still eager cop known affectionately to his colleagues as "Blotter" (he's so big he blots out the sun) has found a middle-aged black man standing on a lawn about a block away from the crash watching the jolly police parade and commotion. Blotter, who prides himself on being a rough, tough professional who can recognize a villain when he sees one, asks the man what the hell he's doing standing around and gawking at the police at this time of night. The man, according to Blotter's report, begins to back off and edge "furtively" away, telling Blotter, as he does so, that he has no intention of answering any questions when the cops are raising such a racket and running around like chickens with their heads cut off.

Blotter is not amused. Few people treat him this way. Nor is he the sort of officer who allows himself to be hamstrung by tiresome legalities. The man is knocked to the ground, choked out, and sat upon. Later Blotter tells the duty sergeant at the station house that the man didn't "pass the Big A." He was therefore put upon for the Being-Rude-to-Blotter Act. In early December Blotter took a three-day holiday without pay.

Meanwhile, back at the Interstate, the K-9 officer and Rex are restless and want to get on with the chase. David, after admiring the view, climbs down from the library roof empty-handed. The police helicopter is reported to be out of service. Several cops crawl out from under a house with nothing to show for their efforts but dirty uniforms which they will pay from their own pockets to have cleaned. The officer who spied the suspect fleeing across the Interstate is now gratefully believed.

Since it's David's suspect and would-be prisoner, "body," "stat," or "number," we await David's decision as to what to do next.

"Cross over the Interstate," he barks.

I'm told by a plump and panting officer on the scene to drive the patrol unit over to the other side and set up one corner of a surveillance quadrant across from the fire station at Cherry and Longmead. David is apparently now running with the dog officer, and the rest of this hunting party, maybe fifteen to twenty cops, are to set the rest of the quadrant and begin searching inside its boundaries.

Except for the sergeant still sitting in the Mercedes, the accident scene empties quickly. I start the car and drive away, slowly realizing that I don't have a clue how to handle this mobile example of police high tech.

The radio seems to be screeching at me to do something. The lights and siren, to my astonishment, somehow come on. The demonic shot-gun is no longer secure and bounces around the front seat. The power brakes feel awkward and almost toss me through the windscreen at the first stop sign. To complicate matters, I have no idea where I'm going.

As I round a corner near the Interstate, the ticket book, the clip-board, the logbook, the portable radio, David's hat, and God knows what else go sliding out the passenger door I'd forgotten to fully close and onto the street. The shotgun would have gone too had I not grasped the stock of the weapon with a last-second, panic-stricken lunge. Shamefully, I pull to the side of the road to gather up my litter.

Luckily I was not unobserved by the police. Two Southend officers, looking for something to do, had come up to assist in the chase. They had just passed the accident scene and were coming to the Interstate when they saw the minimally controlled police car carom to the side of the road and its plain-clothed driver hop out to retrieve a host of police impedimenta.

They drive up as I'm puzzling over what switch controls what func-tion of the machine. I know one of the attending officers and thus sal-vage some self-esteem, since I don't have to go into a long account of who I am, what I am doing, and why I am doing it so badly. Between chuckles, they give me remedial instructions on how to operate a prowl car and direct me to where I am next to appear.

When I eventually arrive at the firehouse, David is standing on the corner chatting with another officer. Maybe ten minutes have passed since I left the section sergeant fondling the Mercedes, but of course it seems like years. William James is right about time stretching out when events conspire to fill it up.

I park the car facing the firehouse and jump thankfully from the jinxed driver's seat to rejoin David at the side of the road. Despite my obvious lack of composure, I say nothing of the reason for my delay—although we certainly talked of it later and it seems not to be the sort of incident my Union City friends are likely ever to forget.

While we are standing there talking, the door of the fire station—25 or so yards away—rolls up and out comes the battalion chief's car. It turns slowly away from us in the dark and moves on down the road.

"That's odd," says David, "wonder what he's up to this time of night."

We soon find out. A few minutes pass in idle chatter before a message from headquarters comes over the air.

"All units involved in the northend chase should be advised that we've just received word from the duty officer in the Cherry Street firehouse that the battalion chief's car has just been taken and driven away by party or parties unknown. It just might tie into that suspect you all have been chasing around up there."

"Shit."

The chase is on again. This time, however, there is very little enthusiasm. The fire chief's car may be quite visible on the road at this time of night but virtually all the on-duty cops in the city are clustered in this little quadrant we've just set up, a quadrant from which our sneaky little suspect just fled. The trail is several minutes old, and as a result very cold. The cops know well that at this time of night a properly motivated driver could be miles away. Moreover, the new prize, a fire chief's shiny car, is unlikely to be greatly valued by our fugitive, who the police rightly believe will dump it as soon as possible.

This is indeed the case. The car is found the next morning, abandoned across town near a sleazy motel. There is not even a usable description of the suspect. Not that it would much matter. But David and I, the two who perhaps had the cloest and longest look at the suspect, disagree and disagree spectacularly about how old he was, how tall he was, how much he weighed, and what he was wearing.

The coup de grace is delivered when David tells me the dog tracked the suspect right up to a window of the fire station but the human handler who was following Rex pulled him off the track in the mistaken belief that no self-respecting car thief on the run would dare break into a manned and operational firehouse.

David booked off that night on schedule. No overtime, no prisoner, no closure, and no justice. "I oughta go out right now and drag some clown in for drunk-n-refusing-to-fight," says David back in the squad room. I feel much the same way. Another member of the squad figures the suspect is now "laughing his ass off about how he's fooled all those dumb-fuck cops." Others mope around, changing out of their uniforms, muttering that the K-9 officer and Rex ought to trade roles. Attached to all of these remarks, however, is a clear, if begrudging, respect for the car thief.

"He's clever, man, he beat a dog."

Impressionist Tales in Perspective

Fieldwork isn't always as eventful as this story indicates (as students of managers, accountants, and computer programmers are quick to point out). Certainly most of my time in the police world was spent in long conversations, looking for something to do, and attending to the routine, tedious, everyday tasks the police are everywhere required to do. Occasionally such mundane matters are interrupted by an exhilarating event, and in those moments I have found myself swept away by them. It is, I think, irresistible to tell of such things. But it seems that fieldworkers rarely do so in print. This is a mistake.

What I have learned from this little episode and its many tellings is that I wasn't as smart or as detached in the field as I thought I was and had, in fact, presented myself as being in my confessional writings. I was frightened but thrilled by the chase, touched by guilt because I was so fearful and slow to emerge from the prowl car after the crash, maddened by my inability to operate the machinery or find my way around an area I had spent considerable time in, frustrated yet crazed with the idea of capturing the little car thief, puzzled by the confusion on the scene, surprised by the actions (or inactions) of both myself and some of my colleagues, and, in general, somewhat ashamed but mostly amused by the buffoonery of the night shift.

Intellectually, telling of the incident sharply reminds me that the backstage reality of policing is considerably more individualized, chaotic, fragmentary, and disorganized than my realist writings indicate. When the chips are down, for example, the police don't seem to trust either their technology or each other, often get caught in whirlwinds of confusion and sometimes enjoy the foolery that results, mistake identities with some regularity, and follow their own highly personalized instincts by relying on whatever crime-busting lore can be called up by the passing situation. Much of my work stresses the banal, ho-hum and commonplace reality of police work featuring sore feet (and seat), monotony, easing behavior, and the oversimplified common-denominator policeman's own view of things. Cops are concerned about bad weather, cups of coffee, and awful supervision. They show a sense of occupational solidarity that would probably make a Zulu proud. But they also care about their own safety and their own individual place in the scheme of things. Moreover, the desire to catch a crook is a widely distributed one. Irish playwright Brendan Behan catches the spirit of my tale with the remark that he'd never seen a situation so bad that the presence of the police didn't make it worse.[9]

Impressionist tales are the "kitchen sink" reports of past events that took place in the field. They allow fieldworkers to dump all sorts of odd facts and speculations into a shaggy narrative. Indeed, the well-told tale will always go behind the bare bones and embellish, elaborate, and fill in little details as the mood and moment strike. Certainly in my written telling of this story I've hedged here and there, added an extraneous point or two, polished up some descriptions, and left others out from previous tellings. Storytelling of the impressionist sort seems to rest on the recall of forgotten details and the editing of remembered ones.

One conventional and strategic definition of fieldwork is The "method that throws the researcher directly into the life-worlds under investigation and requires the careful recording (through fieldnotes) of the problematic and routine features of that world" (Denzin, 1981). Such a view raises the analytic position of fieldnotes and the recording of observations, conversations, and so forth to a very high, almost sacred level. But rest assured, nowhere in my fieldnotes does this story appear in a form even remotely comparable to the shape, tone, concern for detail, background information, or personal posturing that I've given it here. My fieldnotes, hastily composed the morning after the incident, contain a terse two-page descriptive statement typed in fractured syntax and devoid of much other than what I took then to be the incidental highlights of the episode. Nor do I even consider very interesting the relationship (or lack thereof) between the production of the tale as retold here and its various intermediate versions in the forms of fieldnotes, diary entries, and drafts.

Fieldwork, at its core, is a long social process of coming to terms with a culture. It is a process that begins before one enters the field and continues long after one leaves it. The working out of understandings may be symbolized by fieldnotes, but the intellectual activities that support such understandings are unlikely to be found in the daily records. The great dependency commonly

117

claimed to exist between fieldnotes and fieldworkers is not and cannot be so very great at all.[10]

The heavy glop of material we refer to as fieldnotes is necessarily incomplete and insufficient. It represents the recorded memory of a study perhaps, but it is only a tiny fraction of the fieldworker's own memory of the research period. More importantly, coming to understand a culture in a way even remotely similar to that of those that live within it is a continuous and, if the fieldworker is careful, a deepening interpretive process. Theoretical abstractions will not allow a fieldworker to get to the so-called heart of a culture any more quickly or better than natives do. Culture is not to be found in some discrete set of observations that can somehow be summed up numerically and organized narratively to provide full understanding. Events and conversations of the past are forever being reinterpreted in light of new understandings and continuing dialogue with the studied.

What a fieldworker learns over time is an interpretive skill relative to the culture of interest. It is perhaps more akin to learning to play a musical instrument than to solving a puzzle. What the fieldworker learns is how to appreciate the world in a different key. Early experiences and understandings of the world studied (and their representation in fieldnotes) are not data per se but rather primitive approximations of the writer's later knowledge and perspectives of those studied—a little like the beginning pianist's two-finger playing of *Twinkle, Twinkle, Little Star.*

Nowhere is this so apparent as when impressionist tales are told. They draw attention not only to the culture of study but also to the way of fieldworker's location and experience in the field help him produce a text to interpret. To tell my story in its mannered way, to characterize the various figures running through the tale in disorderly fashion, and to hold the dramatization up for scrutiny suggests, if nothing else, that I have come to claim a degree of interpretive authority in the police worlds in which I have lived. I can, for example, interpret this tale in a vast number of ways (as I am sure the reader can also) but I nonetheless regard the story as something of a paradigmatic scene of the police life on which my understanding can be put to test by its representation.

More important, perhaps, is the fact that I immodestly believe I have passed on in the tale itself a slice of the unruly police life as real, if not more real, than in some of my realist accounts. Stories, by their ability to condense, exemplify, and evoke a world, are as valid a device for transmitting cultural understandings as any other researcher-produced concoction. The fact that they can do so without recourse to disciplinary hedges makes them in some ways very appealing, since they can be read and appreciated by a general audience. This is, of course, a plea for the inclusion of more impressionist tales in our published fieldwork materials.

Coda

Impressionist tales typically highlight the episodic, complex, and ambivalent realities that are frozen and perhaps made too pat and ordered by realist or confessional conventions. Impressionist tales, with their silent disavowal of grand theorizing, their radical grasping for the particular, eventful, contextual, and unusual, contain an important message. They protest the ultimate superficiality of much of the published research in social science—ethnographic or otherwise. Fieldworkers are sometime conscious that the art they practice is to provide an account of or even paper over a deeply uncertain world. The pen as camera obscura. Impressionist tales of the field bring such matters to light, for they attempt to be as hesitant and open to contingency and interpretation as the concrete social experiences on which they are based.[11]

If knowing a culture is anything like Geertz (1974:45) implies—"grasping a proverb, catching an illusion, or seeing a joke"—it is a most ambivalent matter. Moreover, a culture is not something that can be known once and for all. Fieldworkers may stalk culture and meaning, but these elusive, will-o'-the-wisp targets slip in and out of view, appear in many apparitions, look different from different angles (and to different stalkers), and sometimes move with surprising speed. Knowing a culture, even our own, is a never-ending story.[12]

Writing up fieldwork tales in any or all of the forms discussed here brings this discomfort to the surface. We edit, contemplate, and evaluate the disparate materials we have on hand: the action observed in the field, snippets of conversation, interpretive skills we believe we have developed, documentary evidence collected,

119

stories we have heard, events we have participated in, bits and pieces of the "relevant" literature we have read, counts we have done, native category systems created and textualized, and so on. We assemble these originally unrelated segments into the dim shape of a representation and continue with our editing.

Slowly an analysis takes shape and a paper develops. We may even reach a final delusional state where we think that with perhaps one more rewrite, the paper will rise from mere perfection to beatitude and the representation will at last correspond to the world out there. But because of some wicked editor's deadline, classes that must be taught, the demands of a new project, the family vacation, the illness of a child, the visit of out-of-state friends, or the five minutes we have left to catch a plane, the form and content of the paper freeze. We know that our analysis is not finished, only over.[13]

The magic of telling impressionist tales is that they are always unfinished. With each retelling, we discover more of what we know. Because of their form and their dependence on the audience, meaning will be worked on again and again. By telling our stories and telling them over in different ways, we are admitting to those we trust that our goals are not necessarily fixed, that we are never free of doubt and ambiguity, that our strategic choices in fieldwork are often accidental (guided more by inchoate lore than by a technical logic), that our data to be meaningful require development over time, and that we are far more dependent on the people we study than we can know or say. The rub, of course, is that by such an admission we must recognize that we are flying by the seat of our pants much of the time. There is risk here, but there is also truth.

NOTES

1. When agonizing over what to call the tales of my affection in this chapter, I considered several options. Clifford (1981), for example, writes of surrealism as something of a subversive attitude certain French ethnographers once found attractive, for it valued the unclassified, shuffled conceptual categories, and produced incongruities, rather than reducing them. The idea was to arrange ethnographic materials in ways that made the familiar seem strange to an audience. The Anglo-American tradition in ethnography has been the reverse. Clifford's context is Paris of the

twenties and thirties, during which time he argues ethnography and sur-realism were both emerging and linked by common aesthetics. My use of impressionism rather than surrealism suggests I find images of melting watches, sewing machines on operating tables, or nudes with drawers in their chests to be less associated with the tales of my interest than is the impressionism of an earlier period as described in the text. Other possi-bilities I considered were expressionism and symbolism. Both involved open air painting and both rejected earlier formalist and realist ap-proaches to representation. But both expressionist and symbolist paint-ings are less figurative than impressionist paintings and achieve their effects largely by use of powerful distortions. The aims were apparently more toward capturing an inner or unconscious reality than an outer or conscious one. Consider Munch's *The Shriek* as an early example in this regard. Since the tales of the field I address in this chapter focus more on the sociology of emotion, not its psychology, impressionism seems a better analogy. Recent genres of painting, such as hyper-, super-, and photorealism, appear, in part, to bring to a halt the various trends to-wards obscure, abstract, flat, and vanishing imagery in contemporary painting. Maybe such forms also hold a message for ethnographers. If so, however, it is one beyond my reach.

2. These tales are not meant to capture much more than fragments of the fieldwork experience and are therefore difficult to integrate within a single interpretation. This is perhaps one purpose behind the telling of them, for they allow their teller to escape from the dictates of previous work. They leave the constitutive procedures of ethnographic analysis unarticulated while assembling something of a collage of brief images. For the most part, then, the images of the impressionist tale are presented as they may have appeared at the time to the fieldworker and not as they became known later.

3. Stories as units subject to analysis are beginning to attract attention in a number of social science quarters. Renaldo Rosaldo's (1980, 1986b) inventive use of Ilongot stories has already been mentioned. Martin (1982) also uses natives' stories as units of study in her energetic search for orga-nization cultures. Other researchers find the story itself to be subject to analysis in the manner of Propp (1958). Still others regard the conversa-tional telling of tales as worthy of study (Sachs, 1971). A good source book is Van Dijk (1985).

4. The notions of argumentative and narrative rationality are based on Weick and Browning (1985). Their work is an attempt to tie certain forms of organization to the typical modes of discourse found within them. The logic they apply suggests that more narrative rationality is found where less stratification exists (i.e., all can judge the coherence, adequacy, fidelity, and relevance of a story). Argumentative rationality is

121

found where greater stratification (hierarchy) exists (i.e., some are better judges than others). These forms may be self-serving too, since arguments create winners and losers while narratives do not. Part of the attraction of impressionist tales is just this feature—they illustrate, rather than claim. See also Krieger (1983:173–99) for additional poetic criteria of truth that contrast to the argumentative kind associated with standard social science versions of reliability and validity.

5. For a more critical reading of this classic tale, see Crapanzano (1986), where Geertz is taken to task for ducking out of the essay soon after telling the tale and falling back too easily on realist conventions. Crapanzano's main point is that Geertz's claim to have "cracked the code" governing the role the cockfight plays in Bali is pretentious because it assumes a final interpretation is possible.

6. Fieldworkers, like any other occupational community, tell stories for a number of reasons—to cheer each other up, to persuade people to do certain things or see things in a certain way, to find allies and expose enemies, to brag and drop names, to kill time, or simply to try to make a little sense of the world. The fireside chats of fieldworkers represent something of an oral tradition of the trade, and mythical elaborations of "what really happened" emerged and are passed on. Through informal channels and gossip, fieldworkers hear of Edmund Leach losing his fieldnotes on the way home from Burma, of David Sudnow writing *Passing-On* in only three days while sealed in a bare motel room, or of Erving Goffman spotting and then replacing a Las Vegas blackjack dealer who was cheating the house. The origins and truths of such tales are misty to be sure, but they comprise an endless source of fascination for fieldworkers and no small source of instruction about how the craft is practiced.

7. This is to suggest that a live performance adds something beyond words to an impressionist tale. In telling of fieldwork there is an opening up of the experience in the apparent spontaneity or freshness of the teller's recall. This may be something of an illusion, for the tale itself may have been told many times over. Parts of the story may be thoroughly memorized. Nonetheless, as Goffman (1981:162–95) suggests, listeners will gain a sense that they have special access to the speaker and can hear more in the tale (and the author's stance toward the tale) than would be possible were they to merely read it. I vividly remember, for example, sitting on the floor among a hushed crowd of sociology students at Yale in the winter of 1975 listening to Kai Erickson weave a deeply moving tale of his work in Buffalo Creek and thinking at the time (and long afterward) how lucky I was to be present. Writing up such tales, even by so skilled a writer as Erickson, robs them of much of their warmth. Tyler (1986) ar-

gues that "post-modern ethnography" must find ways to communicate in writing less of the cold ambition that comes from print and more other truths and intimacies that come from speech. This is a tall order.

8. The title for my tale is lifted from *The Spooky Old Tree*, a children's yarn involving the indefatigable Berenstain Bears. In the writing presented here, I try to preserve a spoken narrative and dramatic form that does not destroy all similarities to the way I might tell the story in person. As I suggest later, one of the most useful aspects of impressionist tales is their unfinished character. History and experience work on these tales in innumerable ways. I have never told the tale printed here in precisely the same way before nor can I tell it in exactly the same way again. More reading, writing, research, conversation, or simply living will surely lead to amendment and further understanding. Impressionist tales point to the discomforting fact that we are unable to do much more than partially describe what it is we know or do. We know more than we can say and will know even more after saying it.

9. A sketchy background of police studies would be instructive here. Early ethnographic writing on the American police gave the impression of ceaseless activity of an often violent sort (Westley, 1970; Skolnick, 1966). The police in these realist tales were besieged, busy, and hostile. As time passed, however, fieldworkers began to stress the more mundane and commonplace in police work; it was, after all, an occupation like others and not, to most policemen, a holy war. It is unlikely that police work itself shifted drastically over this period. Rather, as Downes and Rock (1982) argue, the early fieldworkers considered the occupational and organizational features of the work to be descriptively uninteresting compared to the more interesting stuff of police talk and the violence of the street. The rhapsody of crime fighting is still heard among the police, but as we now know from the second-generation realist tales, it is heard mostly in the coffee holes and station houses. And, I might add, in the impressionist tales of police researchers for whom occasions of violence, crook chasing, and "real police work" are very rare indeed. One wonders if the early police ethnographers told tales of the boredom and aimlessness associated with their work since these characteristics were so underplayed in their writings?

10. This is, of course, not an argument for doing away with fieldnotes. Where else would we find such a rich storehouse of materials to tickle and otherwise stimulate memories of fieldwork. It is an argument for keeping in perspective the place and value of fieldnotes. To put it bluntly, fieldnotes are gnomic, shorthand reconstructions of events, observations, and conversations that took place in the field. They are composed well after the fact as inexact notes to oneself and represent simply

one of many levels of textualization set off by experience. To disentangle the interpretive procedures at work as one moves across levels is problematic to say the least. To reinterpret fieldnotes requires knowing something about what was taken for granted when the notes were written—difficult enough for the writer to deal with, let alone another reader. Early notes from the field are particularly troublesome in this regard, because the writers themselves may no longer know or feel what they did when they first assembled the notes. Little wonder that fieldnotes are the secret papers of social research.

11. With this polemic paragraph I only wish to remind the reader that our theories of the social world deal with the most ephemeral, delicate, and elusive of matters. It is easy to slip away and start granting abstract entities (like culture, signs, rules, structures, etc.) status as iconic significations. Theories are always metaphoric and therefore precarious. From my perspective, the only effective antidote for the airsickness caused by theoretical flights is periodic returns to the field. As a theoretician I never get sucked in by informants, overinvolved in their worlds, misclassify my data, screw up an interview, piss off a gatekeeper, misread meanings members put on events, or become bored, lost, or underfed or overfed with information. As a fieldworker I am never free of these problems. It is humbling but it is the closest thing to church a theoretical atheist is likely to find.

12. The importance of this point can not be overstated. Culture is not something neatly wrapped up and given to people as a sort of gift for living. Rather, culture is earned, something each person must somehow gropingly reach for and recognize on his own. Turner (1981:140) makes the point: "We never cease to learn our own culture, which is always changing, let alone other cultures." That much of this cultural learning goes on late in life is a sobering notion for fieldworkers who want to understand it all in as short a time as possible.

13. This point suggests that external occurrences mark the completion of a manuscript for an author. My experience supports this position, but there are arguments to be made for internal occurrences as well. Some feel, psychologists for example, that a work is done at the point of physical and mental exhaustion, when an author literally depletes all the resources available to him. Others feel, economists perhaps, that a work is done only when an author discovers something else more satisfying and worthwhile for him to do, when the further tinkering, testing, and adjusting of a manuscript is no longer adequately compensated for by his continued interest in the work. As I near the end of this manuscript, all these accounts make good sense.

Fieldwork, Culture, and Ethnography Revisited

> What is necessary is more critical discussion by or for eth-
> nographers of each other's works, which in paying attention to
> rhetoric would not lose sight of the goal of constructing system-
> atic knowledge of other cultures.
>
> George E. Marcus and Dick Cushman

My concern throughout this book has been with the literary and
rhetorical devices used to represent the results of fieldwork. Ethnography may still be archaic in terms of its technology, requiring
only a fieldworker, time, a bunch of people to talk with, and some
writing materials. But ethnography has also become very sophisticated in terms of its emerging understandings of the practical,
philosophical, and epistemological problems facing those who
choose to study the social world. There is, in fact, some reason to
believe that fieldworkers are the leading edge of a movement to
reorient and redirect theoretical, methodological, and empirical
aims and practices in all the social sciences except, perhaps, the
dismal one. There is an almost giddy excitement among some
fieldworkers who believe the worm has finally turned. The narrative, semiotic, particularist, and self-aware standards now emerging from ethnography are being treated seriously, and if they have
not been adopted, they are at least exerting considerable influence
on a number of previously hostile and self-satisfied champions of
a behavioral science governed by the rule of social physics.[1]

Within the folds of anthropology and sociology certain changes
are also afoot as a result of some of the newer, more experimental
forms of ethnographic expression. Writers of realist tales, as suggested in earlier chapters, no longer treat observation alone with
the same respect as previous generations did. Characterization of

informants is more acceptable these days, as is a more personal writing style, with the author less inclined to hide in third-party conventions. Confessionals, too, are less likely to simply recount the conditions of fieldwork. They are increasingly serving as vehicles for their authors to launch into self-reflective encounters with hermeneutic and representational issues. Impressionist tales are finding their way into more fieldwork accounts and are less likely to be associated only with the informal chatter of fieldworkers in the faculty club taking a time-out from their more serious work.

It would be easy, of course, to see the three reporting formats I have presented here as fitting an evolutionary progression of sorts—from realist, to confessional, to impressionist tales. While there is a grain of truth in such a view, it is only a grain. The three forms exist side by side. There is no temporal connection. Realist tales are unlikely to vanish from the scene, even though some of their more extreme and troublesome conventions are changing. Realism in fieldwork reports remains a laudable and thoroughly respectable goal. As I mentioned in the Preface, we need now more than ever precise, complex, concrete images of one another if we are to continue to occupy this planet as a species. We are perhaps less fascinated or repulsed today by representations of the exotic as found, for example, in the somewhat dated manners-and-customs ethnographies of anthropology or in the still popular skin-and-sin ethnographies of sociology baring deviant subcultures. But ethnographers continue to be drawn to strange places with the intention of making them familiar.

Fieldworkers are also being drawn increasingly to familiar places with the slightly ironic intention of making them strange—as the burgeoning number of ethnographic studies of our own institutions and groups suggests: the coke dealer as small businessman (Adler, 1985); the computer hacker as Bohemian artist (Turkel, 1984); the independent trucker as corporate victim (Agar, 1985); the fundamentalist Christian school as a haven for indifferent students and a blessing for parents who fear the secular influence of public schools on their children (Peshkin, 1986); the congressman as tribal chief or flunky (Weatherford, 1981); or the drunk driver as media fiction (Gusfield, 1981). These are all important and close-to-home studies that deflate stereotypes and help us see the world with fresh vision.

An important trend for both realist and confessional tales is the changing notion of culture itself (Clifford and Marcus, 1986). Much current ethnographic writing depicts culture as something that is contested, emergent, and ambiguous, particularly when the writing is attached to studies of groups and organizations deep inside complex industrial societies (e.g., Pettigrew, 1985; Schein, 1985; Crapanzano, 1985; Feldman, 1986). Holistic perspectives of culture with their toe-bone-connected-to-the-foot-bone logic have given way to representations of culture in flux, whose natives may have as much difficulty knowing it and living in it as the fieldworker. Cultural representations are left open and are subject to debate by fieldworkers and informants alike. This is not because the methods at our disposal are imprecise or weak, but because such ambiguity is an accurate characterization of lived cultural experience. Representations should presumably be commensurate with the obscurity and shifting nature of the cultural materials themselves.[2]

More Tales of the Field

The three forms of representing fieldwork and its results that I have considered thus far do not exhaust the domain. The presentation of social reality is in a creative period now and much innovation is taking place. Of these additional forms of ethnographic expression, four are notable and suggest some of the new directions fieldworkers appear to be taking. Brief notes follow.[3]

Critical Tales

Fieldwork studies are often, particularly in sociology, strategically situated to shed light on larger social, political, symbolic, or economic issues. In industrialized societies, and for that matter, in virtually all societies, it is increasingly difficult to argue that fieldwork alone is sufficient to properly grasp the life situation of a studied group. Much criticism of ethnography has, in fact, been directed at what is seen by some as its parochial, romantic, and limited vision—its blindness to the political economy in which all groups must swim to survive (e.g., Hall and Jefferson, 1976; Harris, 1979; Hammersley and Atkinson, 1983). While among tellers of critical tales there is an appreciation for the unique strengths of fieldwork, there is also a sense that the groups studied need to be selected with more care on the grounds of what they might reveal about larger issues, particularly those concerning the political and economic workings of capitalist societies (Marcus, 1986).

Critical tales often have a Marxist edge and a concern for representing social structure as seen through the eyes of disadvantaged groups in advanced (and not-so-advanced) capitalist countries. Willis (1977) is a superb example of realist ethnography embedded within a Marxist framework. The ethnographic materials comprise only a part, about half, of the text. The key to the writing is Willis's self-conscious and tactical choice to intensively study a working-class secondary school in northern England where he suspects the reproductive mechanisms of the class system required by capitalism—dependent, in Willis's view, on strong backs, weak minds, and submissive spirits—will be most visible. He finds his suspicions confirmed, although in the process he is apparently made aware of a more creative and energetic proletariat than his theory led him to expect.[4]

Another splendid work in the same tradition is June Nash's (1979) historical and contemporary account of Bolivian tin miners, memorably titled *We Eat the Mines and the Mines Eat Us.* The theme of this work is an old standby for ethnographers, the confrontation of the old with the new, but the writing is fresh and avoids finessing the questions of power, economy, history, and exploitation. Unlike many other tales of the field, where the presented reality appears to be merely the unintended consequence of interacting people sharing natural problems, so that the reality belongs to no one in particular, the authors of critical tales make it clear just who they think owns and operates the tools of reality production.[5]

Such work need not always take a Marxist slant. The mark of a critical tale is, again, the conscious selection of a strategically situated culture in which to locate one's fieldwork. Hochschild's (1983) imaginative work on the sociology of emotions is also an engaging example of a critical tale. Her work is part fieldwork, part literature review, and part depth psychology, and it blurs traditional ethnographic boundaries. Here the author spent a good deal of participant-observation and interview time among flight attendants. The Delta Airlines "stews" were a consciously targeted group, mostly women, who she rightly thought would be engaged in some problematic emotional work—"Service with a smile." Powell (1985) manages the same trick in the culture-producing business with his fieldwork (and wider-reaching examination of the industry and its records) in academic publishing houses. Millman (1976) is another example in which fieldwork occupies only a part of the textual representation of the studied scene—in this case the topical concerns were the sociology and economics of medical practice as revealed by a sometimes shockingly close look at the decision-making rules of heart surgeons. Finally, Thomas (1985) uses some high-flying macrotheory of the labor process to inform his acute ethnography of lettuce workers in the fields of California. There is an interaction effect as well for his ethnography helps reassess and reorder the macrotheory with which he began his study.

In all this work, what Giddens (1979) regards as the central problem of sociology—the merging of structural (theory of action) and interactional (theory of meaning) traditions—is also the central problem for authors. The critical tales also point to the increasing tendency of fieldworkers to poke their heads into the disciplinary closets of economists, historians, political scientists, and psychologists, as well as their own. No longer content to leave their realist tales in the hands of other specialists to somewhat whimsically interpret as the mood strikes them (which has, in fact, been seldom); ethnographers are themselves now eager to see what help, if any, other disciplines can offer them when they try to provide a larger context for their own field materials. To some degree fieldworkers have always played this poaching role in social science, although it is perhaps a more aggressive and confident role now than it was in the past. Erickson's (1976) moving account of the Buffalo Creek disaster is a superb example in this regard.

There is, of course, something of a crusading spirit behind many critical tales. The authors often call their fieldworker ancestors to task for not paying enough attention to the political, social, and economic surroundings of the group represented in an ethnography. The criticism, often justified, is nonetheless akin to the complaints of missionaries and colonialists who viewed the early anthropologists as godless, unpatriotic folk who cared not a whit for the souls of those they studied and were content to leave the groups of their interest unchanged and no better off (perhaps worse off) by their presence. At any rate, the tellers of critical tales of the field are unlikely to suffer similar accusations. There is little celebration of the status quo (or romancing of the past) to be found among them.[6]

Formal Tales

Like the tellers of critical tales, the formalists of ethnography are also out to build, test, generalize, and otherwise exhibit theory. Less concerned with the political economy of a fieldwork site, the tellers of formal tales push a much narrower view of ethnography under labels such as ethnomethodology, semiotics, symbolic inter-actionism, conversational analysis, ethnosemantics, sociolinguistics, ethnoscience, various forms of structuralism, and so forth. The analystic goals, while many and diverse, include the derivation of generalizations through inductive and inferential logic. Representations of persons, places, activities, belief systems, and activities, when not the specific target of study, are limited and enter the formal tale only to provide a context for the textualized data under review. The formalists are the specialists of the ethnographic trade and they are on the make.[7]

The problems they face, of course, are many. Foremost among them is the fact that the programmatic research agendas suggested by the promoters of particular theoretical slants are often difficult for untrained or general fieldworkers to fully adopt and embrace. Formal theory, after all, may make a field setting little more than a mock-science laboratory. It therefore conflicts with some honorable fieldwork traditions. While many formal theories have proven helpful when one is making interpretive sense of the fieldwork evidence, there is a cautious resistance to the invocations of Lévi-Strauss, Garfinkel, Eco, Barthes, Mary Douglas, Leach, or Foucault. Moreover, fieldworker representations produced by some of the patron saints of modern theory may be well beyond the ordinary skills of fieldworkers who find it difficult to trace a brilliant analysis back for those features that might allow them to replicate such virtuosity. When I try, for example, to do a frame analysis as I imagine Goffman (1974) might, my results feel and look rather awkward and stilted, if not downright stupid. While this is surely partly my own doing, I suspect part of it also lies with the fact that Goffman knew more than he could say to the rest of us.

Formal tales must also reckon with the textualization problems discussed earlier in the book. To put a theoretical scheme to work crunching text requires text to first be put in crunchable form. Fieldworkers wishing to tell formal tales must first create a text that travels. Events must be specified, simplified, patterned, and to a large degree stripped of their context if they are to travel well and serve as fodder for formal theory. Such is true for all descriptions, of course, but theory itself can be a formidable taskmaster. Ultimately the theory may provide an illuminating reading of the text (or, more conventionally, the data), but even if it does, this does not mean it is the only reading possible (see Manning, 1987).

There is finally the troublesome problem that the members of the studied culture so artfully portrayed in good formal tales appear as they do in good critical tales: as rather automated figures who are pushed and pulled according to whatever theoretical scheme animates the tale. Theory is soverign, and therefore forces that are tacit, hidden, unconscious or falsely conscious, implicit, taken for granted, or ideological rule the day. There is more than a little theology involved whenever people are said to be acting on the basis of unseen and unknown forces. Whether they blame it on the devil, the sign, the id, the universal myth, low-protein diets, or the running dogs of capitalism, fieldworkers must tread softly when telling formal tales, for in the end, all representations are contestable. Formal tales alone can not protect us from the wind.

Literary Tales

Academic disciplines do not have a monopoly on the cultural representation trade. Nor is fieldwork the exclusive, protected-by-patent business of anthropologists or sociologists alone. Journalists in many guises make use of intense and sustained fieldwork as a way of coming to terms with the social worlds they investigate. The distinctive stamp of a literary tale is not, however, the particular brand of fieldwork that lies behind it, but the author's

131

explicit borrowing of fiction-writing techniques to tell the story. Literary tales combine a reporter's sense of what is noteworthy (newsworthy) with a novelist's sense of narration. Dense characterization, dramatic plots, flashbacks (and flashforwards), and alternative points of view are illustrative techniques. Stylistic contrasts mark the genre, rather than substantive ones. While literary tales occasionally overlap with other forms of ethnography, the genre is sufficiently distinct, powerful and currently vigorous to warrant separate attention.[8]

Literary tales are spiked by a number of conventions. Some popular ones include scene-by-scene reconstructions of dramatic and mundane events, extensive use of dialogue and monologue to establish character, direct representations of the character's emotional and subjective points of view, strong story lines organized around themes of general social interest, and explicit claims made by the author for the transparency and immediacy of the writing.[9] Tom Wolfe (1973:28) expresses the ambition and attraction of literary tales in the following way: "Hey, come here! This is the way people are living now—just the way I'm going to show you! It may astound you, disgust you, delight you or arouse your contempt or make you laugh. . . . Nevertheless, this is what it's like. It's all right here! You won't be bored! Take a look!"

Literary tales are meant to provide an emotional charge to the reader. The reality is not sliced, diced, and served up analytically, but is put forward theatrically without great concern for interpreting the recreated world for the audience. Intense, well-crafted sketches crowd the literary tales so that readers are placed, for example, at the dinner table with a devout but beleaguered Hasidic family in the wilds of Brooklyn (Harris, 1985); among hardpressed midwestern families facing foreclosure on their farms (Kramer, 1979); in a cell with the doomed of death row in a bleak prairie prison (Capote, 1966); backpacking with articulate environmentalists up-country in Alaska (McPhee, 1977); or hanging out with field geologists on the precipice of time (McPhee, 1980). The scenes and action move swiftly. Vignettes are backed up by pertinent facts drawn from a grab bag of sources and thrown together into occasional bursts of sociology, social history, or cultural critique. But by and large, writers of literary tales are careful to stick to their stories and not tell their readers what to think of

132

the presented material. "Being there" is both the means and the end of the writing.

Two kinds of authorial poses stand behind literary tales. The most popular one is the half-hidden pose in which the writer speaks directly through the characters of the tale or as an offstage narrator telling what the characters of the tale are doing and thinking. The implicit claim behind such a style is that the authors have so fully penetrated and understood the world of their subjects that they are now competent to see and speak for them. Thus Tom Wolfe (1979) can tell us what the astronauts are thinking as they sit perched on the pinhead of an enormous rocket awaiting the fire down below; or Joseph Wambaugh (1984) can tell us what goes through a frightened cop's mind as he sits in a dark San Diego canyon seeking the armed bandits who prey on illegal aliens as they make their desperate dash across the invisible international line; or Peter Mathiessen (1962) can tell us what a battle feels like for a Kurelu warrior whose accurately hurled spear has just penetrated the breast of an enemy. Tellings such as these are often accomplished by an interior monologue or simulated dialogue suggestive of an almost perfect identity supposedly achieved by the author with the subjects of study.[10]

The second stance is more artful and tricky, for it involves the writer's use of self as the register and filter of worldly happenings. Consider here, for example, Jane Kramer (1978) evoking the passing of cowboys through her own efforts to locate one in the bleak and dusty panhandle of Oklahoma; or Thomas Bass (1985) meditating of the meaning of theoretical physics while playing roulette in Las Vegas with a computer in his shoe; or Norman Mailer (1979) bringing forth the dark side of the American dream in Mormon Utah through his relentless wanderings and restless conversations with relatives and friends of self-condemned killer Gary Gilmore. Tales such as these suggest that there are no external frames of reference available (of culture, of morals) that are any more compelling or shared than the author's own. Perspectives multiply, for the personal voice allows the writer to play off one world against another, to wander around recording everyday habits, gestures, and customs from different points of view, to turn the self into a character of the story, or more generally, to simply toy with irony.

Regardless of whether or not the author is present in the text, literary tales leave no doubt that a single, creative, and willful voice is shaping the work. There is something of a free-spirited authenticity to literary tales that other tales of the field lack. Because the author is not tethered to an institutional pole, claims of pure and open inquiry are embodied in the work. Literary tales are not written for tenure, grants, or a Ph.D. Writers of literary tales present their topical concerns on the basis of personal appeal and curiosity. These are unfettered by disciplinary logics or academic career aspirations. Involvement, receptivity, and what seems to be an openness to experience are the means of getting a story rather than the means to shape-up a theory or satisfy the dictates of received traditions. The attraction of such a stance, coupled with the excitement that can be whipped up as the story is represented in writing, is considerable.

Critics of literary tales provide familiar carping themes. There is either too much or too little of the author in the tale. There is no way of knowing whether the author really got it right. There is too much unlicensed interpretive work in the text, and hence the author's credibility must be questioned. The howl of the Wolfe (1973:11) can be shrill: "The bastards are making it up!" Lacking institutional credentials, writers of literary tales are perhaps somewhat more vulnerable to such indictments than other tellers of tales.

Yet accusations of this sort are little different from the slightly more mannerly barbs and zingers hurled by critics of the day at Malinowski, Evans-Pritchard, Becker, or Geertz. The response must necessarily be the same. Authors of literary tales must marshal out their confessions. Such confessions are often published in the form of a sympathetic interview with the author wherein a text or technique is defended and readers are assured that the writer's own true-to-life experience, closeness to subject matter, and native-approved text adequately vouch for the veracity of the tale. But literary tales can be taken to task on other grounds. Three matters are somewhat worrisome to ethnographers.

First, writers of literary tales appear perfectly content to allow their accounts to stand alone with little or no mention of previous work in the same area or a similar one. The representations are typically cast as discoveries and come forth in something of a scholarly vacuum. McClure (1981), for example, presents a lengthy and lively portrait of the Liverpool police (ca. 1976–77). The writing is spirited, engaged and, as far as I can tell, truthful. Yet against this portrait stands a very sound body of ethnographic work devoted to the police in some very similar contexts (e.g., Manning, 1977; Rubenstein, 1973; Cain, 1973; Westley, 1970; etc.). Readers, while absorbing all the excruciating details of McClure's vivid account, gain no sense of whether or not the author is familiar with, makes use of, or rejects other work. There is a predatory feel behind some literary tales that leaves the knowledgeable reader somewhat queasy and suspicious.[11]

Second, literary tales can be fluff—merely zippy prose on inconsequential topics. They are liable, then, to the charge of "scoop ethnography." Such a charge, I hasten to add, can also be brought to bear on other tales of hte field, but it is perhaps most commonly attached to literary tales whose tellers must locate and titillate a general audience or disappear from the literary scene. Thus literary tales may concern plot summaries of the yuppie way of life, graphic descriptions of various forms of guru adoration in the zero culture, pastel cities of California, or fast-paced accounts of the latest corporate scandal, evangelical craze, or fat-farm innovation. The self-serving, pandering, and ad hoc character of some literary tales may provide an immediate audience, but it virtually cancels out any lasting ethnographic interest beyond that of style. The problem, of course, is that some of the cultures presented in literary tales are of a most ephemeral and transitory sort, gone almost the instant they are inscribed.

Third, literary tales may be so tied to the representational techniques of realistic fiction that they distort the very reality they seek to capture. The need for action, drama, high-jinx, colorful characters, and purple prose may drive out the calmer, more subtle and sublime features of the studied scene. Ironically, the techniques of social realism have been abandoned by many novelists for some of the same reasons that realist tales no longer hold a monopolistic grip on ethnographic writing. Perhaps the neo-fabulist novels of Borges capture the essence of contemporary reality as effectively as the social manners and mores novels of Balzac did for an earlier time. There is, as Webster (1982) points out, something suspicious about canonizing the narrative conventions of literary tales as eternal verities. Do Tom Wolfe's de-classé spontaneity, bold and joyful punctuation, and flights of turned-on consciousness seem as alluring to us in the 1980s as they did in the 1960s?

Such flaws are not inherently genre specific. As I noted, there are a number of splendid literary tales that more than hold their own when compared to other forms of cultural representation. Moreover, literary tales have now entered the ethnographic scene and the good ones enjoy brisk and justly deserved sales in both the university and airport bookstores. In some ways, they may provoke better writing from the more institutional and stodgy ethnographic writers by providing examples of lush show-and-tell exposition. Literary tales offer the fresh perspectives of some very talented and insightful self-styled ethnographers who are blissfully unconcerned with and free of the historically routinized formats of cultural story telling. The best literary tales display a fascination with language and language use and make the phrase "active reading" more than a cliché. Such possibilities spill over into academic worlds.[12]

Jointly Told Tales

Clifford (1983a) provides some evidence for the increasing popularity of what he calls dialogic and polyphonic authority in fieldwork representations. These modes refer to what he regards as a trend among anthropologists, the production of jointly authored texts (fieldworker and native) in a way that opens up for readers the discursive and shared character of all cultural descriptions. While it seems far from clear that the fieldworker troops are, in fact, following this trend, jointly told tales do recognize a fundamental and deep truth of all forms of fieldwork. Life histories in sociology have a similar goal, where the author provides space for the natives to tell their own tales without the undue interference and wanton translation of the fieldworker (e.g., Shaw, 1930, 1931; Klockers, 1975). With literate and sophisticated informants who possess something of an "ethnographic subtlety" toward their own groups, the jointly told tale may become even more practical (if not always welcome to fieldworkers concerned with their own identity).

As with auto-ethnography of Hayano's (1979) sort, the jointly told tale brings the fieldworker to the brink of ending the game and admitting (in theory anyway) that some natives are as able to represent their culture as is the fieldworker (if not more so). There is, of course, some truth to this, but, as always, it is a partial one.

Most self-respecting cultural members have no interest in representing their culture to others (writing is, after all, a peculiar activity that is hardly as much fun as it is cracked up to be). Those that do have such interests will have particular versions of their cultures to present and these, like all cultural portraits, are likely to be particularistic, in flux, and therefore limited. Moreover, when jointly told tales are "negotiated," it is usually the fieldworker who holds the editorial and publishing keys, not the informant (Tyler, 1986). Hence the negotiation is often an unbalanced one so far as the final representation is concerned: informants speak, ethnographers write.

I do not wish to make light of what are some superb and sensitive joint works in ethnography. Crapanzano (1985) provides some disturbing, but remarkable impressionist tales told with "authority dispersed among interlocutors." He makes clear that the heart of ethnography is discourse. The sensitive ear is perhaps more crucial than the sensitive eye. Occasionally, however, work in the let-them-speak school has a contrived and superficial flavor, approaching the proverbial "monologue about a dialogue." The root problem is caught by Tyler (quoted in Marcus and Cushman, 1982:44): "No amount of invoking the 'other' can establish him as the agent of the words or deeds attributed to him in a record of dialogue unless he too, is free to reinterpret it and flesh it out with caveats, apologies, footnotes and explanatory detail."

As with other, less conventional forms of fieldwork reporting, the jointly told tale often means an unruly text that "doesn't read like ethnography." A reader must develop a good deal of tolerance for the ambiguity and difficulty such texts display. But, unlike some of the realist tales, in which it is apparent that the fieldworker's observations and interpretations are being passed off as the native's point of view (and vice versa in the so-called "dictated text" of ethnographic ill repute, in which the native's point of view is passed off as the fieldworker's interpretation), jointly told tales respect the authority of natives and at least attempt to bridge the gap between two meaning systems of equal validity (but not always with equal power).[13]

Reprise

I have covered a good deal of ground in this book. By examining the representational or writing forms fieldworkers follow, my intent has been to draw attention to the fact that the desk or office work of ethnographers is no less important than their fieldwork. Certainly fieldworkers' silence about and sleepy indifference to the writing conventions of their craft has been shattered in recent years, and there is now no going back to more complacent or blissful days. The issues involved in current epistemological debate are not passing fancies and will not go away. The reality of fieldwork itself will no doubt remain chaotic, unpredictable, and always beyond the full control of the fieldworker. But the ways of presenting fieldwork and its results have changed and will continue to change.

The crucial problem of what we so cavalierly call "writing it up" is to balance, harmonize, mediate, or otherwise negotiate a tale of two cultures (the fieldworkers' and the others'). Manning (1979:660) describes this usefully as "avoiding solipsism on the one hand and avoiding positivism on the other." Whether we regard tales of the field told outside the realist stance as subversive or pathbreaking, the tacking back and forth between two cultures (or systems of meaning) will always characterize fieldwork writings. It is possible that we sit on a sort of giant pendulum, gently and invisibly being swung by the intellectual tides from one side to the other. At the moment, the pendulum seems to point us toward a mirror in which we appear to be unclothed and turning over and over our own understandings of fieldwork for inspection. If so, we will no doubt swing back again, and in the mirror will appear others whose thought and action puzzle, instruct, and fascinate us. Conventions will change, new ways of representing the others will be developed, and this blurring of forms will create new ones.

It is difficult to say much more. I have endeavored to show that there is no sovereign method for establishing fieldwork truths. It is murky out there and in here. Self-understanding is not the endpoint of fieldwork as confessionals sometimes suggest. Nor is the brilliant, but necessarily objectified, representation of another culture the endpoint. Impressionist tales dance around both poles and inform, educate, amuse, and evoke in useful ways. Their open-endedness is their strength, for meaning can be worked on again and again and few readers are excluded. But even here, impressionist tales can be used in many ways, not all of them good.

In complex settings, fieldwork, while a vitally important and core activity, is not likely on its own to provide a particularly balanced representation of a culture without being supplemented by diverse readings, broadened reflection, and (gasp) other research techniques. Fieldwork tales of whatever sort are not likely to prove as informative if the problems we wish to study concern population trends in India or the workings of the housing market in Los Angeles. Fieldworkers will have something to say on both these matters, but straight-ahead ethnography is unlikely on its own to say very much. New ways must be developed for representing and using fieldwork when complex problems are attacked.

Old ways of representing and using fieldwork must also become better understood. It is no longer possible to see fieldwork as merely gathering data through cumulative experience. It is unruly, conflict ridden, and always problematic. So too with the harvesting of data in fieldwork representations. Relatively less work has been directed at understanding how, why, for whom, where, and with what consequences ethnographies are written. There are many ways to push this analysis, one of them being the sort of approach I've taken in this book. Another means of understanding ethnography is to examine various existing works against the context of academic institutions and the personal careers within them. I have, by and large, ignored such institutional matters here. They are important, as the following bits of cautionary wisdom argue.

On advice to students of fieldwork, my feelings are traditional. There is, alas, no better training than going out and trying one's hand at realist tales. Sensitivity is required, of course, and students armed with the latest warnings and insights of the epistemological crowd are probably better off than the unarmed—provided their eyes are not glazed over and their minds shut down as a result of soaking up all that nimble scholarship. Putting pen to paper and producing a representation that is persuasive, melodic, empathetic, and aimed at some general insights based on the particular is the real rite of passage into fieldwork circles.

By producing a cultural representation one perhaps earns the right to confess and tell how the representation came into being. Presumably textual consciousness is sufficiently raised these days that a writer can also engage in a bit of self-deflating literary criticism of the sort I've been playing with here. Lastly, an impressionist tale or two might be worked up formally to dazzle or annoy one's colleagues and informants. There is, however, a sense of privilege (and of course risk) associated with publishing one's impressionist tales. Since the refrain "it doesn't read like an ethnography" is patently true, one who writes impressionist tales exclusively had best seek tenure in the English department and not in the anthropology or sociology departments.

What I am saying of course is what I said much earlier in this book: different tales attract different readers. Realist tales are most easily grasped and appreciated by like-minded colleagues. Other social scientists may occasionally dip into them to pursue particular topics but, rest assured, they are not checking out ethnographies from the library for methodological or writing tips. Confessional tales also attract mostly colleagues, especially those curious about the method, stance, problems overcome and perhaps mental health of the author. Confessions are of special interest to students of fieldwork in search of guidance and reassurance. Impressionist tales may have the best chance of attracting the general reader. Yet, these tales risk alienating collegial readers who may not take kindly to the flaunting of ethnographic traditions.

All of this is perhaps too true for our own good. We need to shop around more and encourage narrative ingenuity and novel interpretation as potentially put forward in any and all of the three genres. To deny the matters covered in a classic realist tale because one prefers a lurid confessional or breezy impressionist tale is a little like saying Joan Didion and Virginia Wolfe write novels but Ann Beattie and Jane Austen do not. We need more, not fewer, ways to tell of culture. The value of ethnography from this standpoint is found not in its analysis and interpretation of culture, but in its decision to examine culture in the first place; to conceptualize it, reflect on it, narrate it, and, ultimately, to evaluate it.

Finally, I must close this book. This is no doubt a blessing for the reader taxed by my prose and weary of the disembodied voice of the black-and-white page. Reading about writing is like writing about reading. It can absorb our interest and possibly entertain us, but it too often leaves our practices untouched because it is so remote. Nonetheless, I hope in a small way to have passed on some borrowed wisdom to readers concerned about the deskwork of fieldwork. And perhaps to have widened a few pairs of eyes so that the textual practices discussed here will not go unnoticed. If so, the work here is not finished, only over for awhile.

Hey, have I got a story for you . . .

NOTES

1. Ethnographers are not the only challengers to the rule of social physics. Some homegrown literary critics within social science are emerging and applying their black art to conventional scholarly discourse. McClosky (1985) examines the rhetoric of economics and finds personal, cultural, political, and philosophical commitments everywhere. Edmondson (1984) does the same for some major sociological schools of thought. Ditton (1981) presents a collection of observations on Goffman's writings, some of which delve into his rhetorical and narrative styles. Even a statistician has surfaced in this domain (Lieberson, 1985). All of these analytic probes demonstrate that social science writing, indeed all writing, is rhetorical. In this sense the critical challenge is to identify the rhetoric devices used by writers who insist they do not use them. Such insistence is easy to understand because if, say, economists copped a plea to the charge of the flagrant use of rhetoric, their empirical claims would hardly have the same bite. Anthropologists have of course been at the game longer than most social scientists, and a good deal of their current writing reflects a fairly sophisticated, reflexive attitude toward the presentation of any social reality, including their own (Marcus and Fischer, 1986). The detailed literary analysis of major works (*explication des textes*) in all the social science disciplines is a task urgently needing to be tackled, not only by critics outside the fields, but more importantly by critics within the fields whose voices will carry weight and respectability.

2. A personal example may be worth mentioning in this regard. I once wrote an invited paper on an assigned topic, the reaction of the police to shootings in their midst (Van Maanen, 1980). I found myself soundly criticized by the editors of the volume in which the paper ap-

peared for not presenting a fixed and clear portrait of the police on these matters. My only response, of course, was to suggest to my critics that such sorrowful occurrences were hardly generic, nor were the police themselves in any agreement as to the meanings of the events. My critics were not impressed with my unwillingness to claim closure, focus, confidence, and authority. Such is life in American academic communities, although the cultures associated with them are not as cloistered and resistent to change as they sometimes appear. Changes are afoot here too.

3. My choice of additional tales to address in this last chapter may disappoint some readers whose favorites do not appear on my list. Squeezed for a standard, I stick with those closer to the descriptive wings of ethnography than the prescriptive ones. Ethnographic writings that flow from the applied streams of social science research and practice would include "hired-hand tales," in which fieldworkers study and report on social impact and fix-it questions at the request of others (Roth, 1966); "clinical tales," in which a report is generated on the process and outcome of some improvement program initiated by a client and assisted by the fieldworker (Schein, 1987); and "action tales," in which the fieldworker (as agent of change) reports on the results of a self-help program undertaken in line with a given normative theory (Argyris, Putnam, and Smith, 1985). While it is true that these forms of ethnographic writing are the work of the fieldwork-for-a-fee bunch, it is not true that the tales they tell always reflect the views of their sponsors.

4. In the American edition of the book, Willis adds a confessional appendix not appearing in the original English publication. This appendix is usually self-critical while at the same time it attempts to specify the value of ethnographic studies for Marxist analysis. Another book with similar aims, although written in a much more experimental fashion, is Hebdige's (1979) fieldwork glances at the London style scene.

5. Consider also Buroway's (1979) spirited ethnography of machinists in a Chicago machine shop. Interestingly, Buroway inadvertently stumbled upon the same shop where Donald Roy (1952, 1954, 1958) had labored some thirty years previously, thus giving Buroway's tale an unusual and enlightening historical thrust. What is most striking is how little had changed in the shop across time.

6. The roots of critical tales run deep. In anthropology, the Manchester School of Max Gluckman set off a long run of critical ethnography aimed at uncovering the workings of political and legal systems (see Kuper, 1977:147–66). Perhaps the most famous critical tale is Leach (1954). In sociology, Gouldner's *Patterns of Industrial Bureaucracy* (1954) is a vintage but paradigmatic critical tale.

7. My discussion of ethnographic formalism would be incomplete

unless I noted Gregory Bateson's still peculiar attempt to unravel *Naven* (1936), the ambiguous and altogether bizarre New Guinea ceremony involving transvestism, simulated incest, and other apparent reversals of normal behavior. Bateson's work, while certainly singular, does represent a sort of prototypical formal tale in its self-imposed limitation of range. Other far more restrictive ways of drawing boundaries are found in Spradley's (1970) componential analysis, Cicourel's (1968) cognitively oriented sociology; Mars's (1982) use of Mary Douglas's grid-and-group categories, and Schneider's (1968) symbolic treatment of American kinship patterns.

8. What I call literary tales are close to tales with several other less graceful labels: new journalism, parajournalism, personal journalism, and subjective journalism. The best accounts of the basics of the genre are found in Wolfe (1973:3–52), Bellamy (1982:vi–xv), Webster (1982: 103–8), and Sims (1984:3–26). The fieldwork that lies behind these literary tales is often extensive but of a most straightforward sort—"get close to the subject and stay there." Exemplars include the eighteen months Hunter Thompson (1966) ran with the Hell's Angels; the two years Mark Kramer (1983) spent with a surgical operating team; or the ten months Tracey Kidder (1981) spent following the work of a computer design group. Needless to say, not all literary tales involve such dedicated fieldwork, but the better ones do, it seems.

9. Bellamy (1982:xii) suggests that literary tales marry the aesthetics and methodology of the eighteenth and nineteenth century novel (e.g., Fielding, Austen, Dickens, Melville) to the modus operandi of the big-city, police-beat reporter. This seems broadly accurate, although the criteria put forward for truth claims in the literary tale seem more similar to the fieldworker's "personal experience" standard than the reporter's "two people told me so" standard. The genre, in this light, is hardly new. Good early examples (before the phrase "new journalism" was coined in the early 1970s) include Mark Twain's *Innocents Abroad* (1869), George Orwell's *Down and Out in Paris and London* (1933), and John Hersey's *Hiroshima* (1946).

10. The bravado shown by some writers may stretch reader credibility in the same way that realist tales have become somehow less believable and true over the years. One difference, however, is that the literary tales make less use of composites and purport to speak only for an individual rather than for an entire people or group. Presumably this restriction of voice carries somewhat more authority, if less range. There is also the fact that most literary tales are not about distant preliterate people but about close-to-home people (and events) at least partly familiar to a reader whose own memory, knowledge, and experience provide the truth

test. Indeed, it is the reader's presumed understanding that all this actually happened that gives the genre its powerful punch (Sims, 1984: 14–16).

11. Methods, of course, are not irrelevant to such suspicions. Writers of literary tales seldom remark on the significance of their presence on the scenes they represent, and this is in some instances a bothersome problem to fieldworkers in addition to the common concerns for reactivity in any situation. It is, for example, very difficult to imagine that as famous and dandy a writer as Tom Wolfe was merely a fashionable but unobtrusive fly on the wall in the classic uptown parlor scene of *Radical Chic* (1970), or that Tracey Kidder did not in any way influence the raising of the Souweines' roofbeams in *House* (1985). Since writers of ethnographic tales have begun to break their silence on these matters, it is seemingly time for writers of literary tales to do so too—especially when their accounts so clearly rest on intimacy.

12. Consider, in this regard, the way some literary tales are punctuated and organized; the way they flow through time and space, use extended dialogue rather than short quotes, explicitly call up emotional states, smells, noises, and other scenic properties, and provide interior monologues for others. Writers of literary tales invent wild hyphenated expressions that break up habituated thought (e.g., I-mmersion, break-fast, re-search), heighten excitement through dramatic reconstructions, and, perhaps most rare in scholarly ethnographies, tease readers by self-aware displays of humor. Such practices are unwelcome in academic discourse, and are viewed as exhibiting bad taste, if not bad writing. This hyper-formality and lack of experimentation in academic writing is unfortunate and dulls both the representations and the mind.

13. In this regard, Whyte's (1984) plea for "active collaboration" between informant and fieldworker is refreshing. While making this plea, Whyte also discloses that he worked so closely together with "Doc" (probably sociology's most famous informant) that he is no longer sure which ideas in *Street Corner Society* are his and which are Doc's. Not all fieldworkers feel this way, of course. As noted in chapter 4, the romanticized notion of rapport is taken by some to be merely a negotiated settlement, the result of a continuous push and pull between fieldworker and informant. Such a settlement determines what can and cannot be learned in the setting. Distrust of natives' accounts is probably as frequent these days as trust. Convincing jointly told tales will hardly come from interrogatory fieldwork where "hidden secrets" are to be forced from informants. It has been some time since the rack has been seen as an instrument of truth.

Epilogue
2010

This closing essay is cobbled together from the two-penny nails of talks and papers I've delivered over the last few years to a variety of academic groups more or less unfamiliar with the past and present of ethnography. My intention in podium presentations and paperwork is always to try to pass on a bit of the imaginative, inventive, and slightly subversive spirit that animates the best of ethnographic writing. Good intentions however are usually just that. What I think is often carried away by many if not most of those who hear or read what I have to say is just how hard it is to successfully complete an ethnographic project from inchoate beginnings to readerly ends. This writing, alas, will not offer much solace in this regard. Ethnography has always been tough. But I do think the some of the challenges—empirical, conceptual, textual—shift with time. Some old problems fade, new ones appear, and these are the matters that occupy me here.

To my mind, the most dramatic shift since *Tales of the Field* was published more than twenty years ago has been the surge and spread of the distinctly open and modern idea of culture as something constructed (and construed)—thick or thin—by all self-identifying groups. Everyone these days, except for those who bowl alone, has a culture, it seems, and more likely multiple cultures from which to draw meaning. Hence we have lively ethnographic accounts of exotics abroad as well as exotics at home, culture as built, sustained, understood, and questioned by identity-inventing Indonesians, motorcycle gangs in Japan, Second Life enthusiasts in the United States, beat policemen on the High Street, elite academics serving on peer-review panels, doormen on the Upper East Side, Wall Street traders from Planet Finance, and those unfortunate earthlings abducted by aliens but mercifully returned to us.[1]

For ethnographers—veterans and wannabes—to whom the study of culture is their presumed raison d'être, their meat-and-potatoes specialty, this creates enormous opportunity. Across disciplines in the social sciences, adjectival ethnography—urban, educational, medical, organizational, legal, and more—continues to grow and diversify. In the humanities, cultural studies programs prosper and expand; writing, journalism, and communications programs treat ethnography as a form of creative nonfiction while providing media ethnographies of their own; ethnomusicologists offer field methods courses; and historians ponder the conditions under which the curious and problematic practice of people of one kind studying people of another kind arises in various times and places. All this increases the topical choices, narrative structures, conceptual alternatives, fieldwork practices, epistemological commitments, and analytic tools available to and used by ethnographers. In short, ethnography has escaped well beyond the relatively insular and mannerly anthropological and sociological quarters where it was hatched and has now carved out small but vibrant niches across the social sciences and the humanities.

This, of course, raises immediately the question of how any single person can keep up with what is now an enormous, increasingly differentiated, and expanding literature. The full measure of the ethnography industry now includes the ceaseless production of authoritative monographs, exhaustive reviews of the literature(s), method manuals, encyclopedias of concepts and theories, meta-critical expositions, themed anthologies, handbooks of door-stopping weight, established and quasi-established journal publications, formal presentations of talks and papers presided over by umpteen academic societies, online publications, blogs, topical chat-rooms, message boards, forums, social networking sites, and on and on. The answer then to how a single person can keep up without gagging is that he or she can't, for the potentially relevant materials are overwhelming, and new theories, new problems, new topics, new concepts, and new critiques of older work multiply with each passing year. It seems the best one can do is to selectively pursue and cultivate an ever-diminishing proportion of the potentially relevant work that comes one's way and assume an attitude of benign neglect toward the rest.

This is to say that the broad survey approach I undertook in *Tales* would now be an undertaking of a scale and complexity unimaginable to me. The ethnography-of-ethnography (or "anything-you-can-do-I-can-do-meta") attitude I took when writing *Tales* was admittedly a period conceit but a relatively modest one compared to the massive one it would be today, so segmented and enlarged the field. What I do wish to do in this brief epilogue is simply comment on a few ways ethnographers of an anthropological and sociological sort now think about and carry out their work. Some changes are apparent, some less so, but ethnography remains—to give away my conclusion—a recognizable enterprise, and not all of what once seemed so solid has melted to air.

This discursive, tagged-on probe into ethnography then and now begins with a quick look back at the broad literary perspective I relied on in *Tales* and considers why this perspective remains restricted, if not ignored, by many social scientists. I next consider how ethnographic work in the field and at the writing desk—as shaped and informed by an empirical as well as a conceptual context—have shifted (or not) over the years. I include here an expeditious look at the emergence of several new genres or tale-telling practices that were marginalized and neglected in *Tales*. I end by suggesting where a certain coherence and stability seem to me still in place despite the diversity of norms and forms swirling around ethnographic practices.

On Reading & Writing

The ordinary truth of any research trade—ethnographic or other-wise—is that we traffic in communications, and communications implies that we intend to alter the views of our readers. From this perspective, our task is rhetorical. We attempt to convince others that we've uncovered something of note, made unusual sense of something, or, in weak form, simply represented something well. This is to say that our writing is both explicitly and implicitly de-signed to persuade others that we know what we're talking about and they ought therefore to pay attention to what we are saying.

Things get interesting here because, when it comes to writing, the literature across a good part if not most of the social sciences is relatively silent. While findings, theories, and methods are well inscribed, little attention is given to just how these various writings persuade. Since some writings generate a good deal more reader response (altered views) than others, it seems reasonable to ask why this might be so and inquire as to what authorial styles (and stances) lie behind such success (and failure).

147

Ethnographers have of course been worrying about such matters for some time. As chronicled in *Tales*, canonical works have been pilloried (and defended), narrative experiments developed (and deplored), representational forms altered (and critiqued), field-work pretensions revealed (and reasserted), and theoretical nets shredded (and rewoven). *Tales* was published in what was perhaps the high watermark of textual criticism and debate in high-church ethnographic circles. While the tides have yet to retreat on some on these debates, the trade stumbles on—and even expands—despite (or, maybe, because of) the relatively acute textual awareness among many practitioners. Raising the textual consciousness of others in the social sciences located outside ethnographic circles, however, seems to me more like trying to raise the Titanic, for it often generates a "why bother" response. There remains a wide-spread reluctance to look seriously at writing as anything other than a restrained, straight-ahead, and rather tedious burden—a mop-up, resolutely analytic, after-the-facts-have-been-determined activity having little to do with narrative conventions in a field or authorial choice and style. This is both myopic and unfortunate but perhaps understandable.[2]

Looking to the social sciences generally, a question about how a text generates certain reader responses still appears to many as curious and beyond the pale because it is not clear what examining texts might mean. Textual study is something of a blind spot, since most of us are trained to read through our texts to what they say about the world they present and not to examine them for the compositional features they display. After all, few social scientists have any training or aptitude for analyzing metaphors, deciphering tropes, recognizing voice, or examining rhetorical ploys. Literary practices are terra incognita. Syntax is not about grammar but more likely to be something a smoker or a French wine connoisseur might pay, and lexicons are not special vocabularies but right-wing political pundits. Were it otherwise, we'd be going about our work in literature departments.

Yet, even if we knew something about and cared about such matters, the close analysis of text might still seem strange for it would contradict what we think we ought to be doing. We should be off doing studies or examining the relevant social research literature(s) for what they have to say that might inform and direct our scholarly interests and projects. Those who want to sit back and detect the use of irony and satire in an ethnographic report or examine the plots and subplots (if any) in population ecology or network studies would seem a bit odd. Social scientists should be out doing research, not in the library doing some amateurish or silly "lit crit" on the words and works of our trade.[3]

Even if these reservations were overcome, such work might still seem at first blush a bit embarrassing and hardly worth the effort. It is one thing to attempt to decode the narrative structure, characterization techniques, plotlines, and authorial voice in the work of Jane Austen, Saul Bellow, Thomas Pynchon, or Gabriel García Márquez (or any other acknowledged star of the literary scene), but it is another matter entirely to worry about the same things in the prosaic and seemingly rule-governed work of social researchers who, informed by current theory, presumably get their effects by constructing texts bursting with facts drawn from the use of well-established methods and put forth in clear, unadorned language exhibiting something close to a style of no style.

It may also be that this silence and lack of curiosity rest on a vague but unexamined feeling that if we did start looking closely at the ways our major and minor works are put together, we might not like what we find—a fear that if we looked closely at our use of imagery, phrasing, allusion, analogy, and claims of authority, we might discover some literary chicanery or authorial trickery that would undercut our ability to make any claims at all about the worth (and truth) of our findings and theories. If style were shown to play an important persuasive role in research reports, a corrosive relativism might overcome us, making us players in a mere game of words, trapped in the same "prison house of language" thought to be occupied by poets, novelists, and not-so-cunning memoirists. From this perspective, it is best to imitate the poor ostrich and not look.

Of course if I took any of these claims seriously, *Tales* would never have been written. Surely it is not too difficult to accomplish at least a modest literary reading of research texts. We might perhaps become better readers in the process. Reading is, after all, a good deal of what we do as reputed scholars. More to the point, most of us would readily admit that we spend as much if not more time writing and endlessly rewriting our research reports— ethnographic or otherwise—than we do gathering the empirical materials on which our writings are presumably based. Since writ-

149

ing and reading are such a large part of our research endeavors, to not look closely at such everyday work seems foolish.[4] As to the claim that we have no "real writers" in our midst and thus need not worry about how authors generate their texts, experience and evidence suggest otherwise. Indeed we have a number of quite convincing and stylish writers in our field who have put forth some highly persuasive prose. A short list of influential writers might include Pierre Bourdieu, Erving Goffman, Michel Foucault, Anthony Giddens, Clifford Geertz—and a long list of others who are more or less specific to readers in particular subfields of the social sciences. These are powerful writers and some of them are no doubt responsible for drawing us into the field in the first place. Blame them, perhaps, but their writings have altered the way we see the world.

Misguided too is the worry that if we examine the rhetoric displayed in our texts, it will somehow sink the ship and deep-six its cargo. We need not be so cautious. To seriously take this position is akin to arguing that literary criticism will destroy the novel. Literary criticism has been around for ages, and the texts addressed and at least partially opened up by such study remain works of value even if we now read them more knowledgably and skeptically than in times past and attach a wider range of meanings to the inscribed. This I think has certainly proved to be the case in ethnography over the past thirty or so years. Certainly good and bad criticism can be found, but it is at least arguable that criticism has in a variety of ways improved (or at least changed) the novel and I would claim ethnography too.

There are, then, good reasons for looking closely at writing practices whatever the field of study. And these reasons stand behind and ground all that I have to say moving forward. While I focus on textual change and stability in ethnography, I do think a similar sort of approach to other fields would prove instructive and valuable: if a literary perspective helps us better understand what is going on in one domain, it might help in others as well.

Fieldwork, Headwork, and Textwork

As put forth in *Tales*, ethnography is first and foremost a social practice concerned with the study and representation of culture (with a distinctly smaller *c* these days). It is also an interpretive craft focused far more on "how" and "why" than on "how much" or "how many." It remains a field many claim to be the most scientific of the humanities and the most humanistic of the sciences. As such, it exists somewhere in academic limbo (or purgatory) as a storytelling institution possessing a good deal of scholarly legitimacy whose works are commissioned and approved by the leading educational institutions of the day.

Ethnography has long claimed a sort of informative or documentary status—"bringing back the news"—by the fact that somebody actually goes out beyond the ivory towers of employment, libraries, classrooms, and offices to more or less "live with and live like" someone else. At the end of the day, the ability to convince readers that what they are reading is an authentic tale written by someone personally knowledgeable about how things are done at some place, at some time, among some people is the foundation on which rests anything else ethnography tries to do—to critique, to theorize, to edify, to surprise, to amuse, to annoy, or to comfort.

These are ironclad matters, pretty much given, not up for grabs. One becomes an ethnographer by going out and doing it (and writing it up). Fieldwork of the immersive sort is by and large definitional of the trade. If one cannot do lengthy and sustained fieldwork among others who are often initially recalcitrant and suspicious of those who come uninvited into their lives, one has no business doing ethnography (and is perhaps best advised to take up a pleasant academic career in economic sociology or experimental social psychology).

However, it is becoming increasingly obvious that fieldwork practices are biographically and contextually varied—stunningly so. Studies differ in terms of working style, place, pace, time, and evidentiary approaches, although all rely on some form of lengthy participant-observation, now a rather tired and stock if oxymoronic phrase that indexes one of the most impressive ways yet invented to make ourselves uncomfortable.[5] Fieldwork is a technique of gathering research material by subjecting the self—body, belief, personality, emotions, cognitions—to a set of contingencies that play on others such that over time—usually a long time—one can more or less see, hear, feel, and come to understand the kinds of responses others display (and withhold) in particular social situations.

In any hard discipline, be it ethnography, engineering, gardening, or auto repair, the learner must submit to things that have their own intractable ways, an authoritative structure that commands respect. For fieldworkers, this means subjecting one's self to at least a part the life situation of others, after getting there by one (often sneak) means or another. While ethnographers can leave the field whenever they want to, on the scene they must customarily act like this is not true. In many respects, the legendary—if too frequently overhyped—ethnographic sympathy and empathy often comes from the experience of taking close to the same shit others take day-in and day-out (or, if not taking it directly, hanging out with others who do). Even when studying professionals, societal elites, or high-ranking organizational members, the fieldworker inevitably must come to terms with the situational dictates and pressures put on, expressed, and presumably felt by those studied.

In the field, one must cut his or her life down (sometimes to the bone). In many respects, ethnographic fieldworkers remove themselves from their usual routines, havens, pleasures, familiar haunts, and social contexts such that the fieldwork site provides a social world. The assumption here is that to get at this world, one has to need it. This is not easy and to varying degrees requires fieldworkers to question if not tear down at least part of their own systems of belief and their preconceptions about themselves and the various communities from which they come. There are few shortcuts and no ways to learn one's way around an unfamiliar social world without being there and banking on the kindness of strangers.[6]

At the most concrete and practical level, ethnographers come to see the world as others do not just because they want to scrupulously document what goes on among the group being studied or because the social benefits of doing so somehow outweigh the costs (and preclude expulsion), but because seeing the world as others do is the only way of staying and being in that world for any length of time with those particular people. Of course, spending a year or so in some alien community with people doing a great many unfamiliar things in unfamiliar ways does not lend itself to great subtlety in pinning down their interests, identities, beliefs, knowledge, or values. A good deal of caution is exercised these days surrounding claims to have a handle on what we still call— perhaps a bit more reservedly than in the past—"the native's point of view."[7] Ethnographic authority of the classical sort thrived in part under a cloak of distance and difference. Natives never knew what was written about them. Today they do, and we write far more circumspectly as a result, or risk being upbraided and run out of town.[8]

Often shaping fieldwork in the past, and to a degree, a precept that still holds today, is the counterintuitive idea that to become culturally astute and knowledgeable in a studied domain requires one to begin work in a state of blissful innocence if not near ignorance. The position is that one's learning, insight, sensitivity, and eventual powers to represent are advanced by being spectacularly clueless at the outset of a study. Fieldwork may appear romantic and adventurous from the outside but on the inside there is a good deal of childlike if not blind wandering about in the field. Cultural oversights, misunderstandings, embarrassments, ineptitudes are common. Relationships based on a certain kind of rapport form only with time, patience, and luck. Fieldnotes are always incomplete, filled in later by memory of an accurate or quixotic sort. Choices of topics, frameworks, and substantive domains emerge only after considerable thought and experimentation. Analysis never ends. And all writing is of course rewriting and rewriting and rewriting. In short, learning in and out of the field is uneven, usually unforeseen, and rests more on a logic of discovery and happenstance than a logic of verification and plan. It is anything but predictable or linear. The unbearable slowness of ethnography—from "getting in" to "getting out" to "writing it up"—is thus an enduring feature of the work.

Why the devil anyone would put him- or herself in such a seemingly woeful and uncertain situation is of course a question that a good many social scientists continue to ask. And blue-in-the-face ethnographers continue to argue that if one wants to know, for example, "how things work" in a given society, community, organization, or social group, there is no other way except through hard-slogging fieldwork, through ceaseless interpretation of what one is learning in and out of the field, and through the careful production of texts to convey such interpretation (and the grounds on which it stands) to others. "How things work" is of course a cultural and hence often disputed matter that inevitably requires grappling with the meanings (and meaningful forms) those studied make use of as they go about their everyday activities—the ever-mysterious and elusive native's point of view. Yet "culture," like all keywords in the social sciences, is a term that meanders and is thus

153

continually being reconceptualized and reworked as old problems persist and new ones appear.

"Culture" is certainly one of the more contentious and complex words in our lexicon. Like the term "force" to a physicist or "life" to a biologist, or even "god" to a theologian, "culture" to the ethnographer is multivocal, highly ambiguous, shape-shifting, and difficult if not impossible to pin down. When put into use, contradictions abound. Culture is taken by some of its most distinguished students as cause and consequence, as material and immaterial, as coherent and fragmented, as grand and humble, as visible (to some) and invisible (to many). In anthropology and sociology, the term has had a long, distinguished, yet sharply contested career, and today, a few of the more prominent and vocal students of culture suggest the concept is exhausted and, hence, should be duly honored but packed up and retired.

Or should it? One of the charming but endlessly frustrating things about culture is that everybody uses the term, albeit in vastly different ways. The notion of culture as used by ethnographers today is more a loose, sensitizing concept than a strict, theoretical one. It signals a conviction that agency and action (be it word or deed) rest on social meanings that range from the rather bounded and particularistic to more or less institutionalized and broad. Over the past several decades, however, ethnographers of all varieties have been paying far more attention to the former than the latter. Certainly the view of culture as an integrated, shared system of interlocking ideas, routines, signs, and values passed on more or less seamlessly from generation to generation has withered away (thankfully) as have most notions of communities, states, villages, organizations, or social groups generally as tightly bound "cultural islands" and the evolutionary theories of culture generated by such notions. But as long as meanings are taken to be central to accounts of human activity and meanings are seen as coming forth— somehow, someway—from human interaction, it is most unclear what conceptual framework might step up to replace culture as a way to imagine and think about such matters as "how things work." In terms of understanding how things get done by people on the ground in the social worlds we are—or become—familiar with, culture and the meaning-making and remaking processes associated with the concept, however trimmed down and inevitably flawed, still seem to me indispensable.[9]

"Culture" simply refers to the meanings and practices produced, sustained, and altered through interaction. Ethnography is the study and representation of culture as used by particular people, in particular places, at particular times. Viewed as a process, culture calls attention to those meanings that are being contested in a rough-and-tumble fashion and are thus continually being renegotiated and redefined. More important perhaps is not what culture is (and the semantic elasticity and debate surrounding the concept) but—following pragmatic principles—what culture does. And what it does most critically is the work of defining words, ideas, things, symbols, groups, identities, activities, and so forth. We all live our lives in terms of the definitions that culture creates. These definitions however are far from consensual. The view of culture I now take—a shift since *Tales* appeared—is a distributive and deterritorialized one that would contest the idea of culture as necessarily a bounded, coherent entity of collective sharing. As drifting clusters of meaning, culture can be seen as comprehensible and distinct even though it may also display indeterminacy, indifference, discord, ambivalence, and considerable range. Much more important these days than in times past, culture should be understood as residing largely within a sphere of social relationships and only indirectly tied to place.[10]

What I am trying to do in a neat and tidy way—to conceptualize, contextualize, and communicate current notions of culture and cultural processes—is a bit of both ethnographic headwork and textwork. My headwork, such as it is, comes from my reading of the ethnographic literature, my fieldwork experiences and memories, my understandings and interests in organization studies, my ethnographic tastes, my sense of what I want this piece of writing to convey, and an almost infinite list of other constraining (and liberating) sources, some obvious to me, some not. Headwork is of course always a part—a huge part—of any project. One could not pick up rocks without some sort of theory to guide them.

I use the term "headwork" here to refer to the conceptual work that informs ethnographic fieldwork and its various representational practices. This is a matter I left rather unexplored in *Tales*, although such work is no doubt most obvious when we are composing (or reading) ethnography. While it may be true that when the narrative pleasures of ethnography are great enough—meticulous detail, drama, surprise, irony—no one asks for conceptual niceties, and the analytic frames, aims, and implications are over-looked by readers (although surely not absent). But, given the shrill call these days to ethnographers of all sorts to be "theoretically informed and informing," it seems to me that ethnography is expected to do a lot more heavy lifting of an abstract and analytic sort than has been required of it in the past. This is perhaps in part to give theory-obsessed and cherry-picking readers beyond ethnographic circles something to hang onto and take away, but it is also, in part, an odd result of the opened-up (yet trimmed down) version of culture I just put forth. A good story with only a pinch of theory and an odd concept tossed in here and there will no longer do.

Here pragmatism offers aid. Ethnography's focus on the "empirical" alongside its "I-witnessing" ideal—meaning its intense reliance on personalized seeing, hearing, experiencing in specific social settings—has always generated something of a hostility to generalizations and abstractions not connected to immersion in situated detail. This is certainly in keeping with pragmatists such as John Dewey, William James, and Charles Sanders Peirce, who favor fallibilism and theoretical pluralism when trying to work up accounts for how a part of the world might operate. They suggest that some theories work better than others depending on the particular problems addressed and the equally particular situations and times in which they are used. While we are accustomed to the rule that we should allow our research questions to determine our methods, pragmatism suggests that we should also allow our questions to determine our theories. This is not a claim that all theories are equally valid or that research questions are themselves pre-theoretical. It is simply the recognition that one need not stake out a theoretical claim on how the world is before beginning a research project.[11]

This view of theory resonates well with the ethnographic research process both in the field and at the writing desk. It may lead at times to a rather shameless eclecticism as various theories are drawn on to explain and perhaps generalize certain matters and as the specific nuts and bolts of various theorists are selectively put to use. No overarching theory required. Use only what fits such that analytic concepts and empirical data meet and adjust to one another. A recent example of this kind of theoretical cocktail is found in Jakob Krause-Jensen's organizational ethnography, *Flexible*

Firm (2010), a splendid account of several "cultural projects" undertaken inside the globalizing Danish electronics firm Bang and Olufsen. The writing offers up passing reflections on theories of magic, ritual, resistance, ideology, labor process, identity, control, and power coming from a broad set of social theorists—the usual suspects—including Foucault, Turner, Weber, Bourdieu, Barth, Giddens, Geertz, and Goffman. There are many theoretical muses at play here but the author's touch is subtle and his engagement with theory critical, sharp, and original. Much the same could be said of another organizational ethnography, Michel Anteby's *Moral Gray Zones* (2008). This is a work that looks closely at a dying occupational community formed among craftsmen working for (or retired from) a French manufacturing firm. In the monograph, Anteby quite smoothly (and cleverly) mixes and matches various theories that are, on the surface at least, incompatible (e.g., functional, symbolic, new [and old] institutionalism, structural, exchange) to account for his field materials.

This laser like use of highly selective social theory forecasts a rather gloomy future if one is awaiting, like the good member of a cargo cult, the arrival, elaboration, and celebration of *Le grand paradigme* in cultural (or organizational) theory. Pragmatists and ethnographers would certainly argue that there are many truths to be found that can help shape and order social life. But there is, alas, no requirement that such truths be universal or even consistent with one another. I am reminded here of the master of contextualization, Erving Goffman, who was often taken to task by critics for being too specific, too carried away by particulars, too ready to wrap a concept around every situation he analyzed. He responded bluntly but eloquently to those who took his work to be "untheoretical" by saying that it is "better perhaps [to have] different coats to clothe the children well then a single, splendid tent in which they all shiver" (Goffman, 1961:xiv).

The point here is that a good deal of the headwork involved in ethnography is (and has been) in developing concepts, theories, or frameworks that fit one's particular research questions and studied situations. And there is, I submit, a good deal of social theory—indeed a brain-numbing amount—well advanced in the social sciences on which to draw. We read, listen, converse with others in our academic and social circles; we read and ruminate about different but attractive concepts and theories; we sometimes try

157

them out; we judge them in accordance to what is currently going on in our respective fields and then attempt to put them to use in the context of the work we are doing. This usually requires tinkering with them ever so slightly to make for an arguable fit between theory and data. Some work for us, some don't, and we move on.

In practice, theory choices (the rabbits we pull out of our hats) rest as much on taste as fit. And taste in ethnography, as elsewhere, results from what is no doubt a complex interaction involving ethnographers, their readings, their disciplinary orientations, their mentors, their colleagues, their students, their friends, their critics, and their readers, who are increasingly their subjects too. The process is altogether decentered and beyond the grasp of any one interested group to fully monitor or control. The majority of us are no doubt most comfortable working analytic lines that follow the traditions in which we were trained and are thus committed generationally and institutionally to certain broad perspectives, research etiquettes, and topical, if not stylistic, preferences.

Such lines are helpful, to be sure, and inform theoretical and substantive choices, but, as mentioned earlier, ethnographic approaches in the post–*Tales of the Field* world have multiplied and spread far and wide such that today notable work can come from ethnographers located across a wide range of applied and multidisciplinary fields—women's studies, management, nursing, criminal justice, computer science, accounting (gulp), social work, and other fields, both large and small, too numerous (and rapidly growing) to list. Each develops more or less distinguishable analytic and substantive interests and traditions, thus widening the ethnographic landscape. And each manages somehow to occasionally create fresh and persuasive work for at least some readers (and its share of stale and unconvincing ones too).

What makes for a persuasive and fresh ethnography brings me to what was at the core of *Tales*, ethnographic composition and its genres. Textual awareness and self-consciousness has spread to the point where ethnographers would surely agree that the raw materials of cultural representation (and I might add theory making) are terms, idioms, labels, frames, phrases, categories, sentences, stories—words, not worlds; maps, not territories; representations, not realities. Since ethnography remains something of an art, science, and craft rolled into one, the virtues and felicities of stylistic writing and the narrative conventions and experiments that carry ethnography to readers continue to be of more than passing concern.

I use the term "textwork" as a suturing together of two words meant to convey that writing is a labor-intensive task and represents a good deal of what we do as intrepid ethnographers. As with fieldwork and headwork, textwork involves choices, innumerable ones concerned with such things as voice, authorial presence (or absence), analogies and metaphors, allusions, professional dialect and jargon, imagery, interpretive moves, tone, empirical or theoretical emphasis, truth claims (or lack thereof), figures of speech, and so on. As I argued and tried to demonstrate in *Tales*, some of these choices cohere such that recognizable but contrasting ways of treating and representing culture and cultural processes can be discerned.

Stuffing ethnographic writings into three categories is of course a bit fanciful and strained—both then and now. The categories are anything but pure, and as I said before and will now say again, most ethnographic writings mix and match various styles (and do so increasingly). But I do think—surprise, surprise—my three categories have held up reasonably well. One category, realism, is certainly still with us if in slightly modified forms. Another category, confessional tales, are fewer in number, perhaps, but reflexive confessional tales are now rather routinely attached to or blended into the ethnography itself rather than split apart and plunked down in secluded appendixes, turgid and one-off method chapters, or separate, follow-up monographs seemingly intended to humanize the initial ethnographic report (and reporter).[12] Impressionist tales, my third category, are still around and perhaps more popular than ever as a result of growth in the cultural representation business and the continuation of experimentation with ethnographic forms that has more or less been part of the trade from its beginnings.

A few broad shifts are however apparent across all genres. Ethnography is less confined to single-site studies of supposedly bounded or conveniently distinct and isolated peoples (the cultural island approach).[13] What Marcus (1998) calls "multi-site ethnography" is on the rise. Consider both Christena Nippert-Eng's (1995) terrific study of integration and separation of home and work, and Louise Lamphere and colleagues' (1992) treatment of how new immigrants from Southeast Asia are faring in several communities and workplaces across the United States. Of illustrative note here too is Louisa Schein's (2000) work with the Miao in reform-era China exploring how ethnicity is constructed and re-constructed in state institutions, among cultural elites, and by the Miao themselves.

There is also a good deal of inventive textwork that allows a far greater role for the ethnographic subject than in times past. What I set off as a subgenre, jointly-told tales, has expanded considerably. A fine example is Ruth Behar's (2003) emotionally riveting tale of Esperanza, a Mexican street peddler crossing back and forth across the U.S. border, told largely in her own voice. Another il-lustration is Paul Rabinow's (1996) voice-giving strategy in *Making PCR*, where celebrity biotech researchers and entrepreneurs seem almost to take over the text. Notable too is George Marcus and Fernando Mascarenhas's (2005) textually inventive, collaborative (and provocative) ethnography exploring (among other things) the life of the Marquis (coauthor, Fernando) in Portugal.

While less obviously and intentionally experimental, realist tales these days also provide more room for the often disparate voices of those studied. Thus, the indignity of speaking for others that some ethnographers feel is perhaps reduced. An elegant illustra-tion of just this is Carrie Lane's (2011) *A Company of One*, a multi-sited ethnography exploring "self-managed careers" as told through the voices of job-seeking high-tech workers in Dallas, Texas, circa 2001–2. Throughout the monograph, authorial commentary is intermingled with lengthy self-fashioning observations made by a number of unemployed engineers and managers, a few of whom we get to know rather well as we read. More generally, it seems to me that fewer "common denominator people" are to be found in recent ethnographic texts.

In some ways, the career paths of those we study are on some-thing of a roll—from subjects to informants to members to in-terlocutors to (maybe someday) coauthors.[14] I am impressed here with John Weeks's splendid work in *Unpopular Culture* (2006), in which employees of a large British bank—clerks and executives—are given voice, and some of them, mostly managers, are presented as up to much the same mischief as the ethnographer, namely, trying to ferret out and grasp the elusive culture and cultural pro-cesses in the firm. The ends sought by each may differ since some of Weeks's interlocutors—referred to as "lay ethnographers"—seek not only to understand and represent but also to "manage" culture for particular purposes—"to shape-up the firm," "to discover the core values," "to engage and excite the workforce," and so on. Until fairly recently, culture as explored by ethnographers in organizational settings was largely mute, so to speak. The common native understanding of culture was tied to local practices—expressed as "the way we do things around here" and seen by organizational members as virtually impossible to objectify. But, as Weeks's study suggests, we are now operating in an age in which both member and ethnographer may well share a conceptual vocabulary.

This posits something of a problem for ethnography (and not one limited to the organizational variety), for what is "emic" to the ethnographer is "etic" to those studied, and it becomes something of a struggle for both to understand the differences and understand the other. There is irony too in Weeks's rendering when we learn that within this most utilitarian and instrumental of social organizations—a hard-headed, no-nonsense financial business firm—the upper-level managers, human resource specialists, organizational consultants, and even the CEO are seemingly caught up in projects such as "building a shared culture," "articulating a vision," and "communicating corporate values." Weeks's bankers are not alone at trying their hand at cultural engineering. Gideon Kunda (1992) was one of the first organizational ethnographers to draw attention to such explicit enchantment efforts.

As the above studies suggest, the representational burden of ethnography has become heavier, messier, and less easily located in time and space, and innovations in tale telling are on the rise. The faith in ethnographic holism—always something of a fiction akin to Newton's frictionless space—has continued to retreat along with all those quaint claims of writers to have captured the "spirit" of a people, the "ethos" of a university, or the "core values" of an organization. There is less closure and general portraiture in ethnography these days than in times past.

This lack of closure is particularly apparent in ethnographic work concerned with representations of both personal and social identity—a growing and fashionable concern across many fields. Attempting to depict in writing what it is like to be somebody else—arguably, ethnography's main claim to fame—has never been easy, but today it seems almost Herculean given the problematic nature

161

of identity in the contemporary world. A certain instability, rup-
ture, uncertainty, and fluidity of meaning attends then to some of
the best of contemporary identity-focused ethnographies.[15]

One strength of ethnography has always been to position individuals in a specific social setting, placing them in a context where
action takes place. But this setting is no longer, if ever, exclusively
local or whole. Organizations, for example, are venues of inter-
linked relations—local, national, transnational. They are then at
the crossroads of ideas, knowledge, interests, and values. They are
spheres of interaction where meanings of various origins converge,
disappear, amplify, mix, blend, and often clash. They are also, arguably, becoming more complicated, diffuse, fragmented as organizational forms and managerial strategies shift in response to
the changing political economy in which they operate—what the
acronym-crazed business press regards as a VUCCA world: Vola-
tile, Uncertain, Chaotic, Complex, and Ambiguous. Paul Bate
(1997:1157) suggests—rightly I think—that there are now fewer
"Grand Hotels" to study where all is under one roof as, presumably, there once were. Inscribing culture in the contemporary
context—our post-modern, post-industrial, post-bureaucratic, post-
structural, post-toasty world—suggests we must now work in many
social contexts where an assumed (rightly or wrongly) coherence
has been shattered and replaced by a polyphonic pluralism of
meaning and interpretation.[16]

In this regard, a general cautionary note might well be pinned
to the less-than-snazzy jackets of contemporary ethnographers. We
know from our own social lives that spending a good deal of time
in close proximity with others—our families, our work groups, our
companions at the pub—is as likely to create differences as similarities. People living face-to-face also spend time back-to-back.
Disagreements among close associates and friends are often as
common as agreements. Thus in line with the downsizing and
shrink-wrapping of the culture concept as is apparent in contemporary ethnographic accounts—organizational or otherwise—when
the phrase "the native's point of view" is considered and put forth,
the first question a savvy and critical writer or reader should ask is
"which native?"

Making cultural analysis still messier is the "shaken confidence" or "epistemological hypochondria" that Geertz (1988:71)
famously suggested has attached itself to ethnography. Most eth-

nographers would now agree that their textwork owes a good deal of its persuasive power to contingent social, historical, narrative, and political conditions, and no meta-argument, reflexive turn, or navel-gazing can effectively question these contingencies. Yet we soldier on knowing that any particular ethnography must still make its points by pretty much the same means that were available before these contingencies were recognized and absorbed—by putting forth evidence; providing interpretations (and defending them); borrowing, inventing, and elaborating concepts and analogies; invoking authorities; working through examples; marshaling one's tropes; and on (and on). While the nature of ethnographic evidence, interpretation, authority, and style may have changed—more modestly, I think, than radically—the appeal of any single work remains tied to the specific arguments made in a given text and referenced to particular, not general, substantive, methodological, and narrative matters. Changes in attitude and reader response are of course possible and what is persuasive to one generation may look foolish to the next, since each generation on coming of age has some stake in showing their ancestors—dead or alive—to be airheads. But ethnography soldiers on not because its findings, facts, methods, truths, and genres remain the same, but because, even in the midst of change, some audience continues to look to it for the close study and account of what an identifiable group of people, more or less stuck in historical and situational circumstances they did not entirely create, are up to. How do they live? What do they do? How do they get by?

Questions such as these are not likely to fade away anytime soon. They are questions, however, that accommodate—if not encourage—a good deal of topical variety, methodological imagination, and stylistic diversity. Moreover, as younger researchers routinely and rightly question older definitions and representations of culture here, there, and everywhere, more subject matter is created and more opportunities can be taken to breach traditional disciplinary and substantive boundaries. Ethnographers must now rather self-consciously select, defend, blend, stretch, and combine various ethnographic templates or genres (e.g., realist and confessional tales, literary and advocacy tales, critical and post-structural tales, etc.) when constructing, for example, a career-making (or breaking) dissertation project or when presenting their work to colleagues, reviewers, or editors whose appreciation and knowledge of ethnographic means and products may be sketchy and feeble (or traditional and unbending).

Such matters present challenges, to be sure. Yet there remains among many ethnographers, perhaps most, a general indifference if not distain for the seemingly endless efforts of social scientists to develop methodological rigor, orthodox and rigid reporting templates, a spare, flat, detached (and boring) writing style, and a set of relentlessly fixed and focused analytic interests that must be articulated before a study begins. Ethnography, by contrast, proposes a relatively open and pragmatic model of social research. It has come into play in a number of fields of study where cultural representation, if not self-consciousness, has largely been absent (e.g., public policy, medicine, design, diagnostics, marketing), and has more or less proved its mettle in these fields, expanding as a result. Theory remains something of an ambiguous, polymorphous term, taking on different import, meaning, and value in different ethnographic circles. While I have suggested that theory is on the move, there is enormous variation in the theories that are moving and being put to use. "Whatever works" seems to be the animating spirit. It seems safe to say that there are now fewer rules for ethnographers to follow but more work to be done. This, to me at least, seems far preferable to a situation of less work and more rules.

This is not, however, a state of affairs that warrants joyful celebration and dancing in the streets. A predicament surfaces because students today (novices or veterans) must negotiate with their teachers (and editors) over the nature of what was once the so-called standard model of ethnography—the single-site, year in the field, one-tribe-one-scribe realist tale. On top of this, more work is coming from beyond the usual ethnographic parade grounds of anthropology and sociology, some of which is impervious to all but the most simplistic of ethnographic tales.

With the spread of cultural discourse, a form of "do-it-yourself" ethnography has surfaced. Such work often rests on hurried and rudimentary ("blitzkrieg") fieldwork and is devoid of interpretive interest and skill. Formal interviews, sample surveys, focus groups, brief periods of observation or, to use the currently popular but altogether murky term, "shadowing" those studied replace lengthy in situ immersion. While we may learn, for example, that someone to whom the researcher spoke said they lived in a "culture of greed" or that their social betters thought little of them, what prompted such a response—when, where, to whom, under what conditions, and so on—never surface in the account. What we get is a vapid classify-and-count portrait of the studied cultural scene that is empirically unsound and conceptually empty. This is not ethnography.

Part of the problem is that ethnography from the outside looks to the uninitiated as a semi-respectable form of hanging out, requiring only a little time and the effort to sally forth with a notebook and pen (or tape recorder) in hand. One goes out, hears and sees and records what people say and do, and returns to report just that. What Diane Forsythe (2001) calls "the invisible work of ethnography" is not apparent to the do-it-yourself crowd, often themselves members of the very group whose cultural processes and projects are of interest to them.[17] By "invisible work," Forsythe largely means the headwork and textwork that stands behind credible ethnographic projects and products. This includes such things as reading and absorbing at least a part of the ethnographic literature (and its debates), undertaking some field training of the sort that prompts reflection and both widens and sharpens cultural sensibilities, cultivating an interpretive (and skeptical) frame of mind, and coming up with a research account that draws on categories, concepts, and forms that are recognizably ethnographic largely by identifying and problematizing the things natives or members take-for-granted. Such invisible work and the skills honed through its labor take years to develop, let alone master.

Ethnography indeed relies heavily on others. But, in the end, it is the ethnographer and not the member or native who develops and takes responsibility for whatever cultural concepts, accounts, and representations mark a study. To position one's self at an angle, to provide a distinctive and rather "cross-eyed," autonomous perspective are what we count on and expect ethnography to do as an intrinsic component of the work. Ethnography is always something of an interpretation of an interpretation because what we call our "data" are constructions of other people's constructions of what they and their compatriots are up to at certain times, in certain places.

Suffice to say, the world has changed, and with it ethnography, whose practices continue to both advance and retreat in light of new problems, new domains of interest, and new practitioners. High-grade ethnography—focused on social worlds light-years from our own or in our own back gardens—can come from students located almost anywhere, inside and outside anthropology or sociology. But, for all, ethnography remains an arduous undertaking, and there are no shortcuts to its production. Such is the game today, and serious (and strong) players in this game require a good deal more textual sophistication than in times past — readers are more diverse, topics (arguably) more complex and nuanced, and the conceptual contexts within which ethnography now operates broader and less forgiving.

Within this world of constant change there are at least three rather distinguishable ethnographic forms or templates (and temptations) now apparent to me that I more or less bypassed when writing *Tales*. Each draws to differing degrees on realist, confessional, and impressionist conventions, and each has something of a traceable history within ethnographic traditions. But the "new" textual categories marked breathlessly below strike me as more than passing fancies, hopelessly blurred genres, or isolated, one-off experiments. These three now seem sufficiently distinct, numerous, and prominent to warrant a stand-alone position within the range of ethnographic tales, a range that probably still remains too restricted.

Structural Tales

This is a template favored by critical scholars who argue — usually with just cause — that many ethnographies suffer from a myopia that sharply delineates behavior at close range while obscuring the proximate and less visible social, political, and economic structures and processes that both engender and sustain lines of behavior. I see structural tales as something of a merging and growth of what I previously called critical and formal tales. They are analytically sophisticated, ambitious, and determinedly conceptual. Like critical tales, they are also something of a back-to-the-future form of ethnography, for the roots of the structural tales run deep in both anthropology and sociology.

Structural tales mix a good deal of engaged and rigorous theoretical reflection with spare, highly focused I-witnessing. They are typically less an ethnography of a specific social group than an ethnography of specific, highly contextualized cultural processes — meaning-making — taking place among those studied. Theoretical and empirical inquires run parallel and are carefully adjusted to one another. This question of "fit" is always tricky and arguable but it allows the choice of the research sites (and sites within sites), the problematic situations selected for study, and the various theoretical concepts put forward to presumably inform and play off one another.

How "fit" is established and justified in the text is however a puzzling, rather circular, and, in the end, entirely rhetorical matter. I am particular fond of a complex structural tale by Andreas Glaeser (2000)—what he refers to as an example of "analytic ethnography." This is a work that looks closely at the West and East Berlin police departments (and their respective critiques of one another) that were merged after the fall of the wall. In his telling of what happened in the early stages of the merger, Glaeser candidly (if ruefully) suggests that the best defense an ethnographer can put forth to a challenge of conceptual choice is simply to claim its "ethnography adequacy" and then insist and try to demonstrate as best one can that the theory or concept "flows" from the field data, "does no violence" to field observations, or in one way or another "captures" the scene. A pragmatic justification might be to suggest that a given concept "works better" than others or is "more helpful" than others. But then we would still be left with the question of "better" or "more helpful" to whom?

Those pushing for a renewed interest in building, borrowing, and elaborating on theory also argue that too narrow a definition of fieldwork, if not fetishizing, denies the legitimacy of social observation beyond the tête-à-tête of interpersonal interaction. Other sources of information are equally important; thus ethnographers must broaden their reach and refuse to reduce ethnography to a representation of perspectives or mentalities—the native's point of view—that are not contextualized by, for example, class, race, gender, and political-economic conditions. Representative and recent work in this tradition include, prominently, Michael Burawoy's (1979, 1999) studies of labor processes at home and abroad; Calvin Morrill's (1995) provocative examination of conflict among top corporate managers; Carol Chetkovich's (1997) grounded analysis of race, gender, and affirmative action in the Oakland Fire Department; and James Tucker's (1999) look at the role played by folk therapy to smooth over disputes in what he calls "post-bureaucratic" organizations.

To be clear, I am not saying that authors of structural tales do not attend to what they witness or bring theory, grand or small, to the front when evidence is scanty. Fieldwork in this domain is as hard-slogging as in any ethnographic domain, but the tales that result are noticeably distinct and keyed to certain disciplinary matters that extend into but also beyond the studied scene. For example, a recent ethnographic work in organizational studies does a thorough job of standing some well-received organizational theory on its head while bringing other theory in, suitably tailored, to bear on the problems at hand. In this work, Stephen Barley and Gideon Kunda (2006) take a close look at high-tech contract workers in the Silicon Valley—of both blue and gold collars—and challenge conventional economic and sociological understandings of contemporary contract work. Theory concerns animate the text, frame the ethnographic snippets put forward, and drive the narrative toward a conclusion that offers what the authors consider to be a more robust—yet highly contextualized—account for contract work than was available before their study.

Structural tales are clearly on the rise, but bridging both the macro–micro and general–particular chasms has never been easy. What is perhaps gained in theoretical acuity is sometimes lost in the coverage of life worlds supposedly governed by larger forces. This is an old critique, of course, and the debate continues with no resolution on the horizon. But what surfaces quite clearly in structural tales is the tight focus and selective character of the cultural representations that appear in the text. The intent is to show how a particular authorial understanding of a local practice or specific social situation travels and illuminates larger matters and thus helps resolve theoretical puzzles posed outside ethnographic circles. Much of the theory seems to reside in a cloud drifting over what is happening on the ground and is identified, pulled down, and used by the ethnographer before, during, or after going to the field to push the inquiry in particular directions. What makes for a structural tale however is not simply a concern for theory—for all ethnographies draw on at least some social theory—but the overall weight such theory carries in the text in terms of the framing, focusing, and generalizing of the ethnographic account.[18]

Post-Structural Tales

There is a kind of rough justice at play in ethnography these days. If structural tales are currently doing well, so too are post-structural ones. Writers of the latter mode read structural tales as conjuring up a dreaded form of holism based too often on out-of-date, discredited, and canned theoretical systems. If structural tales that embrace the big-picture perspective from a cloud (or orbiting satellite) are not trusted in the post-structural camp, neither are the on-the-ground realist, confessional, or impressionist tales, for they are read as slanted (contaminated) by the obscured personal characteristics and interests of the ethnographer, the political and institutional context in which social research is embedded, the topical and narrative conventions of the day, and the relative lack of a deep reflexivity displayed in the work. To the post-structuralist, reality may be a nice place to visit but no one really lives there, since, as Gertrude Stein said of Oakland, "there is no there there." Reality is better treated as a fragile social construction subject to numerous lines of sight and interpretation.

Justification for post-structural tales derives largely from various strains of postmodern (or late-modern) literary criticism and foregrounds language over other social phenomena. Textual acts are seen as persuasive fictions, and the more persuasive they appear to be, the more ideological they become. This form of ethnography has carried a slightly poisonous tag for some time and hostile reactions are still common in certain ethnographic circles. Few ethnographers it seems own up to the label. The gist of such ambivalence is caught well by Graham Watson's (1991) wonderful line: "Make me reflexive—but not yet."

Yet, despite the villainous and tainted image, post-structural tales are multiplying (received of course with mixed reviews). Consider, for example, Carolyn Ellis's (1995) auto-ethnography of feeling; Bruno Latour's (1993) claims that we have never been modern; Stephen Fjellman's (1999) detailed, obsessed romp through Disney World; and Margery Wolf's (1992) thoughtful analysis of a thirty-year-old incident in a Taiwanese village told in succession as a short story, as fieldnotes, and as a scholarly, anthropological report. Perhaps the most innovative—and yet recognizably ethnographic—is Anna Tsing's (1993) interrogation of the ways cultural representation operates on (and among) a marginalized group in the rainforest of Indonesia she calls "the Meratus" (and operates on ethnographers as well).

In all of these works, textual innovation, disorder, the wavering of meaning, and open-endedness are obvious. But three thematic features also stand out. First, there is typically an emphasis on those times and places where stable identities break down and the boundaries that structure identity collapse. Second, there is a focus on what Eco (1986) calls "hyperreality," times and settings in which life is exaggerated and signifiers lack clear referents. Third, there is something of an apocalyptic flair in post-structural tales representing newness, novelty, and an end-to-the-world-as-we-know-it sensibility. Three fine examples of work that embodies at least some of these features are Matthew Desmond's (2007) arresting account of wildland firefighters, Susan Davis's (1997) image-busting, behind-the-scenes analysis of Sea World, and Donna Haraway's (1989) ringing feminist manifesto on the role of women in science.

The literary features of post-structural work come forth strikingly in their textual self-consciousness and purposeful incompleteness and uncertainty. Unlike other forms of ethnography, post-structural tales frequently emphasize and play up what the authors don't (quite) know rather than what they do. The goal remains recognizably ethnographic—to represent affectively and credibly the interaction between individuals and the social worlds they inhabit—but neither the individuals nor their social worlds are treated as if they are fixed, dependable entities, possessed of any natural, inherent qualities. All is in flux.

It follows then that post-structural tales are inevitably inconclusive. Indeed, from a post-structural author's perspective, any work is unfinished without consideration of the critical and differentially positioned responses to the text by specific readers. Texts are therefore always partial. This is perhaps one reason why we might call post-structural work a form of ethnography from another planet. But, however we regard such work, it does represent the outward-looking, experimental rim of ethnographic practice—in terms of both topical choice and textual style. In a sense, those working in this mode are doing what we might call ethnographic research and development.

Advocacy Tales

A confession is appropriate here since I am at a bit of a loss as to what to label work that falls in this domain. Advocacy Tales could just as well be called "Moral Tales," "Normative Tales," "Reform Tales," or even "Judgmental Tales." Whatever they are called, however, the marker should capture those ethnographies that attempt to address some of what the authors see as the major wrongs in the world.

While sometimes criticized for a "save-the-world" missionary zeal, advocacy ethnography of the sort I have in mind has produced some quite good work. Consider, for example, Hugh Gusterson's (2004) biting (and terrifying) portrait of the American weapon design community; Jennifer Howard-Grenville's (2007) nuanced treatment of would-be environmental activists employed as engineers by a large and successful computer chip manufacturer; Timothy Diamond's (1992) heartbreaking plea for change in America's nursing home organizations; Malcolm Young's (1991) informed and devastating critique of the British police; and Vicki Smith's (2002) harsh treatment of corporate restructuring and downsizing in the "new economy."

These works are sometimes superficially similar to structural tales in that they generally articulate a broad grievance: that others suffer unjustly, often unknowingly, and are hard-pressed to do something about it. But they differ greatly from structural tales in the sense that righting wrongs is what motivates and animates the text. The seeming formality and precision of a structural work gives way to vigor and potency in the well-told advocacy tale. The most prominent difference lies in the emphasis advocacy tales place in the text on the necessity for change and a studied consideration for just how it might be accomplished. Theory is carried much lighter in advocacy than structural tales and is likely to be inserted more for its pragmatic usefulness than for whatever explanatory or authoritative power it might provide. A main theme advanced by this work follows the old sociological maxim that good work should "comfort the troubled and trouble the comfortable."

Advocacy tales put forth a strong, clear point of view in which no doubt is left in the reader as to what side the ethnographer is on. Such a moral stance is carried throughout the writing and not restricted to occasional asides regarding reform-minded policy implications or bland change recommendations in the concluding pages of a monograph (or concluding paragraphs of a research article). The entire point of the ethnography—from beginning to end—is to take on certain evils in the world, show what they have done (and are doing), and tell us what might be done about them. The prose is both moral and normative, taking up many causes, including antiracist, profeminist, anticolonial, and environmental ones.

The point here is less to enumerate the ethnographies in this domain than to merely to mark their noticeable presence at the moment. Ethnographic work—like all other social sciences—has always had an applied wing and can easily be seen as something of a tool to help identify and perhaps help solve human problems. Certainly the legendary, tireless, loud, and loquacious Margaret Mead is prototypical in this regard, as her *Letters from the Field* (2001) makes clear. While some may decry such an open advocacy stance on the grounds that it puts ethnographers squarely into an activist role and thus reserves the famous charity, sensitivity, and empathy they are said to cultivate and express for only those whose cause they wish to support, others would surely point out, and rightly so, that ethnography has always served some groups better than others, and making this explicit in the text is well established—if infrequently promoted or practiced—within the trade.

Plus ça change, plus c'est pareil

Thus far I have said little about the ends of ethnography. Such ends merit some attention before drawing this retrospective to a close. As I see it, among other things, ethnography aims to reduce puzzlement—of the ethnographer as well as the reader. What readers learn in a well put together tale is what particular people, in particular places, at particular times are doing, and what it may mean to them. Richard Shweder (1991:23) calls ethnographers "merchants of astonishment" whenever they deliver surprise and wonder to their readers. First-rate ethnography—where the use of evidence is judicious, conceptual frames fresh, and the writing clear and engaging—seldom fails to offer up a number of critical, ironic insights into the world(s) studied. Its representational aims are met (or not) largely by the curiosity generated by the text and the unfamiliarity of readers with the social worlds studied—translating, as it were, what goes on in one cultural context to readers who live in another. Its critical and ironic characteristics are established against what it is those studied and those reading think is or should be going on in the world examined but (woe) is not.

Surprise of course runs the gamut between the mild to the wild. Instances of both can be found, for example, in the ethnographies of science as when, on the modest end, Susan Silbey (2009) reports that scientific laboratories are not at all like most of us imagine them to be (or terribly safe either) and, on the spectacular end, Bruno Latour and Steve Woolgar (1979) show that when the mundane and everyday practices of scientists in the lab are followed closely, the hallowed "scientific method" is more myth than reality. Or, to take another pair of ethnographies, consider, at the eye-opening end, Kate Kellogg's (2011) study of several high-status surgical units where many residents fiercely resisted a change that would have reduced their work hours with no monetary consequence from 120 hours per week to 80 and, at the shocking end, Marcia Millman's (1977) account of frequent pushing and shoving matches occurring in surgical theaters among medical specialists and the routine covering-up of serious medical errors.

The point here is that without close and detailed studies of these worlds, our conceptions of them would be pitifully inadequate. Ethnography shines a light, sometimes a very strange light, on what people are up to, and such doings are rarely if ever predictable or in line with what "current theory" or "the experts," "the elders," "the state," "the law," or what sometimes even "the natives" themselves might say. The appeal of ethnography may then be greatest—in what seems to me a rather timid and stodgy academic world—to those who believe not all learning comes from books and articles, from well-formulated theories and methods, from our revered ancestors, from those in high positions including the already tenured in our fields and our department chairs.

There is of course risk in such undertakings. We know well that the standards of excellence in all fields of endeavor are power laden and anything but Platonic ideals. Most scholarly work, ethnographic or otherwise, generates little interest or excitement and rarely gets much attention even in the domain in which it is hatched. True that ethnography is demanding, is painfully slow, is not particularly journal friendly, takes one away from the university and one's friends, and its crude and unruly methods guarantee no surprising or striking results. But the value of doing ethnography is not for any career rewards—such as they are today—that might result.

To strike a personal note (full disclosure here), I am too washed away by the enlightenment project to not hold deeply and almost religiously that there is something emancipating about knowledge for its own sake, learning something—as ethnography promises— we did not know. Thus, for me, the point and purpose of ethnography is to render the actual—to figure out what is going on in some part of the world and get the word(s) out the best we can. How we go about meeting these ends has of course changed in numerous ways over the years since *Tales* appeared. These shifts have been the main focus of my attention. But, to close out this looking-back-on-*Tales*-from-where-I-sit-today, I want now to examine a few areas that in the midst of change have more or less stayed the same. I have four in mind.

First, ethnography remains relatively free from technical jargon and high-wire abstraction. While polysyllabic postmodernism is not altogether absent in ethnographic accounts, it is infrequent.[19] In what might be called mainstream realism, still the most frequent form of ethnographic tale, concepts are borrowed largely from broad public discourse and, for better or worse, an anti-theory bias is still apparent. Representation by "merchants of astonishment" rather than generalization by "human nature experts" remains the primary authorial pose in the trade, emphasizing the venerable aesthetic of unexpected discovery. Surprise, irony, frame breaking, and a pluck-and-luck pragmatism still shape the analytic domain of ethnography.

Second, because of this relative freedom from a thoroughly specialized vocabulary and a privileged conceptual apparatus, ethnography continues to carry a slight literary air compared to other forms of social science writing. It remains I think a less congealed, passive-verb-and-voiced, congested form of discourse, thus suggesting that a textual self-consciousness has been with us for quite some time. This I think keeps the nonspecialist interested in what we do and occasionally pushes certain forms of ethnography into the trade or general-reader domain, bringing the seemingly distant and alien or proximate but puzzling worlds we study to readers beyond the warrens of our own research guilds.

Third, ethnography maintains an almost obsessive focus on the empirical. The witnessing ideal continues to generate some hostility to abstractions not connected to immersion in situated detail. Other forms of data are acceptable, of course, and responsible scholarship requires a sort of interdisciplinary contextualization of the settings in which we work. But these other forms of evidence and argument are acceptable only (sigh) as a concession to practicality. This signals the struggle structural tales have had over the years, a struggle that continues today despite a recognizable broadening of ethnographic genres.

Finally, there still is not much of a technique attached to ethnography despite fifty-plus years of trying to develop a standard methodology (or at least much of a methodology that gets behind and beyond the simple cautionary stories of seasoned veterans). Ethnography it seems cannot and will not be made safe for science, leaving it trapped as it were between the humanities and sciences. This I don't decry or find terribly worrisome, for a standard methodology would effectively neuter or perhaps destroy the still-present Columbian spirit that marks the trade as broadly inquisitive and adventurous—bringing back the news of what and how certain identifiable people are doing these days, whether they are located at the far ends of the world or across the street. In this respect, ethnography is still a relatively artistic, improvised, and situated form of social research where the lasting tenets of research design, theoretical aims, canned concepts, and technical writing have yet to leave a heavy mark. In the end, this is the way I think it should be, for a persuasive and widely read ethnography will always be something of a mess, a mystery, and a miracle.

NOTES

1. This spread of the culture concept shows up occasionally in the most unlikely places. For example, Milton Friedman, the patron saint of free marketers and hard-lined economic rationalists, when asked by a reporter why he thought the University of Chicago economics department had been so productive and prominent over the years, responded without a trace of irony that it was not the hardy individualists who were attracted to the department nor the rewards put in place to motivate them, but rather, in his words, "the culture of the place" that was responsible for the group's success (*Economist*, July 13,1996:72).

2. C. P. Snow (1993) famously suggested that a "gulf of incomprehension" separated "scientists" from "literary intellectuals." The same gulf separates many social scientists of an interpretive bent from those of a more positivist orientation. In rough form, those in the interpretive camp, where most ethnographers pitch their tents, acknowledge—although not always in print—that their empirical, analytic, and narrative orientations are influenced by their own social location, identity, political preferences, training, and so forth. Those in the positive camp do not. Stephen Jay Gould (2003:141), examining the writing styles of the two camps, notes: "Scientists tend to assert that although brevity and clarity should certainly be fostered, verbal style plays no role in the study of material reality." He then goes on to demolish such claims.

3. To be fair, some social scientists—beyond anthropology—have be-

gun these "lit crit" efforts. It is a tiny literature but instructive. In my own field, organization studies, there are a few who have taken a literary turn but the pickings are slim. Some useful works include Golden-Biddle and Locke (1993), Czarniawska (1997), and Martin Kilduff's (1993) witty but careful look at March and Simon's (1958) *Organizations*, the foundational text of the field. It is worth noting, however, these authors are also well versed in the ethnographic literature and critique, and while not always having produced ethnographic work, they are appreciative.

4. A cautionary note is of course appropriate when it comes to examining one's own writing compared to the writing of others. Narrative reflexivity is a marvelous skill as is clever deconstruction work. But peeking behind one's own authorial curtain can also create worries about losing whatever ability or magic one has to produce readable and, with luck, persuasive prose. Extreme reflexivity can perhaps lead one to give it up and stop writing entirely as suggested by those fearful of close reading or, worse, lead one to blissfully forge ahead thinking one is a genius. The best advice I can give is simply "lighten up."

5. Fieldwork, along with the participant observation it involves, is mystifying largely because it suggests to those who have not done such work a rather straightforward and clear-cut methodology about which there is wide consensus. Yet, as noted in the text, it covers quite different ways of data collection and, hence, leads to different kinds of knowledge and understanding. More mystifying however is that the term neatly elides the critical role of the real participants in the group, organization, community, or society under study, the "locals" whose decision it really is as to what kind of access, participation, and experience the fieldworker will be allowed (see, for example, Spradley, 1980; Barley, 1989; Shaffir and Stebbins [eds.], 1991). As I once suggested in the context of my police studies, while I was watching the watchers, they were watching me. The results of their studies no doubt influenced mine. Awareness of such matters—particularly among anthropologists—surfaced dramatically during what Marcus (2007) tags the "reflexive turn" of the 1980s such that today most worthy ethnographies provide at least some meditations—often deep meditations—on the conditions of their production, thus providing the material and, to a degree, a structure for all confessional tales.

6. I do recognize that a prestige of place has long been associated with ethnography. In anthropology, what Gupta and Ferguson (1997) refer to as a "hierarchy of purity" still stands within the trade such that some field sites are taken as more ethnographic and hence more legitimate than others. The question of "where and with whom are you going to do your research?" remains a significant and telling question, and the reply "across the street" is not likely to generate an enthusiastic response from many colleagues. Fieldwork conducted close to home is sometimes seen

as frivolous—akin to tending one's garden—and some notable figures in anthropology have gone out of their way in the past to stigmatize the practice. Geertz (1995:102), for example, remarks that ethnography in one's own society was once known de-risively as "gas station anthropology." This has of course created a good deal of opportunity for the ethnographically inclined without proper credentials—myself among them—to contribute to various interdisciplinary and substantive fields. Anthropologists have never been totally absent from these fields—including my own—but the numbers are few and the status of their at-home work within the discipline still remains to some rather suspect. This was slowly changing when *Tales* was originally published but has since quickened its pace.

7. Ethnographers are not mind readers nor do they have any special technique to plumb the depths of consciousness in others. Yet careful readers continue to expect that an ethnography not only put forward what the native does all day but what the native makes of it too. This is a touchy business. Perhaps the most common technique for producing the native's point of view is by using closely edited quotations along with culturally specific and frequently used terms, categories, slang, jokes, and the like (all passed on in the local vernacular) to convey to readers that the views put forward are not those of the ethnographer but are rather authentic and representative remarks and perspectives transcribed straight from the respective native sources. As I noted in *Tales*, there is a good deal of epistemological angst generated on this matter and it hasn't gone away. In many ways, the "native's point of view" remains as difficult for ethnographers to pin down as the notion of culture. But the debate continues to turn more on how such a perspective is to be put forth in a text than on whether or not it belongs in one. How one gets at it remains an issue, of course. But ethnographers do have a storehouse of raw materials—words and deeds—on which to draw when rendering the native's point of view. On this matter, Geertz (1986:373) is succinct: "Whatever sense we have of how things stand with someone else's inner life, we gain it through their expressions, not through some magical intrusion into their consciousness."

8. A handy little book edited by Caroline Brettell called *When They Read What We Write* (1993) might well be placed in the ethnographer's backpack (or laptop bag). Current caution and wariness no doubt arises in part because some ethnographers at the outset of projects—most often those undertaken close to home—are well aware that they have already acquired, and hence are accustomed to, and share at least some if not a good deal of the culture they are going to the field to study. It also reflects the troubles that come with working in league with sometimes remarkably patient but understandably chary and occasionally hostile members of the group studied who know quite well that ethnographers, as pesky social researchers, are out to interpret what they say and do in ways they

might not find agreeable. When close to home, it seems the longer one stays in the field, the more suspicious become the studied. When far away, the reverse seems to hold. Of course grumbling about the difficulty of doing ethnography while doing it is a rather well established narrative ploy in the ethnographer's textual playbook.

9. I realize that some influential recent work on culture argues that we might be best off avoiding that hyper-referential word altogether and write more specifically about knowledge, practice, tradition, technology, discourse, ideology, or habitus. There is much to be said for such a tactic that would perhaps relieve us of some of the unease surrounding the totalitarian overtones and perverse idealism that sometimes surround the use of the term "culture." But similar problems are raised by other concepts such that redefining or deleting "culture" from our vocabulary would merely bypass rather than solve analytic difficulties. Kuper (1999) argues that such difficulties become most acute when culture or any other stand-in term shifts from something to be represented, interpreted, or even explained to a source of stand-alone explanation — beyond established social institutions and political or economic conditions — for why people think and act as they do. As I argue later in the text, the increasing use of social theory in shaping ethnographic writings is one response to these difficulties suggesting that the best — and most responsible — ethnographies are inevitably interdisciplinary. This ethnographic broadening is effectively preached and practiced by Nash (1993), di Leonardo (1998), and Burawoy and Verdery (1999).

10. Breaking the tie between culture and place, so often assumed to be tight, is becoming increasingly common in ethnographic reports, particular those that look closely at groups seemingly caught up by global forces. Although I will not touch much on these matters, globalization refers to the apparent intensification of worldwide social relations which link distant localities in such a way that local happenings are shaped by events many miles away (and vice versa). Clifford (1997), among others, argues that the world has changed, and changed dramatically, as a result of globalization. Culture and therefore identity are no longer stable but are now fluid, more or less consciously constructed. Ethnography must now offer a variety of discordant voices, never come to rest, and never "essentialize" (a favorite term of abuse) a people or a culture. Just how globalization is playing out in different parts of the world is of increasing interest to ethnographers generally. Examples of how various aspects of globalization might be treated ethnographically include Appadurai (1997), Passaro (1997), Zabusky (1995), Fox (1991), and Featherstone (1990). A related example of this loosening of place and culture is found in Edgar Schein's (2003) historical look at a onetime huge and highly successful organization that rapidly declined and collapsed but whose apparently

honored ways of doing things were carried by former employees into different organizations following the fall. The work is appropriately titled *DEC is Dead, Long Live DEC*.

11. I am indebted here to my colleague Chris Winship, who reminded me over coffee of the role pragmatism played in the development of symbolic interaction at the University of Chicago in the 1920s and 1930s. George Herbert Mead, a key figure for interactionists, worked closely with Dewey at Chicago and was a fellow pragmatist. Herbert Blumer, who wrote the foundational text *Symbolic Interactionism* (1969), was a student of Mead's and a supporter of the kind of open-ended fieldwork students were expected to undertake at that time in Chicago—going to urban neighborhoods like cub reporters to learn how those in various ethnic, economic, occupational communities (mostly the downtrodden) were getting on and getting by. The influence of this first Chicago School has waned in sociology (as has pragmatism), but it can still be seen in the work of some, particularly those who head for the field when questions of either an empirical or conceptual sort arise. It seems to me that in pragmatism, ethnographers have a philosophy well worth heeding. See Muller and Winship (2009) for a lively assessment of John Dewey's often neglected contributions to American sociology. For a thoughtful appraisal of the first Chicago School, its roots, and its influence, see Bulmer (1984).

12. Two recent examples of confessional work woven into the body of an ethnographic account are Sudhir Venkatesh's (2008) riveting (and best-selling) *Gang Leader for a Day: A Rogue Sociologist Takes to the Streets*, about crack dealing in Chicago, and Peter Moskos's (2008) *Cop in the Hood: My Year Policing Baltimore's Eastern District*, a look at another crack-infested world through an entirely different lens.

13. This is not to say that single-site studies have vanished. Certainly a single social site, situation, or occurrence can be of as much interest for its unique specificities as for its links, similarities and differences to other sites, situations, and occurrences. Single-site studies however still trigger what seems to be a deep and abiding fear of the particularistic among critics of ethnography who wonder what, if anything, can be learned from a "mere case." The smart-ass but wise answer to this hackneyed but too common question is "all we can." Indeed, some of the best ethnographic studies of the workplace have been delivered—and continue, if less frequently, to be delivered—though small scale, highly bounded, single-site ethnographic studies. See, for example, the classic realist tales of Dalton (1959), Crozier (1964), Jackall (1988), Kunda (1992), and Orr (1996). Nor can any serious student of work life ignore *Banana Time*, the minimalist ethnography of routine work unforgettably inscribed by Donald Roy (1958).

14. While degrading terms such as "primitive," "savage," and "sub-

ject" are long gone from ethnographic texts, how exactly to designate those studied remains problematic. To wit, "native" is now interchangeable with "member" (and sometimes "client"). The term "informant" is still with us but its use fading fast, since it represents an increasingly troublesome if not ugly label for those who aid us in our studies.

15. Some examples of notable ethnographic work in this identity domain include Sherry Ortner's (1999) examination of the mutual dependences and cultural conflicts between mountaineers and Sherpas in the Himalayas, Lawrence Ouellet's (1994) gritty view of the lives of American long-distance truckers, Anne Allison's (1994) close observations of corporate-sponsored Japanese nightlife, Tony Watson's (1994) sympathetic exploration of the everyday predicaments middle managers face in a large British telecommunication company, Vered Vinitzky-Seroussi's (1998) appropriately uncomfortable look at high school reunions, and Michèle Lamont's (2008) penetrating examination of how high-status professors serving on interdisciplinary review committees negotiate their expertise in mixed company.

16. Ethnographic culture, like those studied, is constantly shaping and reshaping itself to adjust to new problems. Perhaps the most vexing of the conceptual and methodological challenges these days concern the increasing scale, range, volatility, and complexity of social life. With increased mobility, globalization, advances in communications technologies, and the apparent end to the stability and permanence once associated (rightly or wrongly) with social life, ethnographies of a "people, places, and faces" sort become more difficult to imagine and realize. Networks (even networks of networks), not sites, may become the new terra incognita of ethnographic interest. See Hannerz (1992) and Faubion and Marcus, eds. (2009) for a look ahead (and look back) on these challenges as viewed from the anthropological perspective. For some intriguing examples of just how scale and complexity can be handled ethnographically, see Christina Garsten (1994), *Apple World: Core and Periphery in a Transnational Organization*, and James Watson, ed. (1997), *Golden Arches East: McDonald's in East Asia*.

17. For a good number of readers outside the field, a trustworthy ethnography is often taken to be simply the straightforward reporting of what people say and do as witnessed by the author, who displays the expected courtesy of staying out of the way when the ethnographic facts are neatly bundled up in writing. Local meanings are taken at face value. Whatever tacit assumptions informing and undergirding such meanings are not sought or welcome in the text. Such a response is tied partly to the sacralization of culture that I think goes with the notion's popularization at large as well as what we might call the cult of authenticity associated with heightened cultural sensitivity and awareness. A widespread misun-

derstanding of ethnography results, and anything other than the native's point of view as supposedly put forward and understood by the native is read as less than the real thing. To wit, the enormous popular appeal of both Michael Lewis's (1989, 2010) man-on-the-spot literary journalism and V. S. Naipaul's (1990, 1998) highly detailed travel writings. Many if not most readers take writings of this sort as indisputably authentic cultural accounts devoid of insidious (or subversive) interpretation. There is, to be sure, interesting and valuable work in these literary domains, but it is not ethnography. Such work offers up no explanation, no theory, no model for the facts put forth, no concepts or categories within which to embed the material, little if any comparative or contextual groundings, and is less than candid about how, where, when, and from whom such materials were gathered. Whatever else it may be, ethnography is an interpretation. It is something *added to* whatever wondrous facts were collected or stumbled on during a lengthy period of fieldwork.

18. It is worth noting that the hallmark of most journal-length ethnography is the stark form of the structural tale. Ethnographic details are necessarily cut back, stories abbreviated, and contextual particulars condensed or eliminated. Theoretical constructs move to the fore with argumentation and sharp, highly selective examples pushing away representation and breath. Attempts to control the meaning readers take away from the materials are rather apparent in pursuit of theoretical advancement in a particular (typically narrow) domain. Structural tales, as put forth in monographs of the sort mentioned in the text, are relatively muted and rich in narrative detail compared to what appears in journals. Journal articles can also be seen as products designed primarily to help establish one's reputation in a particular disciplinary or substantive field that extends well beyond ethnographic circles. For better or worse, the career-making importance of journal-length ethnography for those who want permanent jobs in the academy is unquestioned these days. See, for example, the contrast between journal and book products of organizational ethnography as exemplified by Perlow (1997, 1998), Morrill (1995, 1991), Barker (1993, 1999), and Kellogg (2009, 2011).

19. A possible exception here may be those ethnographic accounts I've labeled post-structural whose authors do seem to occasionally mask and obscure their work by importing specialized vocabularies—with lots of semicolons and terms with high syllable counts—thus constructing a "difficult" or unreadable text for many readers. Yet, I would argue, the grounded character of ethnographic work—fieldwork—usually acts as something of a tether, keeping the writers tied as it were to their respective settings. Remember too that post-structural tales concern "post-structural subjects"—those highly mobile and multiply situated social actors who operate within a swirling, expanding universe of ambiguous signs and

symbols. Numerous perspectives appear in post-structural tales and cultural coherence is more or less absent. Texts are thus less tidy than a Disney theme park (and other forms of ethnographic reporting) since more discordant voices (including the author's), never coming to rest, are heard within them. Readers must work harder than they are accustomed in order to figure out what is going on because the narrative is a fractured one. True, too, those textual practices alleged to be "reader unfriendly" may also be labeled as such due to reader unfamiliarity with the tools of textual analysis put into play by post-structural authors fascinated by language and language use. There are, of course, bad—indeed horrid—post-structural accounts crammed with baffling meta-analysis and pounding waves of self-indulgent reflexivity ("enough about them, let me tell you about me") while annoyingly spare with ethnographic details. The good ones I think curb conceptual flights, are only modestly confessional, and are thick with detail. See, for example, some splendid, reader-friendly post-structural tales addressed to students of organizations by Marcus and Hall (1992), Brannen (1992), and the sampler of post-structural accounts by Boje et al. (1996), some of which are informed by ethnographic study.

References

Adams, R. N., and J. J. Preiss, eds. 1960. *Human organization research.* Homewood, IL: Dorsey.

Adler, P. A. 1985. *Wheeling and dealing.* New York: Columbia University Press.

Adler, P. S., and P. A. Adler. 1987a. *Membership roles in field research.* Newbury Park, CA: Sage.

———. 1987b. The past and the future of ethnography. *Journal of Contemporary Ethnography* 16:4–24.

Agar, M. 1986. *Speaking of ethnography.* Beverly Hills, CA: Sage.

———. 1985. *Independents declared.* Washington, DC: Smithsonian Institution.

———. 1982. Toward an ethnographic language. *American Anthropologist* 84:779–95.

———. 1980. *The professional stranger.* New York: Academic Press.

———. 1973. *Ripping and running: A formal ethnography of urban heroin addicts.* New York: Seminar Press.

Agee, J., and W. Evans. 1960. *Let us now praise famous men.* Boston: Houghton Mifflin (first published in 1941).

Allison, A. 1994. *Nightwork: Sexuality, pleasure, and corporate masculinity in a Tokyo hostess club.* Chicago: University of Chicago Press.

Anderson, N. 1923. *The hobo.* Chicago: University of Chicago Press.

———. 1983. A stranger at the gate. *Urban Life* 11:396–406.

Anteby, M. 2008. *Moral gray zones: Side productions, identity, and regulation in an aeronautic plant.* Princeton, NJ: Princeton University Press.

Appadurai, A. 1997. Fieldwork in the era of globalization. *Anthropology and Humanism* 22:115–18.

Argyris, C. R. Putnam, and D. M. Smith. 1985. *Action science.* San Francisco: Jossey-Bass.

Atkinson, J. 1982. Anthropology. *Signs* 8:236–58.

References

Back, K. W. 1956. The well-informed informant. *Human Organization* 14:30–33.

Barker, J. R. 1999. *The discipline of teamwork*. Newbury Park, CA: Sage.

———. 1993. Tightening the iron cage: Concertive control in self-managing teams. *Administrative Science Quarterly* 38:408–37.

Barley, N. 1989. *Not a hazardous sport*. New York: Henry Holt.

Barley, S. R., and G. Kunda. 2006. *Gurus, hired guns, and warm bodies: Itinerant experts in the knowledge economy*. Princeton, NJ: Princeton University Press.

Barthes, R. 1972. *Mythologies*. London: Paladin.

Bass, T. A. 1985. *The eudaemonic pie*. Boston: Houghton Mifflin.

Bate, S. P. 1997. Whatever happened to organizational anthropology? *Human Relations* 50:1147–75.

Bateson, G. 1936. *Naven*. Palo Alto, CA: Stanford University Press.

Becker, H. S. 1986a. *Doing things together*. Evanston, IL: Northwestern University Press.

———. 1986b. *Writing for social scientists*. Chicago: University of Chicago Press.

———. 1980. Culture. *Yale Review* 71 (Summer): 513–28.

———. 1970. *Sociological work*. Chicago: Aldine.

———. 1967. Whose side are we on? *Social Problems* 14:239–47.

———. 1951. *Role and career problems of the Chicago public school teacher*. Ph.D. diss., University of Chicago.

Becker, H. S., B. Geer, E. C. Hughes, and A. Strauss. 1961. *Boys in white*. Chicago: University of Chicago Press.

Behar, R. 2003. *Translated woman: Crossing the border with Esperanza*. Boston: Beacon.

Bell, B., and Newby, H. W. 1977. *Doing sociological research*. London: Allen and Unwin.

Bellamy, J. D. 1982. Introduction. In T. Wolfe, ed., *The purple decades*. New York: Farrar, Straus, and Giroux.

Ben-David, J., and T. N. Clark, eds. 1977. *Culture and its creators*. Chicago: University of Chicago Press.

Berger, B. 1968. *Working-class suburb*. Berkeley: University of California Press.

Berreman, G. 1962. *Behind many masks*. Monograph 4. Society for Applied Anthropology. Ithaca, New York: Cornell University Press.

Beynon, H. 1973. *Working for Ford*. London: Penguin.

Bittner, E. 1973. Objectivity and realism in sociology. In G. Psathas, ed., *Phenomenological sociology*. New York: Wiley, 108–25.

——. 1970. *The functions of the police in modern society*. Washington, DC: U.S. Government Printing Office.

Blumer, H. 1969. *Symbolic interactionism*. Englewood Cliffs, NJ: Prentice-Hall.

Boas, F. 1973. The limitations of the comparative method of anthropology. In P. Bohannon and M. Glazer, eds., *Highpoints in anthropology*. New York: Knopf.

——. 1966. *Race, language and culture*. New York: Free Press.

Bogdan, R., and S. H. Taylor. 1975. *Introduction to qualitative research methods*. New York: Wiley.

Boje, D. M., R. Gephart, and T. J. Thatchenkery, eds. 1996. *Postmodern management and organization theory*. Newbury Park, CA: Sage.

Boon, S. A. 1982. *Other tribes, other scribes*. Cambridge: Cambridge University Press.

Bowen, E. S. [pseud. of Laura Bohannan]. 1954. *Return to laughter*. New York: Harper and Row.

Brannen, M. Y. 1992. Bwana Mickey: Constructing cultural consumption at Tokyo Disneyland. In J. T. Tobin, ed., *Re-made in Japan*. New Haven, CT: Yale University Press.

Brettell, C. B., ed. 1993. *When they read what we write*. Westport, CT: Bergin and Garvey.

Briggs, J. 1970. *Never in anger*. Cambridge: Harvard University Press.

Brown, R. H. 1977. *A poetic for sociology*. Cambridge: Cambridge University Press.

Bruner, E. M. 1986. Ethnography as narrative. In V. W. Turner and E. M. Bruner, eds., *The anthropology of experience*. Urbana: University of Illinois Press, 139–55.

Bruyn, S. T. 1966. *The human perspective in sociology*. Englewood Cliffs, NJ: Prentice-Hall.

Bulmer, M. 1984. *The Chicago school of sociology*. Chicago: University of Chicago Press.

——, ed. 1982. *Social research ethics*. London: Macmillan.

Burawoy, M. 1999. *Global ethnography: Connections and imaginations in a postmodern world*. Berkeley: University of California Press.1979.

——. *Manufacturing consent: Changes in the labor process under monopoly capital*. Chicago: University of Chicago Press.

Burawoy, M., and K. Verdery, eds. 1999. *Uncertain transition: Ethnog-*

raphy of change in the postsocialist world. New York: Rowman and Littlefield.

Burgess, R. G. 1983. *In the field*. London: Allen and Unwin.

Burgess, R. G., ed. 1982. *Field research*. London: Allen and Unwin.

Cain, M. 1973. *Society and the policeman's role*. London: Routledge and Kegan Paul.

Canary, R. H., and H. Kozicki, eds. 1978. *The writing of history*. Madison: University of Wisconsin Press.

Capote, Truman. 1966. *In cold blood*. New York: Random House.

Carey, J. T. 1975. *Sociology and public affairs*. Beverly Hills, CA: Sage.

Casagrande, J. B. 1960. *In the company of man*. New York: Harper and Row.

Caven, S. 1966. *Liquor license*. Chicago: Aldine.

Chagnon, N. 1968. *Yanomamo*. New York: Holt, Rinehart and Winston.

Champoulie, J.-M. 1987. Everett C. Hughes and the development of fieldwork in sociology. *Urban Life* 15:3–4, 259–93.

Chatterton, M. 1975. Organizational relationships and processes in police work. Ph.D. diss., University of Manchester.

Chetkovich, C. 1997. *Real heat: Gender and race in the urban fire service*. New Brunswick, NJ: Rutgers University Press.

Cicourel, A. 1968. *The social organization of juvenile justice*. New York: Wiley.

Clarke, M. 1975. Survival in the field. *Theory and Society* 2:63–94.

Clifford, J. 1997. *Routes: Travel and translations in the late twentieth century*. Cambridge, MA: Harvard University Press.

———. 1986a. On ethnographic allegory. In J. Clifford and G. E. Marcus, eds., *Writing culture*. Berkeley: University of California Press, 98–121.

———. 1986b. Partial truths. In J. Clifford and G. E. Marcus, eds., *Writing culture*. Berkeley: University of California Press, 1–26.

———. 1983a. On ethnographic authority. *Representations* 1:118–46.

———. 1983b. Power and dialogue in ethnography: Marcel Griaule's initiation. In G. W. Stocking, ed., *Observers observed*. Madison: University of Wisconsin Press, 121–55.

———. 1981. On ethnographic surrealism. *Comparative Studies in Society and History* 23:539–64.

———. 1980. Fieldwork reciprocity and the making of ethnographic texts. *Man* 15:518–32.

Clifford, J., and G. E. Marcus, eds. 1986. *Writing culture*. Berkeley: University of California Press.

Conklin, H. 1968. Ethnography. In D. L. Sills, ed., *International Encyclopedia of Social Science*, vol. 5. New York: Free Press.

Crapanzano, V. 1986. Hermes' dilemma. In J. Clifford and G. E. Marcus, eds., *Writing culture*. Berkeley: University of California Press.

———. 1985. *Waiting: The whites of South Africa*. New York: Random House.

———. 1980. *Tuhami: Portrait of a Moroccan*. Chicago: University of Chicago Press.

Cressey, P. G. 1932. *The taxi-dance hall*. Chicago: University of Chicago Press.

Crozier, M. 1964. *The bureaucratic phenomenon*. Chicago: University of Chicago Press.

Czarniawska, B. 1997. *Narrating the organization: Dramas of institutional identity*. Chicago: University of Chicago Press.

Dalton, M. 1964. Preconceptions and methods. In P. E. Hammond, ed., *Sociologist at work*. New York: Basic.

———. 1959. *Men who manage: Fusions of feeling and theory in administration*. New York: Wiley.

———. 1951. Informal factors in career achievement. *American Journal of Sociology* 61:407–15.

D'Andrade, R. 1986. Three scientific world views and the covering law model. In D. W. Fiske and R. A. Shweder, eds., *Metatheory in social science*. Chicago: University of Chicago Press, 19–40.

Davis, M. S. 1971. That's interesting. *Philosophy of Social Science* 1:309–44.

Davis, S. G. 1997. *Spectacular nature: Corporate culture and the sea world experience*. Berkeley: University of California Press.

Dégerardo, J.-M. 1969. *The observation of savage peoples*. Translated by F. C. T. Moore. Berkeley: University of California Press (first published in 1800).

Denzin, N. 1981. Contributions of anthropology/sociology to qualitative research methods. In E. Kuhns and S. V. Marorana, eds., *Qualitative methods for institutional research*. San Francisco: Jossey-Bass.

———. 1970. *The research act*. Chicago: Aldine.

Desmond, M. 2007. *On the fireline: Living and dying with wildland firefighters*. Chicago: University of Chicago Press.

Diamond, S., ed. 1980. *Anthropology: Ancestors and heirs*. The Hague: Mouton.

Diamond, T. 1992. *Making gray gold: Narratives of nursing home care*. Chicago: University of Chicago Press.

di Leonardo, M. 1998 *Exotics at home: Anthropologies, others, and American modernity*. Chicago: University of Chicago Press.

Ditton, J. 1981. *The view from Goffman*. London: Macmillan.

——. 1977. *Part-time crime: An ethnography of fiddling and pilferage*. London: Macmillan.

Douglas, J. 1985. *Creative interviewing*. Beverly Hills, CA: Sage.

——. *Investigative social research*. Beverly Hills, CA: Sage.

Douglas, J., ed. 1972. *Research on deviance*. New York: Random House.

Douglas, J., and J. M. Johnson, eds. 1977. *Existential sociology*. Cambridge: Cambridge University Press.

Douglas, M. 1966. *Purity and danger*. London: Routledge and Kegan Paul.

Downes, D., and P. Rock. 1982. *Understanding deviance*. Oxford: Clarendon Press.

Dreher, M. C. 1982. *Working men and ganja*. Philadelphia: Ishi.

Dreyfus, H., and P. Rabinow. 1982. *Michel Foucault: Beyond structuralism and hermeneutics*. Chicago: University of Chicago Press.

Dubois, W. E. B. 1899. *The Philadelphia slum*. Philadelphia: University of Pennsylvania Press.

Dumont, J.-P. 1978. *The Headman and I*. Austin: University of Texas Press.

——. 1976. *Under the rainbow*. Austin: University of Texas Press.

Dwyer, K. 1977. The dialogue of anthropology. *Dialectical Anthropology* 2:143–51.

Easterday, L. D., C. D. Papademas, L. Schorr, and C. Valentine. 1977. The making of a female researcher. *Urban Life* 6:333–48.

Eco, U. 1986. *Travels in Hyperreality*. New York: Harcourt Brace & Co.

Edgerton, R. B. 1979. *Alone together*. Berkeley: University of California Press.

Edmondson, R. 1984. *Rhetoric in sociology*. London: Macmillan.

Ellis, C. 1995. *Final negotiations: A story of love, loss, and chronic illness*. Philadelphia: Temple University Press.

Emerson, R. M., ed. 1983. *Contemporary field research*. Boston: Little, Brown.

Epstein, A. L., ed. 1967. *The craft of anthropology*. London: Tavistock.

Erickson, K. 1976. *Everything in its path*. New York: Simon and Schuster.

Estroff, S. 1985. *Making it crazy*. Berkeley, CA: University of California Press.

Evans-Pritchard, E. E. 1973. Some reminiscences and reflections on fieldwork. *Journal of the Anthropological Society of Oxford* 4:1–12.

———. 1940. *The Nuer*. Oxford: Oxford University Press.

———. 1936. *Witchcraft, oracles, and magic among the Azande*. Oxford: Oxford University Press.

Faris, R. E. L. 1970. *Chicago sociology*. Chicago: University of Chicago Press.

Faubion, J. D., and G. E. Marcus. 2009. *Fieldwork is not what it used to be*. Ithaca, NY: Cornell University Press.

Featherstone, M., ed. 1990. *Global culture*. London: Sage.

Feldman, S. P. 1986. *The culture of monopoly management*. New York: Garland.

Feyerabend, P. 1972. *Against method*. London: New Left Books.

Filstead, W. J. 1970. *Qualitative methodology*. Chicago: Markham.

Firth, R. 1936. *We, the Tikopia*. London: Allen and Unwin.

Fish, S. 1980. *Is there a text in this class?* Cambridge, MA: Harvard University Press.

Fjellman, S. M. 1999. *Vinyl leaves: Walt Disney World and America*. Boulder, CO: Westview.

Forsythe, D. E. 2001. *Studying those who study us*. Palo Alto, CA: Stanford University Press.

Foster, G., ed. 1979. *Long-term field research in social anthropology*. New York: Academic Press.

Fox, R. G., ed. 1991. *Recapturing America: Working in the present*. Santa Fe, NM: School of American Research Press.

Freeman, D. 1983. *Margaret Mead and Samoa*. Cambridge, MA: Harvard University Press.

Freilich, M. 1978. The meaning of sociocultural. In B. Bernado, ed., *The concept and dynamics of culture*. The Hague: Mouton.

———. 1970. *Marginal natives*. New York: Wiley.

Gamst, F. C. 1980. *The hog head: An industrial ethnology of the locomotive engineer*. New York: Holt, Rinehart and Winston.

References

Garsten, C. 1994. *Apple world: Core and periphery in a transnational organization*. Stockholm: Stockholm Studies in Social Anthropology.

Gans, H. J. 1982. The participant-observer as a human being. In R. G. Burgess, ed., *Field Research*. London: Allen and Unwin.

———. 1967. *The Levittowners*. New York: Pantheon.

———. 1962. *The urban villagers*. New York: Free Press.

Garfinkel, H. 1965. *Studies in ethnomethodology*. Englewood Cliffs, NJ: Prentice-Hall.

Geertz, C. 1995. *After the fact*. Cambridge, MA: Harvard University Press.

———. 1988. *Works and lives*. Palo Alto, CA: Stanford University Press.

———. 1986. Making experiences, authoring selves. In V. W. Turner and E. Bruner, eds., *The anthropology of experience*. Urbana: University of Illinois Press. 373–80.

———. 1983. *Local knowledge*. New York: Basic.

———. 1974. From the native's point of view. *Bulletin of the American Academy of Arts and Sciences* 28:27–45.

———. 1973. *The interpretation of cultures*. New York: Basic.

Georges, R. A., and M. O. Jones. 1980. *People studying people*. Berkeley: University of California Press.

Giddens, A. 1979. *Central problems in social theory*. Berkeley: University of California Press.

———. 1976. *The rules of sociological method*. London: Hutchinson.

Glaeser, A. 2000. *Divided in unity: Identity, Germany and the Berlin police*. Chicago: University of Chicago Press.

Glaser, B., and A. Strauss. 1967. *The discovery of grounded theory*. Chicago: Aldine.

Goffman, E. 1981. *Forms of talk*. Philadelphia: University of Pennsylvania Press.

———. 1973. *Frame analysis*. Cambridge: Harvard University Press.

———. 1961. *Asylums*. New York: Anchor.

Golde, P., ed. 1970. *Women in the field*. Chicago: Aldine.

Golden-Biddle, K., and K. Locke. 1992. Appealing work: An investigation of how ethnographic texts convince. *Organization Science* 4:595–616.

Goodenough, W. H. 1971. *Culture, language, and society*. Reading, MA: Addison-Wesley Modular Publications.

Gould, S. J. 2003. *The hedgehog, the fox, and the magister's pox*. New York: Harmony Books.

———. 1987. *Time's arrow, time's cycle*. Cambridge, MA: Harvard University Press.

Gouldner, A. 1954. *Patterns of industrial bureaucracy*. New York: Free Press.

Gregory, K. 1983. Native-view paradigms. *Administrative Science Quarterly* 28:359–76.

Griswald, N. 1987. The fabrication of meaning. *American Journal of Sociology* 92:1077–1117.

Gupta, A., and J. Ferguson, eds. 1997. *Anthropological locations: Boundaries and grounds of a field science*. Berkeley: University of California Press.

Gusfield, J. 1981. *The culture of public problems*. Chicago: University of Chicago Press.

Gusfield, J. R., and J. Machalowicz. 1984. Secular symbolism. *Annual Review of Sociology* 10:417–35.

Gusterson, H. 2004. *People of the bomb: Portraits of America's nuclear complex*. Minneapolis: University of Minnesota Press.

Habenstein, R. W. 1954. The career of the funeral director. Ph.D. diss., University of Chicago.

Habenstein, R. W., ed. 1970. *Pathways to data*. Chicago: Aldine.

Hall, O. 1944. The informal organization of medical practice in an American city. Ph.D. diss., University of Chicago.

Hall, S., and T. Jefferson. 1976. *Resistance through rituals*. London: Hutchinson.

Halle, D. 1984. *America's working man*. Chicago: University of Chicago Press.

Hammersley, M., and P. Atkinson. 1983. *Ethnography*. New York: Tavistock.

Hannerz, U. 1992. *Cultural complexity: Studies in the social organization of meaning*. New York: Columbia University Press.

———. 1969. *Soulside*. New York: Columbia University Press.

Haraway, D. 1989. *Primate visions: Gender, race, and nature in the world of modern science*. New York: Routledge.

Harper, D. 1982. *Good company*. Chicago: University of Chicago Press.

Harris, L. 1985. *Holy days*. New York: Macmillan.

Harris, M. 1979. *Cultural materialism*. New York: Random House.

———. 1968. *The rise of anthropological theory*. New York: Thomas Crowell.

References

Haskell, T. 1977. *The emergence of professional social science.* Urbana: University of Illinois Press.

Hayano, D. M. 1982. *Poker faces.* Berkeley: University of California Press.

———. 1979. Auto-ethnography. *Human Organization* 38:99–104.

Hebdige, R. 1979. *Subcultures.* London: Methuen.

Heider, K. 1976. *Ethnographic film.* Austin: University of Texas Press.

Henry, F., and S. Saberwal, eds. 1969. *Stress and response in fieldwork.* New York: Holt, Rinehart and Winston.

Henry, J. 1963. *Culture against man.* New York: Random House.

Hersey, J. 1946. *Hiroshima.* New York: Vintage.

Hinsley, C. 1983. Ethnographic charisma and scientific routine: Cusing and Fewkes in the American Southwest, 1879–1893. In G. W. Stocking, ed., *Observers observed.* Madison: University of Wisconsin Press.

Hochschild, A. 1983. *The managed heart.* Berkeley: University of California Press.

Horowitz, R. 1983. *Honor and the American dream.* New Brunswick, NJ: Rutgers University Press.

Howard-Grenville, J. 2007. *Corporate culture and environmental practice: Making change at a high-tech manufacturer.* Northampton, MA: Edward Elgar Publishing.

Hughes, E. C. 1974. Who studies whom? *Human Organization* 33:327–34.

———. 1970. *The sociological eye.* 2 vols. Chicago: Aldine.

———. 1960. The place of fieldwork in social science. Introduction to B. H. Junker, *Field Work.* Chicago: University of Chicago Press.

———. 1928. The Chicago Real Estate Board. Ph.D. diss., University of Chicago.

Humphreys, L. 1970. *Tearoom trade.* Chicago: Aldine.

Hunt, J. 1984. The development of rapport through the negotiation of gender in field work among police. *Human Organization* 43:283–96.

Hymes, D., ed. 1972. *Reinventing anthropology.* New York: Pantheon.

Iser, W. 1978. *The act of reading.* Baltimore: Johns Hopkins University Press.

Jacobs, J. 1974. *Fun city: An ethnographic study of a retirement community.* New York: Holt, Rinehart and Winston.

Jackall, R. 1988. *Moral mazes: The world of corporate managers.* New York: Oxford University Press.

Johnson, J. M. 1975. *Doing field research.* New York: Free Press.

Jules-Rosette, B. 1976. The conversion experience. *Journal of Religion in Africa* 7:132–64.

Junker, B. H. 1960. *Field work*. Chicago: University of Chicago Press.

Keating, P., ed. 1976. *Into unknown England, 1866–1913*. Manchester: Manchester University Press.

Kellogg, K. 2011. *Challenging operations: Medical reform and resistance in hospitals*. Chicago: University of Chicago Press.

———. 2009. Operating room: Relational spaces and microinstitutional change in surgery. *American Journal of Sociology* 115 (3): 657–711.

Kidder, T. 1985. *House*. Boston: Little, Brown.

———. 1981. *Soul of the new machine*. Boston: Little, Brown.

Kilduff, M. 1993. Deconstructing organizations. *Academy of Management Review* 18:13–31.

Kimball, S. T., and J. B. Watson, eds. 1972. *Crossing cultural boundaries*. San Francisco: Chandler.

Kirk, J., and M. M. Miller. 1986. *Reliability and validity in qualitative research*. Beverly Hills, CA: Sage.

Klockers, C. 1975. *The professional fence*. New York: Free Press.

Knorr-Cetina, K. 1981. *The manufacture of knowledge*. Oxford: Pergamon.

Konner, M. 1987. *Becoming a doctor*. New York: Viking.

Kramer, J. 1978. *The last cowboy*. New York: Harper and Row.

Kramer, M. 1983. *Invasive procedures*. New York: Harper and Row.

———. 1979. *Three farms*. New York: Harper and Row.

Krause-Jensen, J. 2010. *Flexible firm: The design of culture at Bang & Olufsen*. New York: Berghahn Books.

Krieger, S. 1983. *The mirror dance*. Philadelphia: Temple University Press.

———. 1979. Research and the construction of text. In N. Denzin, ed., *Studies in symbolic interactionism*, vol. 2. Greenwich, CT: JAI Press, 167–87.

Kroeber, T. 1961. *Ishi*. Berkeley: University of California Press.

Kuper, A. 1999. *Culture: The anthropologists' account*. Cambridge, MA: Harvard University Press.

———. 1977. *Anthropology and anthropologists*. London: Routledge and Kegan Paul.

Lakoff, G., and M. Johnson. 1980. *Metaphors we live by*. Chicago: University of Chicago Press.

References

Lamont, M. 2008. *How professors think*. Cambridge, MA: Harvard University Press.

Lamphere, L. 1992. *Structuring diversity: Ethnographic perspectives on the new immigration*. Chicago: University of Chicago Press.

Lane, C. A. 2011. *A company of one: Neoliberal faith and the post-organizational man*. Ithaca, NY: Cornell University Press.

Latour, B. 1993. *We have never been modern*. Translated by Catherine Porter. Cambridge, MA: Harvard University Press.

Latour, B., and S. Woolgar. 1979. *Laboratory life: The construction of scientific facts*. Newbury Park, CA: Sage.

Leach, E. R. 1976. *Culture and communication*. Cambridge: Cambridge University Press.

——. 1954. *Political systems of Highland Burma*. London: G. Bell and Sons.

Leiter, K. 1980. *A primer on ethnomethodology*. New York: Oxford University Press.

Levine, D. N. 1985. *The flight from ambiguity*. Chicago: University of Chicago Press.

Levi-Strauss, C. 1966. *The savage mind*. New York: Free Press.

Lewis, M. 2010. *The big short*. New York: W. W. Norton.

——. 1989. *Liar's poker*. New York: W. W. Norton.

Lieberson, S. 1985. *Making it count*. Berkeley: University of California Press.

Liebow, E. 1967. *Tally's corner*. Boston: Little, Brown.

Lofland, J. 1987. Reflections on a thrice-named journal. *Journal of Contemporary Ethnography* 16:25–40.

——. 1976. *Doing social life*. New York: Wiley.

——. 1974. Styles of reporting qualitative field research. *American Sociologist* 9:101–11.

——. 1971. *Analyzing social settings*. Belmont, CA: Wadsworth.

Lowie, R. 1937. *The history of ethnological theory*. New York: Rinehart.

Lurie, A. 1969. *Imaginary friends*. New York: Bantam.

Lynch, M. 1985. *Art and artifact in laboratory science*. Boston: Routledge and Kegan Paul.

Lynd, R. S., and H. M. Lynd. 1937. *Middletown in transition*. New York: Harcourt, Brace and Co.

——. 1929. *Middletown*. New York: Harcourt, Brace and Co.

McCall, G. J., and J. L. Simmons, eds. 1969. *Issues in participant observation*. Reading, MA: Addison-Wesley.

McClosky, D. N. 1985. *The rhetoric of economics*. Madison: University of Wisconsin Press.

McClure, M. 1981. *Spike Island*. London: Macmillan.

McPhee, J. 1980. *Basin and range*. New York: Farrar, Straus and Giroux.

———. 1977. *Coming into the country*. New York: Farrar, Straus and Giroux.

Mailer, Norman. 1979. *The executioner's song*. Boston: Little, Brown.

Malinowski, B. 1967. *A diary in the strict sense of the term*. New York: Harcourt, Brace and World.

———. [1922] 1961. *Argonauts of the Western Pacific*. New York: E. P. Dutton.

———. 1935. *Coral gardens and their magic*. 2 vols. New York: American Books.

Manning, P. K. 1988. *Signifying calls*. Cambridge, MA: MIT Press.

———. 1987. *Semiotics and fieldwork*. Newbury Park, CA: Sage.

———. 1985. Limits of the semiotic structuralist perspective upon organizational analysis. In N. Denzin, ed., *Studies in symbolic interaction*, vol. 6. Greenwich, CT: JAI Press.

———. 1982. Analytic induction. In R. B. Smith and P. K. Manning, eds., *Social science methods*, vol. 1. New York: Irvington Press.

———. 1980. *The narc's game*. Cambridge, MA: MIT Press.

———. 1979. Metaphors of the field. *Administrative Science Quarterly* 24:425–41.

March, J. G., and H. A. Simon. 1958. *Organizations*. New York: Wiley.

Marcus, G. E. 2007. Ethnography two decades after writing culture: From the experimental to the baroque. *Anthropological Quarterly* 80:1127–1145.

———. 1998. *Ethnography through thick and thin*. Princeton, NJ: Princeton University Press.

———. 1986. Contemporary problems of ethnography in the modern world system. In J. Clifford and G. E. Marcus, eds., *Writing cultures*. Berkeley: University of California Press.

———. 1980. Rhetoric and the ethnographic genre in anthropological research. *Current Anthropology* 21:507–10.

———, ed. 1983. *Elites*. Albuquerque: University of New Mexico Press.

Marcus, G. E., and D. Cushman. 1982. Ethnographies as text. *Annual Review of Anthropology* 11:25–69.

References

Marcus, G. E., and M. Fischer. 1986. *Anthropology as cultural critique.* Chicago: University of Chicago Press.

Marcus, G. E., and P. D. Hall. 1992. *Lives in trust: The fortunes of dynastic families in late twentieth century america.* Boulder, CO: Westview Press.

Marcus, G. E., and F. Mascarenhas. 2005. *Ocasião: The marquis and the anthropologist.* Walnut Creek, CA: Rowman & Littlefield.

Mars, G. 1982. *Cheats at work.* London: Allen and Unwin.

Mars, G., and M. Nicod. 1984. *The world of waiters.* London: Allen and Unwin.

Martin, J. 1982. Stories and scripts in organizational settings. In A. Hastorf and A. Isen, eds., *Cognitive social psychology.* Amsterdam: Elsevier.

Matthews, F. H. 1977. *Quest for an American sociology.* Montreal: McGill-Queen's University Press.

Matthiessen, P. 1962. *Under the mountain wall.* London: Penguin.

Maybury-Lewis, D. H. P. 1965. *The savage and the innocent.* London: Evans.

Mead, M. 2001. *Letters from the field, 1925–1975.* New York: Harper-Collins.

———. 1928. *Coming of age in Samoa.* New York: Morrow.

Miles, M., and A. Huberman. 1984. *Qualitative data analysis.* Beverly Hills, CA: Sage.

Millman, M. 1976. *The unkindest cut.* Chicago: Aldine.

Miner, H. 1956. Body ritual among the Nacirema. *American Anthropologist* 58:503–7.

Mitchell, G. D. 1968. *A hundred years of sociology.* Chicago: Aldine.

Mitchell, W. J., ed. 1981. *On narrative.* Chicago: University of Chicago Press.

Morrill, C. 1995. *The executive way: Conflict management in corporations.* Chicago: University of Chicago Press.

———. 1991. Conflict management, honor and organizational change. *American Journal of Sociology* 97:585–621.

Moskos, P. 2008. *Cop in the hood: My year policing Baltimore's Eastern District.* Princeton, NJ: Princeton University Press.

Mulkay, M. M. 1985. *The world and the world.* London: Allen and Unwin.

Muller, C., and C. Winship. 2009. Revisiting Dewey. Working paper, Department of Sociology, Harvard University.

Mullins, N. C. 1973. *Theories and theory groups in contemporary American sociology*. New York: Harper and Row.

Myerhoff, B. 1980. *Number our days*. New York: Simon and Schuster.

Nader, L. 1969. Up the anthropologist. In D. Hymes, ed., *Reinventing Anthropology*. New York: Pantheon, 284–311.

Naipaul, V. S. 1998. *Beyond belief: Islamic excursions among the converted people*. New York: Vintage.

———. 1990. *India: A million mutinies now*. London: Heinemann.

Naroll, R. and R. Cohen, eds. 1970. *Handbook of method in cultural anthropology*. New York: Columbia University Press.

Nash, D., and R. Weintraub. 1972. The emergence of self-consciousness in ethnography. *Current Anthropology* 13:527–42.

Nash, J. 1993. *Crafts in the world market*. Albany: State University of New York Press.

———. 1979. *We eat the mines and the mines eat us*. New York: Columbia University Press.

Needham, R. 1984. *Exemplars*. Berkeley: University of California Press.

Nelson, J., and D. N. McClosky, eds. 1986. *The rhetoric in the human sciences*. Madison: University of Wisconsin Press.

Nippert-Eng, C. E. 1995. *Home and work: Negotiating boundaries through everyday life*. Chicago: University of Chicago Press.

Nisbet, R. 1976. *Sociology as an art form*. New York: Oxford University Press.

Orr, J. 1996. *Talking about machines: An ethnography of a modern job*. Ithaca, NY: Cornell University Press.

Ortner, S. B. 1999. *Life and death on Mt. Everest: Sherpas and Himalayan mountaineering*. Princeton, NJ: Princeton University Press.

Orwell, G. 1933. *Down and out in Paris and London*. London: Penguin.

Ouellet, L. J. 1994. *Pedal to the metal: The work lives of truckers*. Philadelphia: Temple University Press.

Palmer, V. 1928. *Field studies in sociology*. Chicago: University of Chicago Press.

Passaro, J., 1997. You can't take the subway to the field. In A. Gupta and J. Ferguson, eds., *Anthropological locations*. Berkeley: University of California Press, 147–162.

Pelto, P. J. 1970. *Anthropological research*. New York: Harper and Row.

Pelto, P. J., and G. H. Pelto. 1973. Ethnography. In J. J. Honigmann, ed., *Handbook of social and cultural anthropology*. Chicago: Rand McNally.

References

Penniman, T. K. 1974. *A hundred years of anthropology*. 3rd ed. New York: Morrow.

Perin, Constance. 1977. *Everything in its place*. Princeton: Princeton University Press.

Perlow, L. 1997. *Finding time: How corporations, individuals, and families can benefit from new work practices*. Ithaca, NY: Cornell University Press.

———. 1998. Boundary control: The social ordering of work and family time in a high-tech corporation. *Administrative Science Quarterly* 43:328–57.

Peshkin, A. 1986. *God's choice*. Chicago: University of Chicago Press.

Pettigrew, A. 1985. *The awakening giant*. London: Macmillan.

Platt, J. 1983. The development of the participant-observation method in sociology. *Journal of the History of the Behavioral Sciences* 19:379–93.

Polsky, N. 1967. *Hustlers, beats and others*. Chicago: Aldine.

Powell, W. 1985. *Getting into print*. Chicago: University of Chicago Press.

Powdermaker, H. 1966. *Stranger and friend*. New York: Norton.

Pratt, M. L. 1986. Fieldwork in common places. In J. Clifford and G. E. Marcus, eds., *Writing culture*. Berkeley: University of California Press, 27–50.

Propp, V. J. 1958. *Morphology of a folktale*. Bloomington: University of Indiana Press.

Punch, M. 1986. *The politics and ethics of fieldwork*. Beverly Hills, CA: Sage.

Rabinow, P. 1996. *Making PCR: A story of biotechnology*. Chicago: University of Chicago Press.

———. 1977. *Reflections on fieldwork in Morocco*. Berkeley: University of California Press.

Rabinow, P., and A. Sullivan, eds. 1979. *Interpretive social science*. Berkeley: University of California Press.

Radcliffe-Brown, A. R. 1958. The method of ethnology and social anthropology. In M. N. Srinivas, ed., *Method in social anthropology*. Chicago: University of Chicago Press.

Rappaport, R. A. 1968. *Pigs for the ancestors*. New Haven: Yale University Press.

Reinharz, S. 1979. *On becoming a social scientist*. San Francisco: Jossey-Bass.

Richman, J. 1983. *Traffic wardens*. Manchester: University of Manchester Press.

Ricoeur, P. 1973. The model of the text. *New Literary History* 5:91–120.

Riemer, J. 1977. Varieties of opportunistic research. *Urban Life* 5:467–77.

Rivers, W. H. R. 1910. The genealogical method of anthropological inquiry. *Social Review* 3:1–12.

Roberts, H., ed. 1981. *Doing feminist research*. London: Routledge and Kegan Paul.

Rock, P. 1979. *The making of symbolic interactionism*. Totowa, NJ: Rowman and Littlefield.

Rohner, R., ed. 1969. *The ethnography of Franz Boas*. Chicago: University of Chicago Press.

Rosaldo, M. A. 1980. The use and abuse of anthropology: Reflections on feminism and cross-cultural understanding. *Signs* 5:389–417.

Rosaldo, M. A., and L. Lamphere, eds. 1974. *Women, culture and society*. Palo Alto, CA: Stanford University Press.

Rosaldo, R. 1986a. From the door of his tent. In J. Clifford and M. E. Marcus, eds., *Writing culture*. Berkeley: University of California Press.

———. 1986b. Ilongot hunting as story and experience. In V. W. Turner and E. M. Bruner, eds., *The anthropology of experience*. Urbana: University of Illinois Press, 97–135.

———. 1980. *Ilongot headhunting, 1883–1974*. Palo Alto, CA: Stanford University Press.

Roth, J. 1966. Hired-hand research. *American Sociologist* 1:190–96.

Roy, D. 1970. The study of southern labor union organizing campaigns. In R. W. Habenstein, ed., *Pathways to data*. Chicago: Aldine.

———. 1958. Banana time. *Human Organization* 18:158–68.

———. 1954. Efficiency and the fix. *American Journal of Sociology* 60:255–66.

———. 1952. Restriction of output in a piecework machine shop. Ph.D. diss., University of Chicago.

Rubinstein, J. 1973. *City police*. New York: Ballantine.

Ruby, J., ed. 1982. *A crack in the mirror: Reflexive perspectives in anthropology*. Philadelphia: University of Pennsylvania Press.

Sachs, H. 1971. Lectures (October 8–December 3). Typescript. University of California, Irvine.

Sahlins, M. 1981. *Historical metaphors and mythical realities*. Ann Arbor: University of Michigan Press.

———. 1976. *Culture and practical reason*. Chicago: University of Chicago Press.

Sanday, P. 1979. The ethnographic paradigm(s). *Administrative Science Quarterly* 24:482–93.

Sass, L. A. 1986. Anthropology's native problems. *Harper's* (May).

Savage, C., and G. Lombard. 1985. *Sons of the machine*. Cambridge, MA: MIT Press.

Schatzman, L., and A. Strauss. 1973. *Field research*. Englewood Cliffs, NJ: Prentice-Hall.

Schein, E. H. 2003. *DEC is dead, long live DEC: The lasting legacy of Digital Equipment Company*. San Francisco: Berrett-Koehler.

———. 1987. *The clinical perspective in field work*. Newbury Park, CA: Sage.

———. 1985. *Organizational culture and leadership*. San Francisco: Jossey-Bass.

Schein, L. 2000. *Minority rules: The Miao and the feminine in China's cultural politics*. Durham, NC: Duke University Press.

Schneider, D. M. 1968. *American kinship*. New York: Free Press.

Scott, M. B. 1968. *The racing game*. Chicago: Aldine.

Shaffir, W. B., and R. A. Stebbins, eds. 1991. *Experiencing fieldwork*. Newbury Park, CA: Sage.

Shaffir, W. B., R. A. Stebbins, and A. Turowetz. 1980. *Fieldwork experience*. New York: St. Martin's Press.

Sharrock, W. W., and R. J. Anderson. 1980. On the demise of the native. Occasional Paper no. 5. Department of Sociology, University of Manchester.

Shaw, C. 1931. *The natural history of a delinquent career*. Chicago: University of Chicago Press.

———. 1930. *The jackroller*. Chicago: University of Chicago Press.

Shore, B. 1982. *Sala'ilua: A Samoan mystery*. New York: Columbia University Press.

Shweder, R. A. 1991. *Thinking through cultures: Expeditions in cultural psychology*. Cambridge, MA: Harvard University Press.

Silbey, S. S. 2009. Taming Prometheus: Talk about safety culture. *Annual Review of Sociology* 35:341–69.

Silverman, D. 1985. *Qualitative methodology and sociology*. Brookfield, VT: Gower.

Sims, N., ed. 1984. *The literary journalists*. New York: Ballantine.

Skolnick, J. 1966. *Justice without trial*. New York: Wiley.

Smith, V. 2002. *Crossing the great divide: Worker risk and opportunity in the new economy*. Ithaca, NY: Cornell University Press.

Snow, C. P. 1993. *The Two Cultures*. 2nd ed., reissue. Cambridge: Cambridge University Press.

Solomon, D. 1952. Career contingencies of Chicago physicians. Ph.D. diss., University of Chicago.

Sontag, S. 1963. A hero of our time. *The New York Review of Books* 1 (7): 6–8.

Sperber, D. 1974. *Rethinking symbolism*. Cambridge: University of Cambridge Press.

Spindler, G. D. 1970. *Being an anthropologist*. New York: Holt, Rinehart and Winston.

Spradley, J. P. 1980. *Participant observation*. New York: Holt, Rinehart and Winston.

———. 1979. *The ethnographic interview*. New York: Holt, Rinehart and Winston.

———. 1970. *You owe yourself a drunk*. Boston: Little, Brown.

Spradley, J. P., and B. J. Mann. 1975. *The cocktail waitress*. New York: Wiley.

Stinchcombe, A. L. 1984. The origins of sociology as a discipline. *Acta Sociologica* 27:51–61.

Stocking, G. W. 1987. *Victorian anthropology*. New York: Free Press.

———. 1983. The ethnographer's magic: Fieldwork in British anthropology from Tyler to Malinowski. In G. W. Stocking, ed., *Observers observed*. Madison: University of Wisconsin Press, 70–118.

———. 1968. *Race, culture, and evolution*. Chicago: University of Chicago Press.

Stocking, G. W., ed. 1983. *Observers observed*. Vol. 1 of *History of Anthropology*. Madison: University of Wisconsin Press.

———. 1974. *A Franz Boas reader*. Chicago: University of Chicago Press.

Stoddart, K. 1985. The presentation of everyday life. *Urban Life* 15:103–21.

Sudnow, D. 1967. *Passing-on*. Englewood Cliffs, NJ: Prentice Hall.

Sutherland, E. H. 1937. *The professional thief*. Chicago: University of Chicago Press.

Swidler, A. 1986. Culture in action. *American Sociological Review* 51:273–86.

References

Tax, S. 1955. From Lafitau to Radcliffe-Brown. In F. Eggan, ed., *Social anthropology of North American tribes*. Chicago: University of Chicago Press.

Thomas, J. 1983a. Chicago sociology. *Urban Life* 11:387–95.

———. 1983b. Toward a critical ethnography. *Urban Life* 11:477–90.

Thomas, R. J. 1985. *Citizenship, gender, and work*. Berkeley: University of California Press.

Thomas, W. I., and D. S. Thomas. 1928. *The child in America*. New York: Knopf.

Thomas, W. I., and F. Znaniecki. 1918–21. *The Polish peasant in Europe and America*. 5 vols. Chicago: University of Chicago Press.

Thompson, H. 1966. *The Hell's Angels*. New York: Ballantine.

Thorne, B. 1983. Political activist as participant observer. In R. M. Emerson, ed., *Contemporary field research*. Boston: Little, Brown.

———. 1980. "You still takin' notes?" *Social Problems* 27:284–97.

Thrasher, F. M. 1926. *The gang*. Chicago: University of Chicago Press.

Traweek, S. 1982. Uptime, downtime, spacetime and power: An ethnography of U.S. and Japanese particle physics. Ph.D. diss., University of California, Santa Cruz.

Tsing, A. L. 1993. *In the realm of the diamond queen*. Princeton, NJ: Princeton University Press.

Tucker, J, 1999. *The therapeutic corporation*. New York: Oxford University Press.

Turkel, S. 1984. *The second self*. New York: Basic.

Turnbull, C. 1972. *The mountain people*. New York: Simon and Schuster.

Turner, V. W. 1981. Social dramas and stories about them. In W. J. Mitchell, ed., *On narrative*. Chicago: University of Chicago Press.

Twain, M. 1965. *Innocents abroad*. New York: New American Library (Signet Classics; first published in 1869).

Tyler, S. A. 1986. Post-modern ethnography. In J. Clifford and G. E. Marcus, eds., *Writing culture*. Berkeley: University of California Press.

Tyler, S. A., ed. 1969. *Cognitive anthropology*. New York: Holt, Rinehart and Winston.

Van Dijk, T. A., ed. 1985. *Handbook of discourse analysis*. 4 vols. New York: Academic Press.

Van Maanen, J. 1984. Making rank. *Urban Life* 13:155–76.

References

——. 1983a. The boss. In M. Punch, ed., *Control in the police organization*. Cambridge, MA: MIT Press.

——. 1983b. Reclaiming qualitative methods for organization theory. In J. Van Maanen, ed., *Qualitative methodology*. Beverly Hills, CA: Sage.

——. 1982. Fieldwork on the beat. In J. Van Maanen, J. Dabbs, and R. Faulkner, *Varieties of qualitative research*. Beverly Hills, CA: Sage.

——. 1981a. Some thought (and afterthoughts) on context, interpretation and organization theory. Manuscript.

——. 1981b. The informant game. *Urban Life* 9:469–94.

——. 1981c. Notes on the production of ethnographic data in an American police agency. In R. Luckham, ed., *Law and Social Enquiry*. Uppsala: Scandinavian Institute for African Studies.

——. 1980. Beyond account. *Annals of American Political and Social Science* 58:458–63.

——. 1979. The fact of fiction in organizational ethnography. *Administrative Science Quarterly* 24:539–50.

——. 1978a. The asshole. In P. K. Manning and J. Van Maanen, eds., *Policing*. New York: Random House.

——. 1978b. On watching the watchers. In P. K. Manning and J. Van Maanen, eds., *Policing*. New York: Random House.

——. 1974. Working the street. In H. Jacob, ed., *The potential for reform of criminal justice*. Beverly Hills, CA: Sage.

——. 1973. Observations on the making of policemen. *Human Organization* 32:407–18.

——, ed. 1983. *Qualitative methods*. Beverly Hills, CA: Sage.

Van Maanen, J., and D. Kolb. 1985. The professional apprentice. In S. B. Bacharach, ed., *Perspectives in organizational sociology*. Greenwich, CT: JAI Press, 1–33.

Venkatesh, S. 2008. *Gang leader for a day: A rogue sociologist takes to the streets*. New York: Penguin.

Vidich, A. J., J. Bensman, and M. R. Stein, eds. 1964. *Reflections on community studies*. New York: Harper and Row.

Vinitzky-Seroussi, V. 1998. *After pomp and circumstance: High school reunion as an autobiographical occasion*. Chicago: University of Chicago Press.

Wagner, R. 1981. *The invention of culture*. Chicago: University of Chicago Press.

References

Wallace, A. 1978. *Rockdale*. New York: Knopf.

Wambaugh, J. 1984. *Lines and shadows*. New York: Bantam.

Warner, W. L. 1941. *Social life of a modern community*. Yankee City Series, vol. 1. New Haven, CT: Yale University Press.

Warren, C. A. B. 1988. *Gender issues in field research*. Newbury Park, CA: Sage.

Warren, C. A. B., and P. K. Rasmussen. 1977. Sex and gender in field research. *Urban Life* 6:349–69.

Watson, C. 1991. Make me reflexive—but not yet: Strategies for managing essential reflexivity in ethnographic discourse. *Journal of Anthropological Research* 43:29–41.

Watson, J. L., ed. 1997. *Golden arches East: McDonald's in East Asia*. Berkeley: University of California Press.

Watson, T. J. 1994. *In search of management: Culture, chaos, and control in managerial work*. London: Routledge.

Wax, M. 1972. Tenting with Malinowski. *American Sociological Review* 37:1–13.

Wax, R. 1979. Gender and age in fieldwork and fieldwork education. *Social Problems* 26:509–22.

———. 1971. *Doing fieldwork*. Chicago: University of Chicago Press.

Weatherford, J. M. 1981. *Tribes on the hill*. New York: Rawson, Wade.

Webster, S. 1982. Dialogue and fiction in ethnography. *Dialectical anthropology* 7:91–114.

Weeks, J. 2006. *Unpopular culture: The ritual of complaint in a British bank*. Chicago: University of Chicago Press.

Weick, K., and L. Browning. 1985. Argument and narration in organizational communication. Manuscript. University of Texas.

Weiner, A. 1976. *Women of value, men of renown*. Austin: University of Texas Press.

Werner, O., and G. M. Schoepfle. 1986. *Systematic fieldwork*. 2 vols. Beverly Hills, CA: Sage.

West, J. 1945. *Plainville, U.S.A.* New York: Columbia University Press.

Westley, W. A. 1970. *Violence and the police*. Cambridge, MA: MIT Press.

———. 1951. *Violence and the police*. Ph.D. diss. University of Chicago.

White, Hayden. 1981. The value of narrativity in the representation of reality. In W. J. T. Mitchell, ed., *On narrative*. Chicago: University of Chicago Press, 1–24.

References

——. 1978. *Tropics of discourse.* Baltimore: Johns Hopkins University Press.

——. 1973. *Metahistory.* Baltimore: Johns Hopkins University Press.

Whyte, W. F. 1984. *Learning from the field.* Beverly Hills, CA: Sage.

——. 1955. *Street corner society* (with method appendix). Chicago: University of Chicago Press (originally published in 1943 without appendix).

Willis, P. 1977. *Learning to labour.* London: Routledge and Kegan Paul. (U.S. edition, New York: Columbia University Press, 1981).

Wolcott, H. 1973. *The man in the principal's office.* New York: Harper and Row.

Wolf, M. 1992. *A thrice told tale: Feminism, postmodernism, and ethnographic responsibility.* Palo Alto, CA: Stanford University Press.

Wolfe, T. 1979. *The right stuff.* New York: Farrar, Straus and Giroux.

——. 1973. *The new journalism.* New York: Harper and Row.

——. 1970. *Radical chic and mau-mauing the flak catchers.* New York: Farrar, Straus and Giroux.

Wuthnow, R., J. D. Hunter, A. Bergensen, and E. Kurzweil. 1984. *Cultural analysis.* London: Routledge and Kegan Paul.

Young, M. 1991. *An inside job: Policing and police culture in Britain.* Oxford: Clarendon Press.

Young, M., and P. Willmott. 1962. *Family and kinship in East London.* London: Penguin.

Zabusky, S. E. 1995. *Launching Europe: An ethnography of European cooperation in space science.* Princeton, NJ: Princeton University Press.

Index

Index

Index

Index